Two Sisters and Their Mother

Translated by Jeanine Herman

Two Sisters and Their Mother
The Anthropology of Incest

Françoise Héritier

ZONE BOOKS · NEW YORK

1999

I wish to express my sincere thanks to Meighan Gale and Ramona Naddaff for their insightful editing of this work and to Françoise Héritier for clarifying many points.

— J.H.

The publisher would like to thank the French Ministry of Culture for its assistance with this translation.

© 1999 Urzone, Inc.
Zone Books
611 Broadway, Suite 608
New York, NY 10012

Originally published in France as *Les Deux soeurs et leur mère: Anthropologie de l'inceste* © 1994 Editions Odile Jacob.

Printed in the United States of America.

Distributed by The MIT Press, Cambridge, Massachusetts, and London, England

Library of Congress Cataloging-in-Publication Data

Héritier, Françoise.
[Deux sœurs et leur mère. English]
Two sisters and their mother : the anthropology of incest / Françoise Héritier ; translated by Jeanine Herman.
p. cm.
Includes bibliographical references.
ISBN 0-942299-33-7 (cloth)
1. Incest. 2. Kinship. 3. Consanguinity. I. Title.
GN480.3.H4613   1999
306.877 — dc21   98-56163
CIP

Contents

For Claude Lévi-Strauss

Introduction

Some enigmatic sentences provide fleeting glimpses into the reasons someone said or wrote them. For instance, when Michel Leiris was asked why he refused to have children, he replied, "Sleeping with their mother afterward would seem like committing incest."[1] A strange thought, but one that no doubt reflected a complex set of ideas and feelings which preoccupied the writer.

Likewise, Florence Delay tells a complex but revealing story in her novel *Riche et légère*. Luz, the narrator, has a half-sister, Dorotea; they share the same father. Their father had a mistress, Constance, who was the daughter of a friend. Constance's family was shocked to learn that she had been the lover of her first cousin (her mother's sister's son), who was also her paternal half-brother. When Luz visits Dorotea in Madrid, she learns that Dorotea and Constance had also been lovers. "That summer, between London and Los Heraldos, Constance stopped in Madrid, in the apartment where I found myself that evening, placed her suitcase beneath the window where I had injured myself, slept in the bed I didn't want to sleep in. Enough time to make someone, my own sister, commit incest, as she did everywhere, as it was in her nature to do."[2]

What kind of incest is this, inasmuch as Constance and Dorotea

9

are obviously not related and their only connection is this: one had been the mistress of the other's father? An incestuous relationship has supposedly been established (but between whom exactly?) in a "love triangle" (without matrimonial alliances) created when a man and his daughter both sleep with the same, unrelated partner.

What, then, is incest? How does one define what is incestuous and what is not ? For most people today, incest involves opposite-sex partners who are close blood relations or relatives by marriage. The examples of incest that most immediately come to mind are sexual relations between father and daughter, mother and son, or brother and sister, but incest can also occur between a man and his wife's daughter or his brother's wife, and so forth.

Yet, in the past, situations that do not conform to this definition were considered incestuous nonetheless. The same holds true for certain contemporary non-Western societies and cultures: the ethnographic literature abounds in descriptions of cases not easily accommodated by our standard representations of incest. For example, among some peoples, the same word designates both incest and adultery as we understand them. How can we explain these different attitudes? Do these societies throw all sexual offenses in the same pot? Are their concepts ill-formed or too lax, or is our own perspective too limited? If these groups place incest and certain forms of adultery under the same rubric, it is not because both are sexual offenses, but perhaps because both are incestuous.

The aim of this book is to establish the existence of a form of incest which, for lack of a better term, I call *incest of the second type* (as opposed to *incest of the first type*, which is the usual but overly narrow definition of incest). Under consideration here is the problem of incest in general and the reasons for prohibiting certain sexual liaisons.

When a society defines sexual prohibitions, what does it

intend to reject and why? What is proscribed and prescribed? To conceive of incest of the second type one must think of the incest prohibition as a means of regulating the circulation of fluids between bodies. The fundamental criterion of incest is the contact between identical bodily fluids. It involves what is most fundamental in human societies: the way our categories of the identical and the different are constructed. Indeed, these categories form the basis for the classification of bodily fluids and the system of prohibition/solicitation governing their circulation.

The opposition between the identical and the different is primary because it is founded on what, in the language of kinship, is most irreducible about the human body: sexual difference. It acts as a checkpoint for nascent human thought; one can neither assimilate it into broader categories nor circumvent it. An archaic thema underlying all intellectual production, it is at the heart of all scientific discourse and of all lay systems of representation. The problematics of the same and the other, the one and the many, the continuous and the discontinuous are derived from it. On a less abstract level, specific values presented in the form of oppositions — hot/cold, light/dark, dry/wet, heavy/light, and so on — connote elements of the world, including the masculine and the feminine and their classification in one or another category. But within the opposition of two sexual categories, each qualified by different values, particularly strong identities of substance characterize certain individuals: pairs of twins, two brothers, two sisters, a father and his sons, a mother and her daughters, as well as, from other perspectives, members of the same lineage, guests at the same table, and so forth.

Naturally, the question remains why the linking of two identicals — two people who share common substance if only in part — is forbidden in numerous societies, particularly those with a wide range of matrimonial prohibitions. The historical and ethnographic data suggest that, beyond local variation, there are only two possible attitudes toward *combination of the identical*, and they derive from the positive or negative effects such combination is thought to produce. When combination of the identical is presumed to engender negative effects, it will be forbidden and juxtapositions or combinations of elements classified as different will instead be sought. Conversely, combination of the identical will be sought in societies or particular situations in which it is thought to produce positive effects. Within a given society such combination may be forbidden in the pairing of bodies, but, for the same fundamental reasons, sought after in medicine. Indeed, when they are forbidden, combinations of the identical are sanctioned by various individual or collective ills, such as sterility, caused by two apparently contradictory modes — dessication and liquefaction. For example, the dehydration harmful to reproduction may be sought to cure purulence.

In order to integrate all known aspects of the incest taboo, it was necessary to broaden the very definition of incest. The idea of incest of the second type came to me as I was reading an article that had been published by Reo Fortune in 1932 in the *Encyclopaedia of the Social Sciences*.[3] Fortune asks in passing why when we speak of incest we always imply heterosexual contact when it might just as well be homosexual. And it is true that such relations have existed and exist between grandfather and grandson, father and son, mother and daughter, if only in the form of fondling, which is nevertheless an incestuous act. Fortune's remark triggered my own inquiry into the possibility of incest of a different nature, between same-sex blood relatives who are not homosexual but who share the same sexual partner.

Since Sumerian antiquity, texts have condemned as incest a mother and daughter sharing the same sexual partner, if both women live together. The Koran is categorical: a man may not have sexual relations with the daughter of a woman he has had as a sexual partner. Stated differently, if a man is married to a woman and has not had sexual relations with her, he may marry her daughter; otherwise, he may not. Can it be said any more clearly that bodily contact and the passage of fluids from one to another is the basis for the taboo?

One of the most interesting features of Deuteronomy and Leviticus is the implicit parallel established between different types of sexual conduct. The verses that prohibit incest of the second type, according to my definition of it, are separated by verses that forbid other sexual behaviors, such as zoophilia, necrophilia, and sodomy. These "reprehensible" behaviors are associated — through the punishment they incur — with illicit unions between relatives by marriage. Based on the level of sanctions set forth in these biblical texts, incest of the second type seems to be considered more serious an offense than that of the first. The most fundamental identity seems to involve gender rather than biological or social relations of consanguinity. Because common substance and identity is greater between a father and son than between a father and daughter, certain societies may treat corporal union between a man and his son's wife or his father's wife as more injurious than sexual relations between a father and daughter, for the father's substance comes into contact with the son's, and vice versa, through the common partner. Incest of the second type is likely at the conceptual origin of the incest prohibition as we know it, that of the first type, and not the reverse.

The Catholic Church, in its very first councils, tried to rationalize certain avoidances of relatives by marriage, that is, the prohibition of incest of the second type. The church used the argument of *una caro* (one flesh): I am you, and being you, I cannot have sexual relations with your blood relative. But, as I see it, it is not because one *is* the other that they constitute one flesh, but

13

because each is the bearer of the other's secretions. If a woman were having sexual relations with both her husband and her husband's brother, secretions of identical stock would meet in her womb, according to the Nuer, who maintain that two male blood relatives' bodily fluids mixing in the same womb cause certain diseases, like hemoptysis and elephantiasis.[4] Our societies, too, are reluctant to link the identical. In *Montaillou*, Emmanuel Le Roy Ladurie described the case of a woman who was ardently pursued by a man whose attentions she discouraged despite her attraction, because she was his first cousin's mistress. This precluded any relationship between them: "The ban on sexual and marital relations between first cousins was so strong in Montaillou that an affair with the mistress of a first cousin was regarded as impure!"[5] You could not "touch carnally" the body of a first cousin, even through the interposed body of a common mistress, because it already "touched you naturally." Here, the prohibition addressed a redoubling of a natural identity through flesh, that is, through sperm emitted and retained in the female body, possibly impregnating it.

All subsequent legislation concerning marriage bans in canon and civil law was modeled on bans of consanguinity, and though this legislation eventually faded, it remained in effect for a long time. For two centuries, the English House of Lords debated whether a man could marry his deceased wife's sister. Behind the argument that a man would be providing a better mother to his children (because she was their aunt), we find implicit the idea that two sisters are essentially the same thing, and that replacing one sister with another amounts to the same. It is not clear *a priori* why a sister would necessarily be a better mother than another woman.

Though most of us are unaware of it, France was governed by the same law until recently. Marriage between a blood relative of the same sex as the deceased relative and the surviving spouse — that is, between a man and his deceased brother's wife or his deceased wife's sister — was legalized only in 1914. Not until the early 1980s were such marriages permissible after divorce, and they are still forbidden between relatives by marriage in direct line of descent (a man may not marry his son's wife, for example, or a woman her mother's husband).

Clearly, there is no fundamental difference between the way Western societies have treated the problem, legally or otherwise, and the way so-called primitive societies have dealt with it. The very arguments used throughout the long British debate on the issue are found in the ethnographic literature, attesting to the universality of the workings of the human mind in similar situations. The study of "primitive" societies helps us to understand our own, yet, conversely, ignorance of our own prevents us from understanding primitive societies.

The anthropologist's concern is to discover the underlying logic of these prohibitions, and numerous theories have been set forth to explain the incest taboo.

In defining incest as "an illicit union between persons who are relatives or relatives by marriage to a degree prohibited by law," Le Grand Littré certainly considered it a social issue. The dictionary judiciously refrained from specifying what it meant by "relatives or relatives by marriage," for this varies with the law and does not pertain to the nature of the phenomenon itself.

A first theory challenges the universal nature of the incest prohibition. It suggests that certain societies, far from prohibiting incest or reserving it for certain social classes, as in ancient Egypt, made the incestuous union an obligation, as in Old Iran.[6] However, the texts that refer to this rule were written six centuries after it was supposedly in effect. Common sense allows us to dismiss this interpretation: if a father could marry his daughter, he would have to have married another woman first, who would provide her. Supposing that this type of incestuous marriage ever existed, it could only have been secondary in relation to a first marriage; consequently, it could not have been obligatory. The idea that incest might have been the rule somewhere (rather than universally forbidden) is groundless.

Theories explaining the incest prohibition can be grouped into two categories. They seek explanation in *final causes* and attempt to answer questions such as: Why does the incest prohibition exist? What end does it serve? What is its use for humanity? Or else they seek explanation in *efficient causes* by asking questions such as: What biological, psychological, or sociological mechanisms cause the prohibition to be respected?

The first "final cause" theory is biological in nature. It explains the incest prohibition through ancestral recognition of the danger constituted by an increase in negative homozygous characteristics. Slow development, smaller size, reduced fertility, a weakened immune system, and shorter life expectancy are the characteristics observed in animals as a result of consanguineous reproduction. Though these ills are far removed from the defects and deformities of popular belief in the malediction of intermarriage, the theory is nevertheless tainted by a hasty transposition of laboratory findings — concerning fruit flies, particularly — to the social reality of men. Moreover, all recessive homozygous traits are not necessarily bad for the group. A number of human societies regularly practice consanguineous union — for example, preferential marriage with the mother's brother's daughter, a first cousin — and have nevertheless survived since the dawn of time. Finally, this theory explains nothing about the prohibition concerning relatives by marriage.

There are also "efficient cause" theories of a biological character. They explain the incest prohibition through man's instinctive, innate repulsion for all incestuous relations. The prohibition, then, would merely be a cultural ritualization of this inborn aversion. Basically, this is nothing more than an elaboration of the popular idea of "the call of blood": we recognize each other immediately because we are bearers of the same blood. In its more contemporary version — the ethological theory of imprinting[7] — the intimacy of the odor of childhood relations is subsequently transformed into an aversion, or at least an avoidance, in most of the animal kingdom, not solely in humans. One might submit the counterexample of human societies that totally separate brothers and sisters in earliest childhood, short-circuiting imprinting, and nevertheless do not practice incest. One might also consider Sir James Frazer's counterargument: Why would a deep human instinct need to be reinforced by law? What nature forbids and punishes does not require a law as well. There is no law obliging people to eat or drink, preventing them from placing their hands in fire, and so on. The very existence of a legal ban would, on the contrary, lead one to infer the existence of a natural instinct toward incest.[8] We know the use Sigmund Freud made of this argument in *Totem and Taboo*.

Freud's theory is a sociological, rather than biological, final cause theory. It is of particular interest in that it accounts for incest of the second type as well as of the first. Through the incest prohibition imposed on other males, the father imposes his domination over all the women of the group, and, among animals, the young males are relegated to the periphery. By eliminating incestuous practices that incite jealousy and competition instead of authority and cooperation, the goal of the incest taboo would thus be to maintain the hierarchy between generations and the discipline necessary for the group's cohesion.[9] Thus, the incest taboo allows society to function without continual crises. Daughters and sisters are also subject to the law of the father, in that they are not forced to distance themselves, as are potential male rivals.

Freud introduces the notions of desire and the Oedipus complex, which arises from the impossibility of fulfilling the desire to kill the father and sexually appropriate the mother. This analysis of the human unconscious may be confirmed by examining populations where true power over the child is exercised by the maternal uncle, not the father. The father is still the one who has, or has had, sexual access to the mother, and the Oedipus complex may certainly develop. Yet, as we shall see, certain ancient texts interpret the incest between Oedipus and Jocasta in another way, which more fully accounts for the primordial nature of incest of the second type without requiring authority and force to maintain familial cohesion and social ties: it is impossible for a son to return to the furrows plowed by his father.

This is not the only final cause theory of incest with a sociological bent. Emile Durkheim was the first to introduce the issue of the body's fluids, but he enclosed it narrowly within the confines of totemism.[10] The incest prohibition is derived from the rule of exogamy, which is founded on a sacred fear of menstrual blood. This fear falls under the more general category of fear of blood, which is rooted in a belief in the consubstantiality of all members of the same clan (a belief of particular interest with respect to incest of the second type). Unintentionally, Durkheim provides the basis for the notion of total consubstantiality, that is, shared identity. In a single clan group, men are identical to each other, just as women are identical to each other. Men and women in the same clan are categorized as different, but in relation to men and women from other clan groups, they have a strong, overall identity of substance.

Claude Lévi-Strauss's theory remains the most convincing. It is founded on this simple reflection: within the small groups that originally made up human societies, the randomness of birth made it highly unlikely for each person to find his appropriate sexual partner. One therefore had to seek a partner from another group. There were only two ways to go about this: either war or exchange, "either marrying-out or being killed-out."[11] "The alternative was between biological families living in juxtaposition and endeavoring to remain closed, self-perpetuating units, overridden by their fears, hatreds, and ignorances, and the systematic establishment, through the incest prohibition, of links of intermarriage between them, thus succeeding to build, out of the artificial bonds of affinity, a true human society, despite, and even in contradiction with, the isolating influence of consanguinity."[12] This theory takes what people say literally, like the incredulous response of the Arapesh to Margaret Mead's question regarding what would happen if men slept with their sisters or took them as wives: "What, you would like to marry your sister! What is the matter with you anyway? Don't you want a brother-in-law? Don't you realize that if you marry another man's sister and another man marries your sister, you will have at least two brothers-in-law, while if you marry your own sister, you will have none? With whom will you hunt, with whom will you garden, whom will you go to visit?"[13]

To show how incest and its prohibition are closely linked in every culture to the totality of representations concerning the individual, social organization, the world, and the relations between these three universes, Lévi-Strauss's theory must be supplemented. The consequences of transgression are not always biological and do not always strike their authors. Instead, for example, the rain may stop, the groundwater may sink, there may be drought, or, on the contrary, the rain may never stop, there may be floods, or there may be wars, infestations, epidemics, and so on.

Moreover, the Lévi-Straussian theory does not account for incest of the second type, particularly the prohibition against a man's sleeping with his first wife's sister—the "two sisters" prohibition that lends this book its title. Indeed, since any woman a man marries cannot be his blood relative (in which case she would be forbidden), her sister cannot be his blood relative either. There is no reason to prohibit her in terms of the incest taboo concerning blood relatives, unless to introduce explanations of an entirely different nature, as, for example, a strategy of alliance that would involve joining with as many partners as possible, rather then immediately renewing an established matrimonial alliance.

In this book I seek to provide a unifying theory that accounts for all aspects of the incest prohibition. By focusing on a neglected area of the incest prohibition, the prohibition of two sisters, the primacy of the symbolic is affirmed, rooted in the most physical element of humanity, namely, the anatomical differences between the sexes. These differences, visible to the eye, as well as the physiological differences or similarities in bodily fluids, have been mulled over in all primitive human groups. The primary categories of the identical and the different stem from the rudimentary observation that has been made by every man and woman and continues to be made by every child: some are like me, others are not. Now, any differential refinement or attribution of values, qualities, and characteristics peculiar to these categories becomes possible. The mechanism that simultaneously engenders and legitimizes the social order and the representation of the world is set in motion.

I have entitled this book *Two Sisters and Their Mother* because so many of the texts on incest that I have encountered speak in the masculine and present these prohibitions primarily in relation to a man, a masculine Ego. The most obvious prohibition of incest of the second type concerns women in three particular situations:

a mother and daughter, two sisters, and sometimes two sisters and their mother. Only in a roundabout way are consanguine women considered a point of reference in texts that speak of the prohibition of sharing a common partner.

The first section of this book is historical, examining the ancient Near East, the Hebrew and Islamic worlds, the Greek and Roman worlds, and the Christian world to the present. The second is ethnographic. Examples from African societies will be analyzed to show the close links between this prohibition and systems of alliance known as semicomplex or complex, which function on the basis of prohibitions, and the relationship between rules concerning marriage and overall systems of representation of bodily fluids in these societies will be demonstrated. In the third, anthropological section, I will examine the logic of the identical and the different, the logic of bodily fluids, or mechanical systems of fluids, the close relationship between the two types of incest, and the preeminence or precedence of the second in relation to the first. I will describe the consequences of incest, meteorological or otherwise, the conceptual links to bodily fluids and to kinships of an apparently different nature, such as milk kinship and spiritual kinship, and links to certain sexual offenses. This is where all the threads of my argument come together and where, ultimately, an analysis of certain contemporary events and documents shows the extent to which the problematics of incest, such as I have established them, govern our behaviors, opinions, and thoughts. At a time when the media publicly asks whether taboos are disappearing, it would be hard to deny their deep-rooted existence. Incestuous acts of all sorts occur; this is a statistical and social truth. But these are not common, ordinary, normal, banal events. As soap operas and certain news items demonstrate, the fantasy of incest — of the second type at least as much as that of the first — is a major driving force of our social imagination.

21

It has been twenty years since I first articulated some of the ideas that form the framework of this book.[14] Over the course of the years, I have refined this work by presenting it before varied but faithful audiences at the Ecole des Hautes Etudes en Sciences Sociales and at the Collège de France. I would like to thank those attentive audiences and one listener in particular, Gérard Jorland, who is no doubt the only person to have heard every word written here. May he consider this book a gift to him.

PART ONE

The Historical Confluences

of Incest

Introduction

If humanity today faces the same biological givens and conceptual problems its most distant ancestors confronted, traces of these phenomena should be found in ancient texts, hidden in the deepest recesses of the crucible forming our representations; they intrigue ethnologists in the field and are difficult to coax out and understand even in our own societies. The prohibition against marrying "two sisters" is present as an imperative that has needed no legitimation, either in secular or canon law, until quite recently. Let us keep in mind that I subsume under this rubric several variants of incest of the second type: a man with two sisters, two brothers with two sisters, a man with his wife's daughter (the substantial identity is between the mother and her daughter), or, symmetrically, a woman with two brothers, a woman with her husband's son, and so forth.

History serves to illustrate and formulate the main lines of a general anthropological theory of incest. My aim is not to produce a historical study, researching every source among the various literatures and documenting each instance of incest in every society that has left a written trace. To find a variety of texts — from various cultures, during different epochs — explicitly dealing with the subject suffices. Relatively few testimonies can adequately illustrate the emergence of the theme, without requiring exhaustive investigation.

Furthermore, I am not seeking to establish a chronological

genealogy of the prohibition pertaining to two sisters and their mother from an evolutionist perspective that would have us as heirs to a long tradition. I believe, on the contrary, that convergent structures have emerged in various places at various times because there are limits imposed on the possibilities of conceptual organization. The possibilities are limited by the most commonplace natural givens: two sexes uniting carnally to reproduce, bodies sensitive to visible attributes, common secretions and others specific to each sex, the succession of generations, a direct relationship between food, the production of substances, and life, and so on. But the possibilities of conceptual organization, though limited, may appear in various guises, from the pure and simple negation of certain elements of the data to complicated architectures. Therefore, while I will not examine the subject historically from an evolutionist perspective, neither will I reduce it to a universal uniformity. One does not find a prohibition pertaining to union with two sisters, or with a mother and her daughter, everywhere. In certain societies, these unions are, on the contrary, sought after. But what is universal is the methodical reflection on the placing into contact of identical or different bodies, of secretions, of identical or different substances, even if the solutions to the problem offered by various human groups vary in form and potency, in nature and intensity.

Several sources mark out this history: the Hittite laws of the second millennium B.C.; Assyrian laws of the great period—the reigns of Sargon II (722–705 B.C.) and Ashurbanipal (668–627 B.C.)—that ended between 612 and 609 B.C. under the Medes; Biblical laws; Greek references; Koranic laws; and Roman law. Finally, examination of a few key texts in the Christian tradition will provide the link to current law.

CHAPTER ONE

Long Ago in the Distant East

To my knowledge, the oldest known legal texts dealing with the various forms of incest are Hittite.[1] As we shall see, there were several categories of incest and several terms to designate them.

One point should be underscored at the outset. As with the Assyrians and the Hebrews, there was a constant: namely, that while cohabitation with a wife's sister was prohibited during the wife's lifetime, it was allowed after her death, though in the Hittite case, it seems to have been merely tolerated. The oldest known source says, "If a man's wife dies and he then marries her sister, there will be no punishment." But, it goes on, "If a man marries the daughter and then lives with her mother and sister as well, he is committing a capital crime." This text calls for two commentaries.

First of all, the line I quote first above speaks only of sisters; the second line introduces, almost surreptitiously, the mother. This seems perfectly logical, since the mother shares an identical substance with her daughter, just as two sisters do. But the two cases are distinct. In the case of the two sisters, there can be re-marriage through the sororate[2] but no cohabitation. In the case of the mother and her daughter, there can be no remarriage with the deceased wife's mother (the text does not even mention the possibility of it), nor can there be sexual cohabitation.

Secondly, the text distinguishes clearly between *antemortem* and *postmortem* situations (vis-à-vis the wife), that is, between sororal polygyny (marrying two sisters at the same time) and sororate (marrying one after the other's death). This distinction is drawn very clearly in numerous human societies and further illustrates our earlier observation that, in certain cases, union with two sisters may in fact be sought after for its beneficial effects. In the French language, for example, there is no established term for a man being permitted to marry or live with a mother and her daughter, or a daughter and her mother, simultaneously or after the death of one of them. All these distinctions, however, are suggested in the Hittite text very economically.

In the Same Place

Article 189 of the Hittite laws governs relations between blood relatives. Subsection 189a prohibits sexual relations between a man and his mother — that is, a female relative of the first ascending generation — while 189b stipulates the same thing in regard to the descending generation, prohibiting sexual relations between a man and his daughter. These prohibitions are stated from the masculine point of view, but this does not mean that the reverse is permitted. That a man may not marry his mother or daughter does not mean that a woman may marry her father or son; on the contrary, such unions are prohibited de facto. Generally, as the law is androcentric, the feminine point of view must be inferred.

Article 190 prohibits sexual relations between a man and his father's wife during the father's lifetime. This is not a matter of consanguinity but of alliance and first-degree relations. Since the preceding article prohibits sexual commerce with one's mother, this article can only be referring to relations with any father's wife who is not Ego's mother.

Article 191 states that "a man may not have relations with

several free women, as well as with their mother, in the same place." "Free" might be taken to mean either "not married" or "not a slave"; based on the context, the first interpretation seems correct. Indeed, it is difficult to see why this situation would be permitted with slaves and why, moreover, the legislator would make a pronouncement on it. "Free" should therefore be taken in the sense of "free of all matrimonial ties." What is important here is the sole appearance of the expression "in the same place."

A man, therefore, may not have a liaison with two sisters, with them and their mother, or with one of them and her mother. If the sisters are indeed second-degree relatives in collateral line and if the sisters and their mother are also first-degree relatives in ascendant line, the man designated as masculine Ego, since the law is stated from his point of view, has *no* degree of kinship with any of them. Consequently, article 191 seems to concern neither consanguineous incest nor incest based on alliance (from the masculine perspective), but an incest prohibition characterized by its focus on "the same place." This act is called *wenzi*.

Article 195 consists of three provisions, one of which is subdivided into two parts. The first provision prohibits relations with the brother's legitimate wife during his lifetime. This is the reverse of the prohibition of two sisters: two brothers may not have relations at the same time with the legitimate wife of one, which is called *seski*. The second provision prohibits relations with the wife's daughter during the wife's lifetime (*salik*). The third, divided into two parts, prohibits any sexual relations with the wife's mother (*salik*) or with the wife's sister during the wife's lifetime (*salik*). The first three cases concern alliance kinship of the first degree, and the last case, of the second degree. As we can see, *salik* is similar to *wenzi*; it involves the same types of people, except that alliance exists between the man and consanguineous women in one case and not in the other.

29

These articles concerning the living wife's sister, mother, and daughter, the brother's wife, and the father's wife, highlight the enigmatic aspect of the *katta-wastai* relationship prohibited by article 191. There is neither consanguinity nor alliance here, since the prohibition concerns sexual commerce in the same place with two sisters and their mother, that is, with women related to each other but not to the man. If they were related to him, this article would be redundant; it would simply be adultery. Generally, adultery is only condemned by Hittite law when implied in a relation of alliance. For a man to be having sexual relations with his daughter-in-law, sister-in-law, or mother-in-law, he has to be married to the mother, the sister, or the daughter. There is no adultery if it is simply a matter of sexual relations between a man and unmarried women. Adultery in this sense is therefore never the primary cause for relations being prohibited by Hittite law. Indeed, article 191 does not stipulate that the prohibition holds only for married men.

This enigmatic article should be compared to two others: article 193, which authorizes a series of levirate remarriages for a widow, that is, with the husband's brother's son, the husband's sister's son, or, finally, the husband's brother; and article 194, which complements it, authorizing a woman's successive remarriage with her deceased husband's son, then grandson, in agnatic descent, that is, through men exclusively.

Now, article 191 is strictly the opposite of articles 193 and 194. In one case, the women are related to each other; in the other, the men are — a man, his son, and his grandson, or a man, his brother, and his nephew. One prohibits sexual relations between a man and related women living in the same place. The others permit a woman's successive remarriages with related men, but only after the preceding husband's death. In both cases, the men or women are related to each other (*untereinander* in the

German translation) but not to those with whom they have a sexual tie (*miteinander*). This type of relationship is prohibited during a spouse's lifetime but permitted after death, because there is an incestuous element in it: identical substance.

We have before us an exemplary case in which the statement conceals the truth: what is prohibited is not for a man to live with two sisters or with a mother and her daughter. What is prohibited is for two sisters, or a mother and daughter — who are of the same nature, of the same flesh, and share a common bodily substance — to allow this identical flesh to touch through a common partner.

In article 195, two types of alliance are forbidden: first, between a man and his brother's wife, which is symmetrical to the prohibition against two sisters, as we have seen (two brothers cannot share the same woman, as in the case of father and son established by an earlier formal prohibition); second, between the husband and his wife's mother, daughter, and sisters during the wife's lifetime. The *salik* case (article 195) is equivalent to the *wenzi* case (article 191), except that the legislator establishes a difference (of degree?) between these two varieties of sexual relations with female blood relatives based on whether a relationship of alliance exists between the protagonists or not.

By specifically prohibiting relations "in the same place," and therefore during the related women's lifetime, article 191 implies that if the first woman with whom one had sexual relations died, a relationship would be possible with her sister. If she in turn died, relations would be possible with their mother. What is said implicitly in this article is that the women are alive; what is said explicitly is that they are related by blood. Conversely, what is said explicitly in articles 193 and 194 is that the men are dead, except the last; what is said implicitly is that they are related by blood.

What does "in the same place" mean then? First of all, that masculine Ego knows that these women are related by blood. If

31

these women live in the same place, in the same village, he will inevitably know their kinship relations. Supposing, on the contrary, that these women are scattered and that he happens to meet, in a remote village, a relative of a woman he has known sexually in his own village; he is unaware of their kinship relation, so the consequences are not the same. First, there is no sanction against him. For this act to be judged *urkil* — unseemly, shameless, socially reprehensible — the guilty party must have knowledge of the women's kinship ties. This knowledge is presumed if he lives in the same place as the women. Where close relatives are concerned, such as the mother, daughter, father's wife, or wife's mother or sister, a man's possession of this knowledge may be assumed in a situation of local endogamy, as among the Hittites. Consequently, the articles concerning these kinship relations do not specify knowing of these ties, but article 191, on the contrary, does. Once again, the law speaks in the masculine, concerns only the essential, and should be taken literally. If one is aware of kinship relations, it is because one is in the same place; reciprocally, if one is in the same place, one cannot be unaware of kinship relations. One may note that the Hittite law does not mention the possibility of a man having knowledge of the consanguineous relations between two women who live at a distance from one another. There is apparently no prohibition here. I infer from this that the putting into contact of the same corporeal identity through a third party has no effect unless the two female bodies related by blood are constantly in each other's presence. The Hittite law, from this point of view, is fundamentally materialist.

According to historians, the Hittite laws have given rise to a series of conflicting interpretations. For some, these laws prohibited love triangles: not only with two sisters, but also the mother. For others, the expression *nu-x-sakki* ("so he knows") suggests that knowledge of the women's relatedness was an aggravating circumstance. For others still, a man's sexual relations with several women related to each other created a familial relationship, as if the women were actually related by marriage to a man who married one of them. Article 191 would then imply that simple sexual relations introduce a relation of alliance with the relatives of each of the partners, de facto. This is why any sexual relations with these relatives is prohibited. This interpretation is indefensible from the strict point of view of Hittite conceptions, which differentiate between marriage and sexual relations, if only by using different terms to refer to them. At no time is kinship by alliance mentioned in the text. Nevertheless, there is something to this interpretation: while a sexual relationship has nothing to do with legal marriage, it conveys the same thing biologically and physiologically: namely, contact and transfer of substance. If a man may not have sexual relations with two sisters and their mother in the same place (and therefore at the same time), it is because the women have the same substantial identity, so that relations with one could contaminate the others. Consequently, this relationship is prohibited not because a sexual liaison is analogous to a matrimonial union, but because a matrimonial union entails carnal relations as well as legal procreation.

Let us return to terminology. *Katta-wastai* denotes a relationship between relatives of the first degree in direct line — that of a man with his mother (in ascending line) or with his daughter (in descending line). But *katta-wastai* is also found in other contexts, where it designates a man's sexual relations with his stepmother *during his father's lifetime*. Why is this relationship *katta-wastai*? It is, because Ego's father, having known Ego's mother, conveys something of her to his second wife, so that if Ego had sexual relations with the latter, he would come into contact with his mother's substance. Through the intermediary of the father's semen, the two women have acquired a certain substantial identity, so that

33

the son, by sleeping with his stepmother, would be sleeping with his own mother. Therefore this would be a *katta-wastai* relationship. Looking at it another way, the son would touch his own father, his own father's innermost substance, which he would encounter in the same womb; vice versa, the father would touch his son's substance.

The same expression is employed again in other articles (187, 188, 199, 200a), which address something entirely different, sodomy, though the translation does not specify whether it is homo- or heterosexual sodomy. In his commentary, however, the translator emphasizes that these articles concern cases where there is no kinship whatsoever between the man and the women, either by blood or alliance, which allows one to assume that the articles concern heterosexual sodomy outside of or within marriage. This is a plausible interpretation. But if one admits that these articles might just as well address homosexual sodomy, the problem is no longer a simple one of kinship. It is clear that the Hittites established an analogy between the various cases implied by the term *katta-wastai*, which covers contact between substances that are forbidden because of too great a similarity (kinship) or too great a difference (sodomy).

Neufeld proposed a systematic analysis of this terminology in *The Hittite Laws*, published in 1951.[3] According to him, *katta-wastai* was the central term, "a term of a general nature used for sexual relations without specific reference to morality." In Neufeld's reading of article 191, *wenzi* is interpreted as "free relations of a base nature, prostitution, fornication, etc." It refers to those sexual impulses that are absolutely primary. One notes, however, that article 191 never mentions prostitution. This is an addition by the exegete in order to justify his interpretation in terms of the absence or presence of moral connotation. Finally, the term *seski*, in Neufeld's reading, groups together "cases of indiscriminate or free sexual relations with cases of 'spending the night' with women, or what actually amounts to prostitution." This term would therefore denote two very different relationships, the indiscriminate relationship between a man and his brother's wife and adultery with a woman who is not necessarily a prostitute.

One might agree with Neufeld about *wenzi* insofar as it is a matter of a man's free, purely sexual relations with several related women whom we may assume to be prostitutes even if the text does not say so, since so many things are implicit and go without saying for the Hittites. Nevertheless, we should keep in mind that when the Hittite lawmaker feels the need to specify something, he does not neglect to do so. Now, a prohibition against a relationship with related prostitutes "in the same place" would be hard to understand. Why specify "in the same place" and omit the fact that they are prostitutes?

In all these cases the women give themselves voluntarily, since the term denoting rape is different; it is *ept* and the act it refers to is also condemnable. All these terms, then, refer to offenses of diminishing gravity, starting with the most serious in the line of direct consanguinity. If the same term denotes both the most serious incest and sodomy, this cannot be accidental; it reveals an implicit relationship between these two acts; and if the terms denoting prostitution and rape are different from one another and from the term that denotes a man's relations with related women, it means that these women are neither prostitutes nor victims of rape.

In Hittite law, incest is thus connoted by sexual relations and not solely by marriage. It implies both consanguinity and alliance, since it implicates individuals related to one another (*miteinander*) in the first degree in direct line, and also concerns relatives by marriage, in the first degree in direct line as well as in collateral line in the first and second degrees, as long as the marriage that

35

established this alliance still exists. It also implies a sexual liaison between a man and women who are related to each other but not to him (*untereinander*).

It is worth noting that no article of the Hittite laws prohibits marriage or sexual union between brothers and sisters. Is this to say that such relations are licit, or else that their prohibition goes without saying? I would be inclined to say the first. If this interpretation is correct, substantial identity would exist only between the father and son, on the one hand, and the mother and daughter, on the other; thus, a brother and sister born of the same parents would not actually have substantial identity. Conversely, two sisters have the same identity, and they have the same identity as their mother, which is why article 191 specifies "two sisters and their mother." Incest of the second type would therefore be considered more serious than that of the first type between collaterals, between brother and sister.

If He Pleases

According to Driver and Miles's translation, Assyrian law stipulates this: "If a man has brought the customary present to his father-in-law's house and his wife has died and his father-in-law has other daughters, if his father-in-law pleases, he may marry a daughter of his father-in-law in place of his dead wife...."[4] In other words, taking the text literally, if he has paid the bride-price and his wife has died, he may marry another of his father-in-law's daughters, with his father-in-law's consent, without having to pay another bride-price. This suggests that these women are worth the same amount, so that the price paid for one includes rights over the others in case of death.

The law continues, "or if he pleases, he may take back the money which he has given" if he does not take one of his deceased wife's sisters. On the other hand, "neither corn nor sheep nor any

36

other thing which is edible shall be given back to him [...] He shall receive only the money."

The bride-price therefore comprises two parts: money and goods (beer, grain, livestock, and so on). As one may have noticed, the husband always has a choice but the father-in-law does not. Though the latter may refuse to give another daughter, he cannot refuse to return the money if he does not have another daughter to give or if the husband decides not to marry one his deceased wife's sisters.

This law seems to have posed serious problems for Assyriologists. To Driver and Miles, specialists in Assyrian law, the text implies that the first marriage was not consummated, otherwise the husband would not be able to take back his gifts legally. All ethnography refutes this interpretation: consummated or not, marriage is sanctioned by a reciprocal transfer of a matrimonial compensation, from a husband to a father in one direction, and from a daughter to a son-in-law in the other. It is this two-way transfer that constitutes a legally sanctioned marriage. The nonconsummation of a marriage may certainly be a reason for divorce. A woman may complain of sexual dissatisfaction, and her parents may then take her back, returning the money portion of the bride-price, but this is absolutely exceptional. One could cite a number of ethnographic examples in which the nonconsummation of the marriage, due to the husband's sexual impotence or the wife's accidental death, is not taken into account and the marriage remains legally valid.

If Driver and Miles's interpretation were correct, why would the text specify that the wife must be dead and omit the consummation of the marriage? The text says that reciprocal transfer has taken place (the money was given and the wife received); that this wife died (it does not say how long afterward); that the men involved have a choice but not the women. Would it then leave

37

implicit whether the marriage was consummated or not? That is unlikely.

To another interpreter, Andries van Praag, whose *Droit matrimonial assyro-babylonien* was published in 1945, the law in question could be applied to a consummated but sterile marriage, one without descendants.[5] Under these conditions, a man could choose either to reclaim his matrimonial compensation in order to obtain another wife, or to take a sister whom he might assume to be more fertile, without having to pay further compensation. This interpretation is certainly plausible, but nothing in the text supports it. Once again, why would the death of the first wife be specified and not her sterility? This hypothesis relies on the code of Hammurabi, the sixth king of Babylon's first dynasty (ca. 2003–1686 B.C.). It includes this law: "If a man has taken a wife and she has not provided him with sons" — daughters do not count — "and the woman has then gone to her fate, her husband is entitled to have the bride-price refunded." This Babylonian law implies *a contrario* that he cannot demand anything if his wife dies after giving him one or more sons.

On the other hand, this additional piece of information regarding the absence of male descendants could well imply the idea of transmission of substance, one via the paternal path to the sons, the other via the uterine path to the daughters. If a man had daughters from his first wife, then sons from his second, there would be no incest between them. On his wife's death, he may reclaim the matrimonial compensation in the event that he has had only daughters, unless he chooses to marry the deceased woman's sister, which would mean that incest no longer exists between the two sisters, there is no longer a mixture of substance between them after one of them dies. A man is able to marry the sister to fulfill the contract because the sisters are in a sense interchangeable. From this sister, his second wife, he may have daughters and sons: the daughters of his first and second wives will have the same substance (that of their mothers); but if he has a son with his second wife, the son's substance is then agnatic, establishing a difference between the father's male and female children.

Van Praag postulates identical solutions to interpreting Babylonian and Assyrian law based on the interconnections between Babylon and Assyria. But he interprets a "marriage without descendants" as a "marriage without sons." Now, a marriage without sons is not, strictly speaking, a marriage without descendants, even if Assyrian law recognizes only agnatic descent, daughters being a good of transfer. Daughters do not count, not due to some sort of misogyny, but due to identical substance, because they have the same substance as their mother, just as sisters do, and because they do not share, or scarcely share, their father's substance.

Scholars have long debated whether it is indeed the son-in-law who may marry one of his father-in-law's daughters in place of his deceased wife, and whether he may or must do so. And yet the text is sufficiently clear. It is hard to see whom it could be besides the son-in-law and his father-in-law, or why the text would have a third man intervene in so clear a relationship. It is difficult to see, furthermore, why it would be an obligation for the son-in-law, since Assyrian law explicitly requires the father-in-law's consent ("if he pleases," the text states) and just as explicitly acknowledges the choice accorded the son-in-law, who may ask for restitution of his bride-price "if he pleases."

Driver and Miles draw a parallel with the next section of the Assyrian code, which states that, if a father pays the bride-price to procure a wife for his son and the latter dies, he then has the right to give this daughter-in-law to another son. This is the opposite of the preceding situation. There, a son-in-law lost his wife and had the right to take one of her sisters if his father-in-law agreed;

here, the father-in-law buys a wife, so to speak, for his son and, having bought this good, is not obliged to return it but may offer it to another son. Driver and Miles argue that just as the father-in-law has the right to give the wife (for whom he paid a bride-price) to another son, if he has received a bride-price for a daughter who has died, his son-in-law has the right to take a sister. While it is better if the father-in-law agrees, it is nonetheless the son-in-law's right.

This parallel, however, actually highlights the *difference* between a husband who loses his wife and a man who loses his son. The former has a choice: he may take an unmarried sister-in-law to be his new wife or he may get his money back in order to find a new wife elsewhere, for there may be reason to doubt the fertility of his dead wife's family members. The latter has no choice: he must keep his daughter-in-law, provided he has someone to give her to. The daughter-in-law's family may prefer to return the matrimonial compensation and ask for their daughter back. They might then marry her off to someone else for a new matrimonial compensation, which, we should recall, includes not only money, which may have to be refunded, but also edible foodstuffs, which do not, and thereby make a sort of profit.

In the first case, all the daughters may have been promised or given. Their father may have already received the matrimonial compensations for them and no longer be in a position to give another daughter to his widowed son-in-law. Or else, were he to return the matrimonial compensation to the family that paid for, say, the youngest daughter, in order to give her to his son-in-law, he would either be showing unparalleled generosity or he would have to ask his son-in-law for a second compensation, which the law explicitly rules out.

For van Praag, this text makes an earlier but lost text on the obligation of sororate (that is, the obligation to marry two sisters) more malleable. Contrary to the prohibition of incest of the second type, van Praag argues, there had been an obligation of institutional sororate, which modifications of the law came to suppress and even forbid. It is true that a whole spectrum of possibilities exists, from prohibition of incest of the second type to its prescription. However, there are few cases in which a single society went from one to the other, unless a great deal of time had passed or there had been such upheaval that the population had been entirely replaced. But then it is not sensible to base an exegesis on the comparison of texts separated by two thousand years.

It is not, therefore, the suppression of an earlier sororate which is revealed in this sentence stating that a father has the right to give his daughter-in-law to another son. On the contrary, it instructs the father not to take back the matrimonial compensation that has been paid, unless he does not have another son to whom to give this woman as a wife. Obviously, it is in the wife's family's interest to reimburse the monetary portion of the bride-price in order to recover their daughter and offer her once again for full compensation, involving both money and edible goods.

According to others, the expression "if he pleases" refers either to the father-in-law in both cases (in other words, the son-in-law would not reclaim his matrimonial compensation unless this pleased his father-in-law), or, on the contrary, all is left entirely to the son-in-law, who chooses between a new wife and reclaiming his money. There is no lack of objections to these various interpretations. First of all, we have no proof at all of the existence of the sororate, in contrast with sororal polygyny and the levirate, where the father gives the wife of his deceased son to another son. In this case, the question is whether he can do this for any of his sons, since most of the time levirate marriage is only possible for the younger brother and his older brother's wife but not the reverse. This is because the older brother–younger brother relationship is more like a father-son relationship than an equal one. A younger brother may marry his father's widow or his older brother's widow, but an older brother may rarely marry his younger brother's widow, just as a father may rarely marry his son's widow. And when this is possible, it is explicitly mentioned. Now, these Assyrian texts speak of a son but do not specify which son.

There is no proof whatsoever of earlier sororate or sororal polygyny. We shall see that they are regarded unfavorably by Leviticus, as they were by earlier Hittite laws, though the first Hittite law expressly declares that no punishment shall be incurred if the first wife is dead, limiting reprobation to sororal polygyny, for which the prescribed punishment is death. The absence of punishment in the case of the sororate is implied by the idea of dissolution by death of the preceding union and, consequently, the definitive bodily separation of the two sisters. Above all, no parallel should be established with the levirate. Under laws of sororate, the woman has in fact been bought, integrated into her family-in-law, and has become its property. The levirate, on the other hand, is never, or rarely, an obligation. It is always, or most often, the option offered a woman to remain with her family-in-law, which she generally does if she has had children.

In patrilineal societies, if a woman has children with her husband, these children belong to the husband. If she leaves her family-in-law and rejoins her own family, she does not bring her children, except a baby she is breast-feeding, which she must return once it has been weaned. If her marriage has been fertile, she generally chooses to be married leviratically by an agnatic member of her deceased husband's family, a younger brother or a nephew, or anyone she can be given to without offending the lineage. Nevertheless she may refuse the levirate if she is unhappy with her family-in-law, does not have children or does not want them, or is in love with another man.

Consequently, the provision of the code giving a father-in-law the right to give his daughter-in-law to another son, apparently without asking anyone's opinion, does not fall under the levirate, strictly speaking. Whether her marriage was consummated or not, fertile or not, a woman belongs to her husband's lineage, which has the right to dispose of her as it sees fit, without her wishes being taken into account. Generally, though, it tends toward the woman's desires. If her marriage has been fecund and she is widowed and marries one of her children's uncles, she may have other children, who would then have the same kinship relations with him as her first children, since a paternal uncle is already the equivalent of a father; thus, nothing would change substantially in her children's status.

During the sixth century B.C., neo-Babylonian documents report marriages with the wife's sister, but do not state whether these were instances of sororate marriage or sororal polygyny. However, inasmuch as the sororate was already possible, these documents may attest that the polygynous union — that is, marriage with the wife's sister during the wife's lifetime — had become licit.

The reader who has followed me through this somewhat arid maze in an attempt to uncover hidden meaning in legal wordings (knowing who is speaking, the father-in-law or the son-in-law; knowing whether "he can" means "he must," "he may" or "he might") has grasped the importance attached to relations with two sisters, and sometimes with a mother and daughter, in Hittite and Assyrian antiquity.

The essential question revolves around marriage. As long as we are dealing with sororal polygyny or the sororate, choices and

43

preferences can be understood in the coolly economical terms of the Assyrian laws. But there is a sidestep, the first step in article 191 of the Hittite laws, which deliberately separates union with two sisters, or with a mother and daughter, from marriage and from adultery. There is no incest between either blood relatives or affines, but between an individual and a series of women related to *each other* but not to *him*. This very incongruity, since there is no economic or social justification for the prohibition but only a spatiotemporal one, leads us to think that this prohibition lies at the heart of our inquiry, for it is an ancient instance of incest of the second type, between blood relatives who do not have sexual relations with each other but share the same partner, introducing an inconceivable carnal intimacy between blood relatives, expressible only by innuendo.

The mode of thought we are trying to penetrate always involves institutional and social trimmings: marriage is what matters. Yet sometimes, as in the Hittite laws, a detail makes meaning shift, allowing a glimpse at the primacy of the symbolic.

CHAPTER TWO

What Do Greek Philosophy,

the Bible, and the Koran Say?

The idea of shared substances — secretions and fluids spread from body to body — raises the possibility of the existence of rules that have meaning only in the symbolic register while being rooted in the purely biological. We have just seen the only clear articulation of an incest prohibition that requires no previous alliance or consanguinity between the protagonists of the incestuous act. The very placement of this legal text amid those prohibiting and suppressing incest between blood relations or affines seems to me to suggest that not only was this text placed there for logical reasons, if these are indeed acts of the same nature, but because it allows one to understand the nature of the prohibition concerning identical individuals (in this case, relatives by marriage), namely, the wife's sister or mother.

Although the incest prohibition was not the object of legal regulation in Greece, strictly speaking, this was nevertheless where the theme of incest knew its greatest popularity and where the idea of two blood relations sharing a single partner was an obsession.

The Greek World, or Horrified Fascination

According to Hellenists, no Greek word explicitly refers to incest. Does this absence imply that incest was not an offense for the Greeks? Nothing could be less certain: the law prohibited marriage between full siblings[1] and siblings with the same mother, that is, between *phrater* and *adelphos*. Moreover, there is the Oedipus tragedy, which has been taken as the perfect model of incest of the first type since Freud. Nevertheless, the law did not prohibit marriage between siblings with the same father or between patrilateral parallel cousins, born of the father's, not the mother's, brothers, as in the marriages of the Danaids and Aegyptus' sons.

In Greek thought, to a certain extent, the father created and imposed the social tie while the mother alone created biological kinship. Is this the reason for the great legal void concerning these notions, though they provide the dramatic force of numerous literary works? The legal governs the social; it is easier to understand the fate of the epicleric daughter than illicit unions involving one's own flesh and blood; these are the topics of dreams, as though only by making its way into a dream could this desire be expressed.

In the second part of this book, where the notion of the identical is analyzed in greater depth, the ethnological data on sexual prohibitions show that it is more common for contact to be prohibited between cousins born of two sisters than between those born of two brothers, between a brother and sister with the same mother than between a brother and sister with the same father. Certainly, being born in the same womb is a factor, but so is being made of the same matter. In Greek thought, according to Aristotle,[2] who could neither ignore nor detach himself completely from the conceptual substratum of his epoch, the mother provides only the physical material, while the father, through sperm-*pneuma*, or "breath," provides form and movement, in other

46

words, life.[3] The anarchic growth and development of material not properly mastered by *pneuma* is even considered to be at the origins of deformity. The contact of identical material between a uterine brother and sister (incest of the first type) or between two sisters or a mother and daughter (incest of the second type) was considered the source of monstrous, irregular developments of feminine matter.

No Greek legal texts on this point have survived, so we must look elsewhere to discover what the Greeks thought about incest in its different forms.

In the *Republic* (571c–d), Plato observes that, during sleep, wherein the "beastly" and "savage" part of the soul is no longer controlled, "there is nothing it will not venture to undertake as being released from all sense of shame and all reason. It does not shrink from attempting to lie with a mother in fancy or with anyone else, man, god or brute. It is ready for any foul deed of blood; it abstains from no food, and, in a word, falls short of no extreme of folly and shamelessness."[4] Plato thereby likens a series of sexual offenses — sodomy, homosexuality, zoophilia, and sorcery (that is, illicit commerce with the gods) — to incest, which he links to murder and food taboos. This should not surprise us: a regulated diet forms the material of maternal flesh as much as the volatile essence of sperm, produced through the concoction of blood, which derives from the absorption of food (according to Aristotle).

In the *Laws* (838a–d) Plato includes a discussion of incest:

ATHENIAN: Even today, as you know, lawless as most men are, they are very effectually deterred from cohabitation with the fair, and not against their own will either, but with their full and entire consent.
MEGILLUS: Of what cases are you thinking?
ATHENIAN: Of persons who have a fair sister or brother [*adelphos*]. The same law, though unwritten, proves a complete safeguard of son

47

or daughter — so that no one lies with them, openly or covertly, or approaches them with any familiarities of that sort — nay the very wish for such congress never so much as enters the mind of the ordinary person.

MEGILLUS: True enough.

ATHENIAN: Well then, you see how all such lusts are extinguished by a mere phrase. [...] The saying that they are all unhallowed, abominations to God, deeds of black shame. The explanation must surely be that no one holds a different language about them. All of us, from our very cradles, are constantly hearing the same report of them from all quarters; we hear it alike from the lips of the buffoon, and again delivered with all the so-called solemnity of tragedy, on those many occasions when the stage presents us with a Thyestes, an Oedipus, or a Macareus, some character who acts the stealthy paramour to a sister and freely sentences himself to death for his crime on discovery.[5]

This text is of interest for two reasons. First, it clearly shows that the incest prohibition comes under "unwritten law" (*nomos agraphos*), that is, law that functions by paralipsis, so deeply rooted is it in people's minds that it need not be expressed. This paraliptical functioning frequently results in the most obvious and basic pieces of information being left out of an argument, because they go without saying. Thus, there may be a missing link between two facts, one of which is the consequence of the first, for a reason that is unspoken but understood by all, requiring no explicit formulation. Incest as an intellectual category, then, has no word to denote it in ancient Greek. It is described as "a deed of black shame," and each type of incest is indicated by an eponym: Oedipus, for incest of the first type in the first degree between a mother and her son; Macareus, for that of the first type in the second degree between a brother and his sister; and Thyestes,

48

for incest of the second type, sleeping with an older brother's wife. The punishment for each crime is the same: death.

Several textual references are also found in Sophocles' *Oedipus the King* (423–25 and 458), Aeschylus' *The Suppliant Maidens* (223–26), Plutarch's *Moralia* (chs. 83 and 101), Dio Chrysostomus (ch. 10.29), Artemidorus' *Oneirocritica* (fragment 79), and Ovid's *Metamorphoses*.[6]

Plutarch explains the absence of written law concerning incest by taking up the Platonic idea that the soul escapes during the night, its bestial and savage part indulging in all sorts of crimes, including incest between blood relations and food taboos, which one dares not mention during the day. There is no need to decree a law, since shame and fear suffice to contain these desires. As in Plato, the prohibition concerns the desire and its expression; consequently, the act is prevented rather than forbidden. In *Moralia* (ch. 83), the soul during sleep is naturally despotic: "'It attempts incest,' and feels a sudden hunger for a great variety of food, acting in lawless fashion, and giving loose rein to the desires which in the daytime the law keeps confined by means of shame and fear."

Similarly, Ovid describes a rite of nonhuman behavior in *Metamorphoses* 7.386–87: "And to the right Cyllene lay, the peak / where fate would have depraved Menephron mate / with his own mother — the incestuous way / of wild beasts."[7]

In Sophocles' *Oedipus the King* (458): "He shall be proved father and brother both / to his own children in his house; to her / that gave him birth, a son and husband both." We know what happens next. While Greece had no specific legal term to denote these familial unions which were *more ferarum*, "in the manner of savage beasts," we see that it condemns them unequivocally in its literary texts. In *Oedipus the King* again (423–25): "the multitude of other evils / establishing a grim equality /

49

between you and your children" certainly alludes to union with the mother.[8]

The idea that incest is not "against nature" but "against culture," that it is absolutely contrary to human nature to commit it, is found in Dio Chrysostomus (10.29): "Oedipus laments being both father and brother to his children, both husband and son to his wife, but cocks are not indignant at this, nor dogs, nor any birds."

In the *Oneirocritica*, Artemidorus devotes a passage to the dream of incest with the mother, which has different meanings depending on various positions of the bodies.[9]

Aeschylus' *The Suppliant Maidens* could be read as a reprobation of marriage between parallel patrilineal cousins: "Settle on the sacred ground like doves clustering together, fearing the winged hawks, who hatefully pollute their very blood." The Danaids were pursued by their patrilineal parallel cousins, the Egyptians; if such a union between cousins was considered so vile, one would be justified to assume marriage between siblings with the same father, and not only with the same mother, would be forbidden *a fortiori*. This type of incest is likened to omophagia, the eating of raw flesh: "Bird consumes bird, how could it be pure?"[10] Now, we know that the law did not forbid marriage between brothers and sisters with the same mother (*adelphos*). It seems hard to imagine, then, that a woman's union with a cousin, even a parallel patrilateral one, would actually be prohibited. But the Danaids' problem is more complicated than this: it is not one woman's union with her first cousin, but fifty sisters with fifty cousins. Therefore in this global, excessive, and hyperbolic union, each of the marriages taken alone does not arouse indignation because it conforms to the rule, whereas the group envisaged collectively brings the sisters' flesh into contact each time, since each is similar to all the others and touches all the others through the intermediary of their husbands, who are like brothers to them. Likewise, each brother encounters his brothers' substance through the intermediary of their wives, who are sisters and treated as identicals, or as a single body. Two such marriages would suffice for "bird to consume bird."

The absence of a specific term to denote incest and the existence of other unions considered "unhallowed" and "abominations" — because they are *more ferarum* — must not lead us to think that the Greeks linked incest, zoophilia, sorcery, and the transgression of food taboos and conclude that they did not have a notion of incest. Marriages between blood relations represent systems of inversion, whether divine (such as the union of Zeus and Hera, full siblings born of Chronos and Rhea) or royal (as in the dynasties of Sparta and Corinth). Far from being models of standard practice, these marriages were exceptions marked by their nonhuman character. Understanding these mythological features, therefore, does not mean that one must postulate primitive endogamy where all consanguineous unions would have been permitted.

The same goes for *epikleros*, the legal institution that obliged a girl without a brother to marry her deceased father's closest relative, so that the inheritance would not leave the family. She was required to marry either her father's brother, which was normally forbidden, or a parallel patrilateral cousin. This does not demonstrate that incest was not prohibited in Greece; rather, it is an exceptional case where what was normally forbidden was permitted against the grain. Therefore we cannot speak of a tension between two contradictory systems, between a desire to return to a primitive endogamy and a true horror of incest attested by *Oedipus the King*, the very prototype of incest of the first type.

As far as incest of the second type is concerned, outside of the

Platonic reference to Thyestes, we find its prototype in the tragedy of Phaedra. Theseus permits himself to love two sisters, Ariadne and Phaedra, but not at the same time, since he abandons
Ariadne (who saved him from the labyrinth) on the island of Naxos
before marrying her sister Phaedra:

"O sister Ariadne! Through love, once more,
You died abandoned on a barren shore"[11]

Here the prohibition against union with two sisters in the
same place and at the same time is respected. But Ariadne has
given Theseus a son, Hippolytus, who is terrified of Phaedra's
love for him. An affair with her during his father's lifetime would
cause two consanguineous men, a father and son, to meet in the
same womb.

Another example of incest of the second type can be found in
book six of Ovid's *Metamorphoses*. (The author, though Latin, is
quoted here because he examines Greek mythology and thought.)
The relationships involve Procne and Philomela, who are sisters,
and Tereus, Procne's husband. The sister-in-law, raped by her
brother-in-law, cries (6.533–41): "What have you done, barbar-
ian! / My father's plea and his fond tears, the love / my sister feels
for you, and, too, my own / virginity; your bonds of marriage —
none / of these could move you. All is now askew. / I am a concubine, and you've become / a bigamist; it's only right for Procne/
to punish me like any enemy. / Why don't you, to complete your
treachery, / tear out my soul? Would you had murdered me /
before this wretched coupling! Then, at least, / my Shade would
be unstained."[12] Through Tereus, Philomela has committed incest
with her sister. She has become her sister's "rival," and Tereus has
become the husband of two sisters.

Further on, Philomela threatens, "But if the gods / of heaven

52

see these things, if deities / still have some power, if my loss of honor / does not mean all is lost, then you — someday — / will pay" (541–44).[13] This quote could not be clearer. Antoninus Liberalis developed an analogous plot in his *Metamorphoses*, except that the two girls' father punishes his son-in-law for having sex with both sisters at once.

In *On the Mysteries* (124), Andocides writes: "Callias married a daughter of Ischomachus but he had not even lived with her for a year, before he took up with her mother [here it is not a matter of two sisters, but of daughter and mother], and he, the most wicked of all men, lived with the mother and the daughter, when a priest of the Mother and the Daughter, and kept them both in his house!" In line 125 he writes, "He felt no shame, nor did he fear the two goddesses, but Ischomachus' daughter thought it better to be dead than alive and seeing what was happening, tried to hang herself." Two accusations weigh upon him: being a priest to two divinities at once, a mother and daughter, to whom he owed respect, and engaging in sexual relations in his home with his wife and his wife's mother, an outrage to the goddesses, as well as mother-daughter incest. Ischomachus' daughter thus attempted to hang herself, but was "taken down and put to bed. When she recovered, she ran away from the house and the mother drove out the daughter. When he in turn had enough of the mother he threw her out, too. She then said she was pregnant by him, but when she gave birth to a son, he denied that the child was his."[14]

This "most wicked of all men" ministered to two goddesses, mother and daughter, and having taken a wife, seduced her mother. His wife was forced to flee, after attempting suicide, which would have put an end to the impossible contact of identical flesh. When the mother was pregnant by him, outside of marriage, he refused to acknowledge his paternity. "After this, gentlemen, he fell in love again with the old battleaxe ... he both received her back

53

into his house and introduced the boy, now a grown lad, to the
Ceryces, declaring he was his son" (127). "Well then, gentlemen,
let us consider whether such a thing has ever happened before
among the Greeks, that a man married a woman, then married
the mother in addition to the daughter" — in the same place and
at the same time — "and the mother drove out the daughter; then,
while living with the mother, he wants to marry the daughter of
Epilycus, so that the granddaughter might drive out the grandmother" (128). We can deduce from this that Epilycus is his first
wife's brother, and thus that Callias, not content with the infa-
mous and base acts already committed, also desired, no doubt at
an advanced age, to marry Epilycus's daughter, who is simultaneously the first wife's niece and his second's granddaughter
(figure 1).

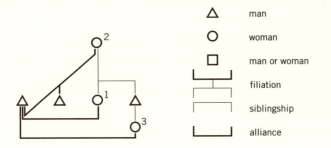

Figure 1.

"Further, what on earth should we call his son? (128). I myself
do not think there is anybody so good at reasoning as to work out
his name" (129) — he is at once his father's son by his mother, his
father's brother-in-law by his father's first wife, and his father's
wife's uncle — "for there are three women with whom his father
will have lived, and he is the son of one, so it is said, brother of

another, and uncle of the third" (129). "Who would he be himself? Oedipus or Aegisthus, or what should we call him?" (129).
The formulation of the question itself is interesting. Oedipus or
Aegisthus? They are emblematic figures of two symmetrical in-
cests on different levels: mother-son incest in one case, father-
daughter incest in the other. The case of Callias' son would be
similar to that of Aegisthus, also born of an incestuous union
between Thyestes and his daughter Pelopia (Thyestes is already
guilty of incest of the second type, as we have seen in Plato);
Pelopia then becomes the wife of his brother Atreus. Given this
relationship, it is difficult to see why there would be doubt as to
whether Callias' son is more like Oedipus or Aegisthus. Aegisthus
is indeed born of father-daughter incest, but he did not kill his
father and marry his mother as Oedipus did. If the text compares
Aegisthus and Oedipus, paraliptically, without having to explain
the comparison, in order better to understand the status of Callias' son, it is by elision and omission of essential points of the
story. Aegisthus is indeed comparable to Oedipus, not because he
is the fruit of consanguineous incest (that is the first part of his
story) but because he is also the lover, then husband, of Clytem-
nestra, the wife of his uterine brother Agamemnon, and finally
the murderer of this same brother. It is through this incest of the
second type, followed by a murder (the second part of his story),
that he is comparable to Oedipus. If Oedipus indeed represents
the prototypical unhappy participant in incest of the first type,
Aegisthus, who is, of course, the fruit of a symmetrical father-
daughter incest, is an absolutely conscious participant, like Callias,
in incest of the second type. The question — Oedipus or Aegisthus? — seems to me to underscore the difference between the
two unnamed types of incest, through a sort of telescoping of the
underlying elements of the comparison:

55

- incest of the first type, mother-son, committed unknowingly by Oedipus
- incest of the first type, father-daughter, committed knowingly by Thyestes, of which Aegisthus is the fruit
- incest of the second type, brother-in-law and sister-in-law, in which Aegisthus is a conscious actor
- murder of the father committed unknowingly by Oedipus
- murder of the uterine brother committed knowingly by Aegisthus

Though the Greek texts that explicitly mention the particular incest I call incest of the second type are not numerous, they are eloquent. As seen through the great classical tragedies and the epics, the Greek world is full of stories of incestuous love, murder, vengeance, and punishment. Incest of the first type is certainly a thematic obsession, but if one looks closely, several literary examples (the Danaids, Procne and Philomela, Callias) show that the idea of incest of the second type is also present in Greek thought; though not explicit, the sharing in common of the same sexual partner by two blood relations of the same sex (and, in the case of the Danaids, the sharing of the same by the multiple) can be found. Hellenists could no doubt provide other examples.

Of course, the prohibition is not inscribed in law, and this particular incest, while rooted in people's minds and imaginations, is barely formulated ("Bird consumes bird, how could it be pure?"). Something is immediately grasped in this metaphor and in well-known stories conjured simply by quoting certain names.

In an entirely different, implacably logical spirit, these situations will be dealt with in Leviticus and Deuteronomy, biblical texts of a legal nature, and in the Talmud.

The Horror of the Same: The Bible and the Talmud

In the biblical world, one man's marriage to two sisters did not seem to incite reprobation, since Jacob married Leah and Rachel in Genesis (29:18–28), while Samson had two sisters as wives in Judges (15:2) (though what may have been allowed with daughters of Philistines may not have been with his own people).

What remains is the amazing story of Jacob, who married Leah and Rachel, daughters of his uncle Laban, his mother's brother. Nothing in this story is simple. In love with Rachel, Jacob worked for his uncle for seven years as a shepherd in order to marry her. On the wedding night, after seven years save one week, Laban substituted his older daughter Leah, who was physically flawed (she had bad eyesight) for his younger one; he offered his son-in-law the younger one as well at the end of the remaining week, provided Jacob work another seven years without pay. Laban gave a servant to each of his daughters. Leah, the unloved (or the "hated" one, as certain translations say) conceived four sons to the great vexation and shame of Rachel, who offered her servant to her husband in order to have a son by her (Gen. 30:3–8). The servant bore Jacob two sons. Leah, who stopped giving birth, offered her servant to Jacob in turn, and this servant also bore two sons. In the "great struggle" between the two sisters, the score was not even. One day, Leah's oldest son, Reuben, found some mandrakes and gave them to his mother. Rachel asked her sister for one, and she agreed, in exchange for a night with Jacob (it was Rachel's turn). Leah thus bought the right to spend the night with her husband. She conceived another son that night, then another son and a daughter. It was only then that "God remembered Rachel...and opened her womb" (Gen. 30:22).[15] She gave birth to Joseph. Rachel was finally a mother, not by proxy.

The case of Jacob marrying two sisters, his cousins, is strange on more than one level. When he saw Rachel at the well and learned from the shepherds that she was Laban's daughter, he watered his uncle's sheep, a gesture symmetrical to Rebekah's watering Isaac's camels and becoming his wife. Then "Jacob told Rachel that he was *her father's brother* and that he was Rebekah's son" (Gen. 29:12). Hearing this, Laban happily welcomed him: "Surely thou art *my bone and my flesh*" (Gen. 29: 14 [emphasis added]).

From this sentence and the preceding variation that describes the kinship relation (Rebekah's son) and the subsequent appellation between the two men (brother), we can infer that the kinship system was matrilineal, probably complete, with appellations of the Crow type, since a woman's brother and her son have a fraternal relationship and this fraternity is expressed by the strong and complete metaphor of flesh and bone. Both flesh and bone are transmitted in uterine line, whereas, in other places and according to other systems of thought, these essential elements that make up the body could be transmitted separately by either of the two parents. This type of kinship system renders the custom of marriage with the female matrilateral cross-cousin, whose status is equivalent to "daughter" for Ego, uncertain, though not impossible.

The geographical distance (Isaac, Rebekah, and her sons live with Abimelech, king of the Philistines, and Isaac sends his son Jacob to find a wife in the country of his mother's father) and the temporal distance (Esau, the older brother, was already forty years old when he married Hittite women, which distressed Rebekah and later prompted Isaac to send Jacob, the younger brother, to marry in the land of the Patriarchs) result in a rupture in mutual knowledge, an absence of familiarity between the two branches of the family: the one descended from Laban, and the one descended from his sister Rebekah and Isaac. Jacob must introduce himself. He is a relative, but he is also a stranger, which perhaps (but only perhaps) suggests that familial estrangement made unions possible that daily contact would have made impossible. Moreover, Jacob was expected to do a substantial amount of work, more fitting for a stranger than a relative, or, inversely, something a relative would ask to do to act like a stranger.

Here we find something of the Hittite law's "in the same place" — which prohibited commerce with two sisters in the same place, since it implied knowledge of kinship ties — but it is given another meaning. Not having been brought up in the same place, blood relatives could now unite. But does this authorize Jacob's relationship with two sisters? If it is not considered totally reprehensible, something about Laban's trickery and this double marriage displeases God, since He makes the infirm and unloved Leah fertile, to the detriment of her sister.

There are several cases in the Bible of a man's union with two sisters at the same time, but under the particular and exceptional circumstances that I have just recounted. Otherwise, Leviticus is categorical: marriage with the sister of the deceased or divorced wife (the sororate) is authorized, while union with two sisters in the same place and at the same time (sororal polygny) is forbidden.

Chapter 18 of Leviticus deals expressly with incest and other sexual offenses, starting with verse 6:

6. None of you shall approach to any that is near of kin to him [i. e., a blood relation], to uncover their nakedness.

7. The nakedness of thy father, or the nakedness of thy mother, shalt thou not uncover: she is thy mother; thou shalt not uncover her nakedness.

8. The nakedness of thy father's wife shalt thou not uncover: it is *thy father's nakedness.*

9. The nakedness of thy sister, the daughter of thy father, or daughter of thy mother, whether she be born at home, or born abroad, even their nakedness thou shalt not uncover.

10. The nakedness of thy son's daughter, or of thy daughter's daughter, even their nakedness thou shalt not uncover: for theirs is *thine own nakedness.*

11. The nakedness of thy father's wife's daughter, begotten of thy father, she is thy sister, thou shalt not uncover her nakedness.

12. Thou shalt not uncover the nakedness of thy father's sister: she is thy father's near kinswoman.

13. Thou shalt not uncover the nakedness of thy mother's sister: for she is *thy mother's near kinswoman.*

14. Thou shalt not uncover the nakedness of thy father's brother, thou shalt not approach to his wife: she is thine aunt.

15. Thou shalt not uncover the nakedness of thy daughter in law: she is thy son's wife; thou shalt not uncover her nakedness.

16. Thou shalt not uncover the nakedness of thy brother's wife: it is *thy brother's nakedness.*

17. Thou shalt not uncover the nakedness of *a woman* and *her daughter,* neither shalt thou take her son's daughter, or her daughter's daughter, to uncover her nakedness; for *they are her near kinswomen*: it is wickedness.

18. Neither shalt thou take a wife to her sister, to vex her, to uncover her nakedness, beside the other in her life time. [Emphases added.][16] (See figure 2.)

I have made it a rule to take the texts literally (having compared several translations in French and English). In these verses from Leviticus that explicitly refer to a number of forbidden women, or implicitly refer to them — as in verse 6, which is valid for a man's daughter, her full sister, or uterine sister (who otherwise would not be prohibited to Ego); Leviticus mentions only the agnatic sister clearly and precisely in verse 11 — what must be understood are the meaning of the expressions "uncovering the nakedness," "the nakedness of thy father," "thine own nakedness,"

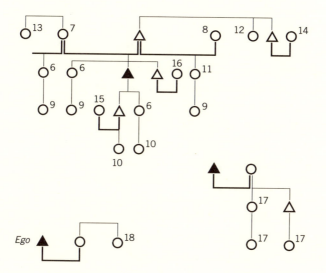

Figure 2.

"thy father's near kinswoman," "thy mother's," "thy brother's," and so on, and the emphatic association of nakedness with one's own flesh.

Why does the father's nakedness, formulated differently in verses 7 and 8, come into play? This is not the expression of a prohibition against sexual relations between the father and the son. What is denounced here is indeed an incest of another type, the existence of which I am attempting to establish. The "nakedness" that one uncovers does not literally signify the body seen or glimpsed, but the *intimacy of the unveiled body*, one's own flesh touched. In sleeping with his mother or his father's wife, Ego "knows" his father's flesh, which is also his own flesh, that of his father's brother, his brother, his son or his daughter. If not for verse 13, which condemns the relationship with the mother's sister, for

61

she is the mother's own flesh, one might think the mother was not forbidden as a blood relation, situated in the general framework of verse 6. While she is her son's blood relation, she is not related to him in the same way as the other female blood relations cited, but as the father's wife. By sleeping with her son, she places the carnal substances and sexual fluids of the father and son into contact with each other. The incest is seen as twofold: to uncover the nakedness of the father's wife, that is, to penetrate her body and leave one's seed there, is to discover the nakedness of the father by encountering the paternal seed.

The verses are quite eloquent if one understands them in this sense: the nakedness of the brother's wife is that of the brother (verse 16), the nakedness of the mother's sister is the "flesh" of the mother (verse 13; double incest of the first type). The crux of these incestuous relationships of the second type — a man's sexual relations with the wives of his blood relations — is a short-circuit, an idea clearly evoked in direct line (incest of the first type) in verse 10. But this case is prototypical of what is ultimately touched in incest of the second type, namely an identical substance and therefore one's own substance: in uncovering the nakedness of his father's wife, of his father's brother, of his brother, of his son, Ego carries out a chain of incestuous acts and, beyond the nakedness of his father, uncovers his own nakedness, which refers to another sexual offense, masturbation, not condemned in Leviticus but forbidden elsewhere.

It is telling that verses 17 and 18 are grouped with the verses we have just analyzed. Verses 17 and 18 no longer concern incestuous acts committed by a man with blood relations, or with the wives of blood relations through agnatic descent, as in the preceding verses, but instead concern forbidden sexual or matrimonial unions with the wife's female relatives and blood relations.

Why this distinction? Like the Hittite law, Leviticus states its decrees from the male viewpoint. Verses 17 and 18 are simply the reciprocal of verse 16. Verse 18, for example, implies that a woman cannot marry her sister's husband; in the same vein, verse 17 implies that a woman cannot sleep with her mother's husband or her grandmother's husband — symmetrically, prohibitions concerning the father's wife or the son's or daughter's granddaughters.

These bans are stated for a man, but they in fact introduce the recognition, or the denial, if one prefers, of a feminine Ego, that is, a woman's point of view. All the preceding bans must be understood in a reciprocal manner for women, which goes without saying, as in verses 16 and 18. By inference, if a man cannot cohabit with his uterine sister's daughter, a woman cannot have sexual relations with her mother's uterine brother.

What, then, makes the enunciation of verses 17 and 18 necessary? Verse 17 is necessary because it does not, strictly speaking, have a reciprocal; verse 18 is necessary because it introduces matrimonial alliance in place of the simple sexual relationship. The formulation is clearly different from that of the other verses: "Neither shalt thou take a wife to her sister, to vex her ... beside the other in her life time." "To vex her" must be understood in the sense of a rival, or "co-wife," whom Ego would present to his wife during her lifetime. One should not conclude too hastily that the incestuous acts forbidden in the preceding verses might no longer be forbidden after the death of the blood relation who created the tie. The reason for the reciprocity is simply obscured: two sisters who share the same sexual partner enter into a mutual relationship with their own flesh by means of this partner. What holds for two sisters also holds for mother and daughter, grandmother and granddaughter. But, just as levirate was the rule, sororate was allowed, hence the necessity to formulate verse 18 in these terms; it was not possible to have a second marriage with one's deceased wife's daughter or granddaughter.

Leviticus seems to proceed by association, coupling verses that follow one another and that, in the very fact of following one another, designate a point of convergence. After verse 18, which concerns the "two sisters," come verses (19–21) that condemn coitus during menstruation (touching impure blood, or placing blood the woman has lost back into her womb?), simple adultery, and infidelity to one's god, a sort of spiritual adultery, by sacrificing one's children to Molech.

That there is a parallel to be made between these verses seems confirmed by the succession of the following verses, in which the condemnation of male homosexuality (verse 22) is immediately followed by a prohibition of zoophilia for men as well as for women (verse 23).

Chapter 18 of Leviticus thus enumerates a series of sexual offenses, first between relatives, then of another nature, through strange associations: homosexuality and zoophilia, adultery and infidelity to one's god, prohibition of two sisters and menstrual impurity. Verse 24 places all these decrees under the same term: abominations that defiled earlier nations. Yet these proscriptions are not moral laws, like Lev. 19:1–37, which, for example, order one not to reap the borders of one's harvest so as to leave something for the poor, not to blaspheme the name of Yahweh, not to oppress (rob) one's neighbor, not to curse the deaf or put stumbling blocks before the blind. Certain commandments, such as not sleeping with a man or a beast, or with a woman who has her period, might have been included here. They were not, because they are linked to the matrimonial laws.

What Leviticus prohibits in chapter 18, it punishes in chapter 20. The gradation of punishments for these crimes follows the same sequence as the various sexual offenses encountered in chapter 18. Lev. 20:10–21 reads:

10. And the man that committeth adultery with another man's wife [...] the adulterer and the adulteress shall surely be put to death.

11. And the man that lieth with his father's wife hath uncovered his father's nakedness: both of them shall surely be put to death; their blood shall be upon them.

12. And if a man lie with his daughter in law, both of them shall surely be put to death: they have wrought confusion; their blood shall be upon them.

13. If a man also lie with mankind, as he lieth with a woman, both of them have committed an abomination: they shall surely be put to death; their blood shall be upon them.

14. And if a man take a wife and her mother, it is wickedness: they shall be burnt with fire, both he and they; that there be no wickedness among you.

15. And if a man lie with a beast, he shall surely be put to death: and ye shall slay the beast.

16. And if a woman approach unto any beast, and lie down thereto, thou shalt kill the woman, and the beast: they shall surely be put to death; their blood shall be upon them.

17. And if a man shall take his sister, his father's daughter, or his mother's daughter, and see her nakedness, and she see his nakedness; it is a wicked thing; and they shall be cut off in the sight of their people: he hath uncovered his sister's nakedness; he shall bear his iniquity.

18. And if a man shall lie with a woman having her sickness, and shall uncover her nakedness; he hath discovered her fountain, and she hath uncovered the fountain of her blood: and both of them shall be cut off from among their people.

19. And thou shalt not uncover the nakedness of thy mother's sister, nor of thy father's sister: for he uncovereth *his near kin*: they shall bear their iniquity. [Emphasis added.]

20. And if a man shall lie with his uncle's wife, he hath uncovered his uncle's nakedness; they shall bear their sin; they shall die childless.

21. And if a man shall take his brother's wife, it is an unclean thing: he hath uncovered his brother's nakedness; they shall be childless.

Here again one may note the alternation of verses on forms of incest and other sexual offenses. We start with adultery. Incest of the second type with the father's wife (verse 11) or the son's wife (verse 12) is followed, not surprisingly, by a verse that condemns homosexuality. Confusion or abomination, these crimes are punished by death, the nature of which is not described. It is the encounter of identicals: father and son are of the same flesh, just as, more generally, two men are of the same nature, which allows one to broaden incest of the second type to include common adultery, on the one hand, and homosexuality, on the other.

Verse 14, which concerns a man's sexual union with a mother and her daughter, is joined to the two verses on zoophilia. The first offense, a prototype of incest of the second type, is called "wickedness," which seems to be more serious than a man's sleeping with female relatives by marriage, such as his father's or son's wife. Indeed, it calls for a death sentence. That the penalty is death by fire is not insignificant, quite the contrary; since the same on the same represents a short-circuit of heat, the damage can only be repaired by the same, that is, fire. It is a sort of homeopathic remedy.

The connection between verses 14 through 16, like that between verses 11 through 13, is not chance. It follows the subterranean and obscure progressions of associative thought, which already appeared in the preceding chapter. To sleep with a mother and her daughter indiscriminately is bestiality, on the same level as the apparently indiscriminate behavior of animals themselves.

Verses 17 through 19 go together in the same way, even if the penalty is not as clearly indicated in verse 19 as in the two verses preceding it. Touching one's sister, one's father's sister, or one's mother's sister, according to verse 17, is like "uncovering one's near kin," touching one's own flesh. "It is a wicked thing, and they shall be cut off." Likewise, in verse 18, sleeping with a woman during her period calls for the same punishment: She touches her own substance, her blood, which he causes to flow back into her. Thus, the woman touches her own flesh, so they must be "cut off."

The similarity of the punishment once again implies the similarity of the sins, consanguineous incest and sexual offense, just as previous parallels were established between incest with women allied in direct line and homosexuality, and between incest with a girl and her mother and bestiality.

Incest of the first type, between blood relations, seems less serious than incest of the second type, since the latter is punishable by death by fire, while the former results in being "cut off," the meaning of which varies among interpreters. According to W. Kornfeld,[17] it is public execution for an offense of a sexual or religious nature, but Edouard Dhorme[18] has described this punishment as public prosecution. This is the case in certain African populations, which punish incest and related sexual offenses such as necrophilia not by execution but by execration. The guilty, or presumed guilty, are stripped and exhibited in the market place, and chickens are sacrificed over their genitals. Then the outcasts are sent into the bush (a near equivalent to being condemned to death). According to Dhorme, public condemnation might involve stoning — especially for women — and therefore, but not necessarily, death.

The concept of being cut off has yet another connotation: sterility. This is how Kornfeld explains the prohibition of leviratic marriages with the brother's wife or father's second wife. Indeed, before the brother's or father's death, it would be adultery. Now, adultery is forbidden and punished by death. What is true during the brother's or father's lifetime continues to be true after their death, but in attenuated fashion. The forbidden contact no longer has the same virulence. It is "defilement" — not "confusion" or "abomination" — which is punished by sterility rather than death.

Furthermore, according to Kornfeld, the expression "their blood shall be upon them" means that the guilty are responsible for their own fate. If they are put to death, they themselves are responsible for their death and not those who execute them. In a way, by committing their sin, they are the ones who make the blood spill from their bodies. They are guilty of their crime and responsible for their death. But this expression might also mean that they have committed sexual offenses that involve placing the identical on the identical. They have touched their own blood; they have placed it on themselves.

In any case, these are perverted acts that Yahweh execrates. Proof is found in the series of maledictions enumerated in Deuteronomy 27:20–26. Cursed are those who sleep with their father's wife, "with any manner of beast," with their sister, or with their wife's mother. Here again, the crime of zoophilia is inserted amid various types of incest, as was done in Leviticus, and we may also be reminded of the bestial impulses of the oneiric soul evoked by Plato.

Deuteronomy 28:21–24 describes the extreme nature of these maledictions. Man is cursed in all his undertakings:

> 21. The Lord shall make the pestilence cleave unto thee, until he have consumed thee from off the land, whither thou goest to possess it.

22. The Lord shall smite thee with a consumption, and with a fever, and with an inflammation, and with an extreme burning, and with the sword, and with blasting, and with mildew; and they shall pursue thee until thou perish.

23. And thy heaven that is over thy head shall be brass, and the earth that is under thee shall be iron.

24. The Lord shall make the rain of thy land powder and dust: from heaven shall it come down upon thee, until thou be destroyed.

All these scourges are characterized by their excessive heat and burning. Sword, or blasting, and mildew are plant pathologies that blight vegetables and make them unfit for consumption. Without rain, the world will be reduced to dust and bear no fruit for the cursed.

Further on we will see that this apocalyptic picture of a world devastated by fire and desiccation is a consequence of the ungodly encounter between two things that are identical in nature (incest) or two things that are totally different in essence (bestiality). In other systems of thought, the consequences of these lapses in behavior were thought instead to produce excessive rains, tornadoes, hurricanes, and floods. For the Hebrews, this machinery dries out human secretions and the earth's moisture.

Locusts consume the fruit of the land, sons and daughters go into captivity, bodies are afflicted "with the botch of Egypt, and with the emerods, and with the scab, and with the itch" (verse 27), which are incurable, and "in the knees, and in the legs, with a sore botch that cannot be healed" (verse 35). Emerods, scab, itch, and botch are skin diseases that indicate ailments within the body's humors: sores and the itch are solidified oozings, the scab an infection caused by worms digging canals beneath the skin, resulting in unhealable wounds.

Numerous other maledictions affect the fruit of man's labor,

69

the fruit of his loins, his freedom to act. Above all, he will be pushed to such extremes of poverty that he will be reduced to endocannibalism: "And thou shalt eat the fruit of thine own body, the flesh of thy sons and of thy daughters [...], in the siege, and in the straitness, wherewith thine enemies shall distress thee" (verse 53). Men and women, even the most delicate, will want to feed on the flesh of their spouses and children.

Therefore, incest and the crimes associated with it cause the disappearance of kinship, family (or sense of family), and solidarity, and give rise to a sinister covetousness and murder. On this disastrous landscape, extreme drought kills animals and plants, everything that emerges from the earth, while making the human body sweat out the humors it should preserve within it.

The laws of Leviticus and Deuteronomy enumerate and condemn the types of incest we are attempting to understand, but further elaboration must be sought on the peripheries of the texts: in their construction and in the real meaning of the words chosen.

Talmudic law repeats and refines Leviticus by insisting particularly on the possibility of union with two sisters. The Talmud adds that after divorcing or repudiating one's wife, marrying her sister is impossible, which was not specified earlier.[19] The Mishnah Yebamoth (ch. 4.13) does not expressly say that a man cannot marry the sister of the wife he is separated from, but implies it through the principle of *expressio unus est suppressio alterius*, "to express one is to suppress the other." Indeed, three cases are provided for: he can marry his wife's sister, if his wife is dead, or if he has divorced her and she dies, or if he has divorced her, she has remarried and she dies. In all cases, a man's wife must be dead in order for him to be able to marry her sister. Remarriage does not suppress the earlier alliance; only death can do so.

The Talmud merely mentions the infraction of sexual congress with a mother and her daughter. It is concerned primarily with the prohibition of two sisters, which it extends to include half-siblings.

Consider, for example, a series of marriages dissolved by death or repudiation. A man marries a woman, then another after the first has died or he has divorced her; his second wife marries another man after his own death or because he has repudiated her in turn; her second husband marries another woman after her death or repudiation once again; this other women marries another man after the death of her preceding husband or his repudiation of her. Suppose a daughter was produced by each of these unions. The daughters of the first (1) and second marriage (2) of Ego's father are agnatic sisters; those of the father's second marriage (2) and the second wife's remarriage with another man (3) are sisters through their mother; those of this remarriage with another man (3) and the subsequent marriage (4) and the remarriage of the widowed or divorced wife of this marriage (5) are sisters through their mother. As a result, the brother of (1) cannot marry (2), whose agnatic brother he is, but can marry (3) with whom he has no tie of kinship although (2) and (3) are sisters. On the other hand, the brother of (2) cannot marry (3) whose half-brother he is through the mother, but he can marry (4) with whom he has no tie of kinship and who is nevertheless the agnatic half-sister of (3). And so on. The Talmud examines ad infinitum all the cases in which it is permitted or not permitted to marry two sisters, by emphasizing the lack of transitivity in these relationships, which testifies to a perfect mastery of the rules of kinship, that is, consanguinity and alliance. (See figure 3.)

These *jeux d'esprit* prove, moreover, that if the (half-) sister of my (half-) sister is not my (half-) sister, it is because we do not share the same blood, the same fluids, the same substance. (1) and (3) do not have substantial identity between them, although they

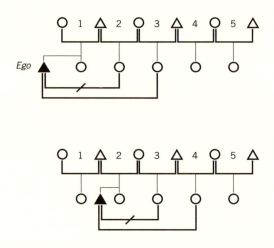

Figure 3.

share the substance of (2), but not in the same way — through their common father for (1) and through their common mother for (3). If a man can successively marry (1), (3), and (5), he can only marry (2) after the death of (1), but then he cannot marry (3); likewise, if he then marries (4) he cannot marry (5). In other words, the prohibition of two sisters during their lifetime is still the rule. (See figure 4.)

The Talmud makes us aware of the particular interest accorded one man's union with two sisters (which could also be two brothers' union with two sisters) as the original form of incest of the second type. To sum up, several cases are possible: the marriage is licit; it is sororal polygyny; the marriage is illicit, if the first marriage is still in effect or the first wife is alive, whatever her fate (repudiated, repudiated and remarried, etc.).

We will not deal with cases in which this marriage is licit, because its effects are supposed to be beneficial, but more partic-

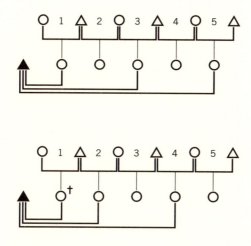

Figure 4.

ularly with the variations around the theme of licitness, when the first marriage is no longer intact but the wife is still alive.

Before closing this chapter, let us consider the Islamic world and its law.

The Koran and Its Subtleties

The Koran provides a text — the first such we have examined here — that obliges the reader to consider not only higher moral principles, but, as I hope to demonstrate, the act of coitus itself, the sexual act, the transfer of fluids from one body to another.

In the Koran, sura 4 (on "Women"), verse 20, stipulates: "You shall not marry the women whom your fathers married: all previous marriages excepted. That was an evil practice, indecent and abominable." Verse 21 adds: "Forbidden to you are your mothers, your daughters, your sisters, your paternal and maternal aunts, the daughters of your brothers and sisters, your foster-mothers,

73

your foster-sisters, the mothers of your wives, the stepdaughters who are in your charge, born of the wives with whom you have lain (it is no offence if you have not consummated your marriage with their mothers), and the wives of your own begotten sons. You are also forbidden to take in marriage two sisters at one and the same time: all previous such marriages excepted."[20]

We are back on familiar territory. Except for the kinship created by milk, which makes its first appearance with the wet nurses, foster-mothers and foster-sisters, the prohibitions quoted above are similar to those we have already encountered, which should not be surprising, at least as far as the Semitic literatures are concerned.

Here again, the point of view is still centered on masculine Ego and follows a generational order. One cannot marry a mother and her daughter, an older sister and her younger one, although for the sake of logical coherence (which would be incompatible with the principle of male primacy) the statement should have read: "It is forbidden for a woman to marry her mother's husband, if this marriage has been consummated, and it is forbidden for a woman to marry her sister's husband." Because this is not possible ideologically, the prohibition of two sisters, as well as that concerning a mother and daughter, are both specifically formulated for a man. But that is where the Koran, in its subtlety, offers us a key to understanding not only these particular prohibitions but the others we have examined as well. The man cannot marry a daughter from his wife's first marriage whom he is raising in his home; he can marry her only if he has not cohabited with her mother ("it is no offence if you have not consummated your marriage"). One may note that these are not the daughters of a woman who was married, divorced, and remarried, daughters he would not have raised in his home.

How should we interpret this? The consummation of the union

in the strict sense is the sexual act and the ensuing circulation of fluids from one body to another, bodies that touch each other and interpenetrate. Co-wives of different origins thus know each other carnally through the intermediary of the common husband, who distributes the same semen to each woman and transports something from each woman to the other. This is not possible when two people share identical substance, and, implicitly, the short-circuit of the identical is supposed to have devastating effects.

Similarly, the ban on taking wives "from your own begotten sons" certainly emphasizes identical male substance in procreation. Koranic law has known variations urged by the Prophet himself, who suppressed filiation by adoption because he was in love with the wife of an adopted son. Since he was the Prophet, his love could be neither incestuous nor adulterous, but as he could not edict a rule for his use alone, such marriages became lawful. Until then all sons, whether by blood or adoption, had been treated in the same way, substantial identity coming from common foods.[21]

Knowing of the Prophet's love, the adoptive son divorced his wife so that the Prophet could marry her: "And when Zayd [the adoptive son] divorced his wife, We gave her to you in marriage, so that it should become legitimate for true believers to wed the wives of their adoptive sons if they divorced them" (sura 33, verse 37). Verse 38 adds: "No blame shall be attached to the Prophet for doing what is sanctioned for him by God." Thus the identity of substance that exists between a father and the son born of his semen is clearly outlined, an identity that does not exist with the adoptive son, or rather an identity previously supposed, in Arab law, to have formed as a result of living together, sharing food, and speaking the same language; this is challenged by the will of the Prophet.

Beyond prohibitions involving consanguinity (mothers, daughters, sisters, aunts, nieces) and alliance (wives' daughters or sisters, sons' wives), there is a prohibition concerning foster mothers and sisters, that is, wet nurses and girls who have had the same wet nurse as Ego. This prohibition is reciprocal; a daughter cannot marry her milk brother, nor a wet nurse her milk son. What, on the other hand, of the relationship between a daughter and her wet nurse's husband? The rule is provided by a saying found in the entire Arab world which governs milk kinship: "Woman's milk comes from man's semen." Consequently, a man may not marry his wife's milk daughters, who have something of his substance.

Since Aristotle, medical writers have not ceased to remark that married women have more abundant periods than young girls, which they explain by the contribution of spermatic substance. In the nineteenth century, Doctor Virey wrote that a man's sperm induced this abundance of menses, to the point that when this contribution became excessive, women were transformed into viragoes, that is, they behaved like men.[22] Another observation, which is the basis of the Muslim saying "Woman's milk comes from man's semen," is that there is no milk until giving birth and no giving birth until coitus.[23] Coitus causes abundant menstrual cycles in married women, semen turning to blood in women's bodies; but when the woman is pregnant, and then breast-feeds, the infusion of semen is transformed into milk.

All of this — particularly the logic governing the movement of secretions — will be considered in the third part of this book. For now, let us simply appreciate the Hittite distinction between women related to each other but not to their partner and the women related to this partner (all of whom were forbidden to him in the same way) and the Koranic distinction between consummated and unconsummated union, which prohibited subsequent alliance with the wife's daughter in the first instance while permitting it in the second.

Among the Hittites, the unity of substance between women is underscored; in the Koran, emphasis is placed on the sexual relationship that brings the feminine identities of the mother and daughter into contact. In each case, the content is the same, and the truth is defined allusively.

CHAPTER THREE

One Flesh

In the religious and legal proscriptions we have considered up until now — from the Hittite laws to Koranic law by way of Greek thought and various Hebraic texts — the taboo against "two sisters" has begun to emerge, testifying both to an implicit logic of identity and difference and to the preeminence of the masculine, since every text we have examined has been stated from the male point of view. The expression "two sister incest" connotes both the substantial identity of two women sharing common ancestry — that is, having either their mother and father in common or just their mother, or, more rarely, only their father in common — and the fundamental asymmetry of relations between the sexes, since this expression is never declined in the feminine. Though it exists, "two brother incest" is not perceived as such but as incest committed by a man with his brother's wife.

Let us continue our historical inquiry in the Christian world, after a brief incursion into Rome.

Rome, or Legality Mocked

In ancient Rome, the ban on marrying within one's kinship was inscribed in law. In direct line, the ban was limitless (although Roman life expectancy made it very unlikely for a great-grandfather to be alive at the same time as his pubescent great-granddaughter). In collateral line, the prohibition also bears on three generations, starting with a common ancestor, namely, six degrees Roman (i.e., to second cousins). These prohibitions concern cognate kinship, that is, kinship uniting persons through chains made up of both men and women. We have inherited the Roman kinship system, so ours is also cognate, despite a slight agnatic inflection evidenced in our handing down the family name through men. But one may inherit from one's mother's ascendants as well as from one's father's, and in the former case, from one's mother's mother's ascendants as well as from one's mother's father's, and so on.

The reprobation of incest, therefore, seems to have been much stronger in Rome than in Greece, inasmuch as the Romans inscribed it in law. Every society chooses what it considers horrifying, whether it is omophagy (the eating of raw flesh) or incest, murder or blasphemy. Nevertheless, there are varying degrees of reprobation depending on the epoch, with periods of tolerance and periods of rejection.

Livy reports that Cloelius, a patrician, provoked a plebeian uprising when he married a cousin who was a degree closer than the seventh Roman (the second cousin of one of his parents), thus shocking the common sensibilities of the population (from 241 to 229 B.C.).[1] (See figure 5.)

Under Roman law, second cousins do not have what is called *conubium*. According to Ourliac and de Malafosse's treatise on law, this is the legal capacity to wed a given person (not the general legal competency to marry). This capacity depends on kinship relations and alliance as well as social conditions.

After the Second Punic War, unions to the sixth degree were allowed, and later those between first cousins (thus, to the fourth degree), who were called *consobrini*. According to Emile Benveniste, the Romans had a semicomplex system of kinship (and

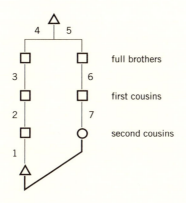

Figure 5.

perhaps of alliance).[2] The evidence he marshals is based on certain lexical features and alliance prohibitions. On the one hand,
the Romans devised terms to denote the mother's brother (*avun-
culus*) and the father's sister (*amita*); on the other, they observed
alliance prohibitions to and including the sixth degree between
blood relations and affines to the same degree.

   This is not the place to discuss semicomplex systems of alliance, which are particularly linked to incest of the second type
because they prohibit two blood relations of the same sex from
having relations with the same partner at the same time and from
marrying a blood relation of the other's husband or wife in a
polygamous union; furthermore, they prohibit two brothers, or a
father and his son (these terms taken in a classificatory sense) —
and, symmetrically, two sisters or a paternal aunt and her brother's
daughter — from seeking a spouse in the same lineage, in a patrilineal regime with an Omaha-type system of appellation. This will
be examined more thoroughly in the second part of this book,

where we will address the relationship between these matrimonial systems and the notion of incest of the second type. Nevertheless, it is impossible to speak of Roman law without mentioning Benveniste's hypothesis, which he developed to explain certain peculiarities of Roman kinship terminology — in particular, the ancient Romans not only devised terms for the mother's brother and the father's sister, they called the father's brother a quasi father (*patruus*) and the mother's sister a quasi mother (*matertera*) — as well as the detailed matrimonial prohibitions that characterize Roman law.

In ancient Roman law, all unions below the sixth degree were incestuous, and guilty parties were thrown from Tarpeian Rock, to the accompaniment of a series of expiations meant to quell the wrath of the gods and ward off various dangers for the community, especially meteorological catastrophes.

Etymologically, the vestals' violation of their vows of chastity was also called "incest." The Romans, too, subsumed under the same semantic category offenses we would consider distinct. The implicit relationship here arises from a quaint bit of logic: the vestal virgin belonged to the goddess and therefore shared in her nature; by sleeping with a mortal, the vestal would allow him to "know" the essence of the divinity.

The moral decadence under the Roman Empire brought about significant legal attenuations, perhaps culminating in the senate resolution of 49 A.D. that authorized marriage between a paternal uncle and his niece. This permitted the emperor, Claudius, to marry Agrippina and caused a scandal, an echo of which is found in Racine's *Brittanicus*: "A less stringent law put Claudius in my bed — and Rome at my feet." It thus became possible to marry to the third degree. Justinian's Institutes later repealed this senate resolution and once again forbade marriage between uncle and niece or aunt and nephew.

In Latin, "alliance" is *adfinitas*, hence the French *rapports d'affinité* in both ethnological language and that of the church. These "relations of affinity" are kinship relations created by matrimonial alliance, ties formed with one's spouse's relatives in the broad sense, but also with the spouses of one's own blood relations.[3] According to Ourliac and de Malafosse, alliance prevented any marriage in direct line. A man could not marry his son's or father's widow any more than a woman could marry her daughter's or mother's widower. Nevertheless, we know of no legal text written before the fall of the Empire that addresses the collateral alliance of a man with his wife's sister or a woman with her husband's brother, after death or divorce.

Roman law authorized cohabitation, particularly when the partners were of disparate social rank and therefore could not marry (class parity was one of the conditions of *conubium*). One could not marry one's slave, but one could have her as a concubine. However, in Justinian's Digest (23.2.56), cohabitation between close relatives is condemned.

At the Council of Elvira in 306 A.D., incest of the second type was mentioned for the first time and would henceforth be inscribed in our own civilization: "If someone, after the death of his wife, has married her sister and if she has been faithful to him, it is decided that he be excluded from communion for five years; unless by chance an infirmity requires he be accorded pardon sooner" (canon 61). The prohibition, then, is permanent, even after his wife's death, since the guilty party must expiate a sin by being deprived of communion for five years, which is incompressible except in the case of illness. While biblical law allowed marrying the wife's sister after the wife's death, it is now proscribed.

This may be read in two ways. One interpretation is that the infirmity has resulted from marrying the wife's sister and is sufficient punishment since it is divine. It would therefore be useless

83

to add spiritual punishment, namely, exclusion from the Christian community. Another interpretation holds that the infirmity itself (a euphemism for impotence) leads to earlier pardon because the marriage with the wife's sister would have been unconsummated. The latter explanation may be the correct one, given the clause "and if she has been faithful to him." In a society where the bonds of marriage were not particularly stable and having children was important, a woman could legitimately leave her impotent husband in order to marry another man. Here, the nonconsummation of the marriage annulled the offense, which consequently required no punishment.

Basil the Great, bishop of Caesarea, justifies this decision by explaining that through marriage, the wedded couple become *una caro*, forming "but one flesh."[4] The husband becomes the wife; therefore, the siblings of one become the siblings of the other. If I am the same substance as my wife, her siblings are mine, her sister is mine, and consequently I cannot marry her under any circumstances. This prohibition of alliance must then be understood as a prohibition of consanguinity.

The argument stops there. Naturally it is valid for all the other relationships prohibited in kinship by alliance, and not only for the wife's sister, though this is the favored example. This is how ecclesiastical interdicts would always be justified from then on.

Nevertheless, further inferences can be made. If the husband "becomes" his wife's flesh and thus enters into a consanguineous relationship with her sister, it must also be true that, from an alternate point of view, the woman "becomes" her husband's flesh; she is incorporated into him. As a result, her husband's blood relations become her own. Additionally, her relationship to her own sister may be seen differently. If it was lawful for her husband to marry her, then there can have been no consanguineous relationship or substantial identity uniting them prior to

84

marriage; consequently, no such relationship or identity united her husband to her sister. But when she becomes her husband's flesh through marriage, he cannot touch her sister; therefore we may infer an identity of substance between the two sisters. The *una caro* argument must be understood in the full subtlety of its implications. Not only do the spouses become one, carnally as well as spiritually, but same-sex blood relations of the spouse also share the spouse's substantial identity.

Likewise, the father's wife has become an integral part of the father; a liaison with her is a liaison with the father, and it is illicit because the son and the father also have the same substance. Consequently, *una caro* implies the substantial identity of blood relations of the same sex, father and son, mother and daughter, two sisters, two brothers. In other words, the principle of *una caro* indirectly reintroduces the substantial identity of blood relations, which was already implicit in the texts we previously examined, but here it is stated (albeit implicitly) from the point of view of relatives by marriage.

The Council of Elvira decree also presupposes a theory of imprinting. Death previously dissolved the ties of marriage; now it would no longer efface the contacts that took place over an individual's lifetime and permeated that individual's substance indelibly.[5] This viewpoint soon became the legal viewpoint in civil law.

In the Theodosian Code (3.12.2) of 355 A.D., we find this: "Although the Ancients believed it lawful for a man to marry his brother's wife after the marriage of his brother had been dissolved, and lawful also for a man, after the death or divorce of his wife, to contract a marriage with a sister of the said wife all men shall abstain from such marriages."[6] In a single statement two symmetrical but structurally different possibilities are presented for a man: to marry his deceased brother's wife or to marry his deceased wife's sister. These statements imply their reciprocal from the feminine point of view *ipso facto*. In one case, two brothers would have had the same woman, in the other, two sisters would have had the same man (figure 6).

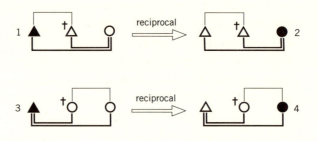

Figure 6.

The code continues, "all men shall abstain from such marriages, and they shall not suppose that legitimate children may be begotten from such a union. For it is established that children so born are spurious." This is the same prohibition as decreed by the Council of Elvira, although the sanction here is of a social nature, since the children are not recognized as legitimate and cannot inherit.

Section 5.5.5 of the Justinian Code of 393 A.D. reinforces this prohibition: "We completely forbid [not merely 'all men shall abstain from'] the right to marry the brother's wife or to couple (or become allied or united) with two sisters, even if the previous marriage has been dissolved in whatever fashion."

Section 3.12.4 of the Theodosian Code of 415 A.D. states: "A man shall be considered as though he had committed incest, if after the death of a former wife he should presume to select her sister for his marriage. A woman, also, shall be held to an equal and similar accountability if after the death of her husband she should presume to aspire to a marriage with his own brother." For the first time, a legal text emphasizes the feminine Ego. Gaius' *Epitome* also expresses the feminine point of view: "It is not permitted for one man to have two sisters, or for one woman to unite with two brothers" (1.4.7). That this occurs successively is not specified, but it is implied by custom.

The Syro-Roman Lawbook states: "No one shall take the wife of his brother. Again, one who has become a widow cannot become a wife of the brother of her husband. Again, a husband whose wife has died cannot take the sister of his wife as his second wife, so to say, two sisters."[7] It is interesting to see the jurist refer to this situation as "two sisters" (*est aliquis diceret duas sorores*), no doubt a standard expression (from a male point of view).

One will doubtless have remarked a few differences between these codes. The Theodosian Code of 355 A.D. prohibits cases 1 and 3 of figure 6, as does the Justinian Code. The Theodosian Code of 415 A.D. speaks only of cases 3 and 2, and *The Syro-Roman Lawbook* deals with cases 1, 2, and 3. Only case 4 is implied.

As diagrammed in figure 6, the development of a single kinship situation may be seen in two different ways for male Ego:

1. If a man cannot marry his brother's widow, it follows that a woman cannot marry her husband's brother: two brothers cannot marry the same woman. Since what is forbidden to men cannot be permitted to women, it follows that two sisters cannot marry the same man and, therefore, that a man cannot marry his wife's sister.

2. If a man cannot marry two sisters, it follows that what is forbidden to a man cannot be permitted to a woman, namely, to marry two brothers. Again, in purely reciprocal fashion, it follows that a woman cannot marry her sister's husband, nor a man his brother's wife.

A woman not being able to marry her sister's husband, transposed under the prohibition against a man marrying two sisters, is central, if obscured, and entirely symmetrical to case 1. Moreover, it is the only case explicitly formulated as "two sisters." Two brothers, two sisters, are the immediately perceptible figures of an identity of substance through the father or mother, or both at once, an identity that lasts a lifetime for these contemporary collaterals. It was impossible in law — in all the laws we have examined — to speak in the name of women as in the name of men, and it is this omission itself, this structural impossibility, that must be put to good use. Only by treating as central the laws stipulating that two sisters cannot touch the same man carnally and two brothers cannot touch the same woman carnally — just as with other consanguineous identicals (father/son, mother/daughter) — can we understand the complete set of prohibitions concerning kinship through marriage.

Only in commentaries referring to jurisprudence or specific cases do we find the fourth possibility exposed.

The commentary in *The Syro-Roman Lawbook*, for example, notes that: "The laws have determined these [rules] because of evil happenings which have occurred through many who have indulged in passion. For instance, a man loved the wife of his brother so that both were against the husband of the wife and killed him through poison" (case 1). In other words, the widow was presumed to have murdered her husband with the complicity of the brother, which presupposes that an illicit liaison existed between them beforehand and that this liaison could not be consecrated by marriage afterward. This is precisely the reason certain African societies prohibit this type of union.

The commentary continues, somewhat redundantly, "again, a wife loved the brother of her husband and they were both against the husband, and killed the husband by poison" (case 2). It then adds, "again, the husband loved the sister of his wife, they were both against the wife and killed the wife of the husband through poison" (case 3). The commentary later considers a fourth case, the symmetrical one of a woman who loved her sister's husband and killed the sister (case 4). Therefore, a previous, attested crime led to the prohibitions against this type of marriage in each of the four possible cases.

Special dispensations were nevertheless made: "If, however, there is no deceit in the midst of such an affair [in other words, if it is proven that there was no previous plot to eliminate the troublesome spouse], then this is what must take place: the husband must bring a petition to the king. On the basis of the order of the king, the husband may take the wife of his brother. In the same way, again, it is right on the basis of the petition and the order of the king that he may take the sister of his wife as a wife. On the basis of this decree, i.e., the order that the king gives, their children shall inherit their properties and possessions. The special dispensations always concern cases 1 and 3 for masculine Ego, leading to reciprocal cases 2 and 4, whereas the logic and underlying meaning of the prohibition would have had dispensations accorded to cases 1 and 4 symmetrically, leading to cases 2 and 3 reciprocally. The ideological force of male primacy in Roman society, as in preceding ones, rendered these contortions of thought necessary, a good example of which has just been provided by *The Syro-Roman Lawbook*.

Dispensations were accorded by the highest public power — in this case, the king — and the children who were born into these unions became legitimate; in other words, the sanction was lifted.

Thus there were two paths: the Christian path of the Council of Elvira, whose argument is spiritual in nature — *una caro* — and the Roman path of the Theodosian and Justinian codes, whose argument is judicial, since proof of one's innocence must be given in order to obtain a royal dispensation. The two branches of European law — that is, canon law and civil law (especially in France) — derive from these two paths.

Under the Roman Republic, marriage between blood relations was thus prohibited to the sixth degree and without limitation in affinity in direct line: it was not possible to marry the spouse of one's grandparents, of one's children, of one's grandchildren, and even beyond, unlikely though that may have been. Later, in the Justinian and Theodosian codes, bans in collateral line appear, notably the famous ban on two sisters. From the late Roman Empire onward, the bans would multiply rather than decrease.

In Saint Augustine's *The City of God*, marriage constitutes "a school of charity" (*seminarium caritatis*), a school of love propagating bonds of affection between families that otherwise would remain foreign to each other (I.7). It follows that alliance between families must not be renewed where links exist already, since love and Christian charity must be spread endlessly. Exogamous law is thus used to further social consolidation. With Saint Augustine, a school of thought develops in which ties of consanguinity transmit what Peter Damian has colorfully called "the smell of kinship."[8] This expression must be understood in an almost literal sense, like "the call of blood." Beyond the implicit idea that we recognize our relatives through the senses and a way of being, there is the idea that this odor is physical, that it has to do not with the immaterial consciousness of kinship but with the body, that it "conveys" the common substance.

Thus, in the twelfth century, blood ties conveyed a "smell of kinship" far beyond the sixth degree: "Nature itself has seen to it that fraternal love recognizes itself to the sixth degree of kinship and exudes a sort of odor of the natural community that exists between relatives."[9] The ban of alliance goes as far as the fourteenth degree Roman, that is, to the seventh degree canon, namely, seven forbidden generations, including that of the apical ancestor. In Byzantium, all marriage was forbidden to the seventh degree Roman inclusive, not only in consanguinity but also in affinity. This number was taken up by the Catholic Church, but as a mode of canonic calculation through branches of collaterality, which ends up doubling it. These two different modes of calculation caused lively controversies in the church, and Peter Damian became famous defending the canonic mode against those who wanted to return to the old interpretation of Roman calculation and thereby reduce the genealogical extension of the bans by half. (See figure 7.)

The question obviously arises as to the sustained effect of these bans. One could conceivably have gone back over seven generations of purely agnatic ties, since in principle men's place of residence varied little, thereby allowing memory to be rooted. On the other hand, establishing this genealogical tree on both sides, through men and women at each of the positions, would become impossible. Nevertheless, this was the rule, absolute in its application since any proof of a kinship tie over fewer than seven generations quite simply annulled the marriage.

For the first time, the Justinian Code extended matrimonial prohibitions to spiritual kinship, in this case, between a godfather and goddaughter. These bans would extend to relationships between parents and godparents, that is, between the child's mother and his godfather, and to adoptive relationships. In earlier Roman law, the obstacle of the fraternity-cousinhood tie established by adoption disappeared in collateral line with emancipation, that is, adulthood. One could thus marry an uncle's adopted children, for example. In the Justinian Code, on the contrary, adoptive children are consanguineous relatives just as natural children are: social kinship takes precedence over biological kinship.[10]

In Byzantium, Leo VI (the Wise) (886–912), the Byzantine

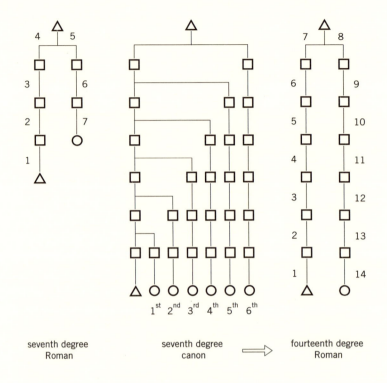

seventh degree
Roman

seventh degree
canon

fourteenth degree
Roman

Figure 7.

emperor who completed the legislative work of Basil I, established in his novel 24 that adoption through the church was to be considered indissoluble and that adoptive kinship be assimilated to natural kinship. The resulting matrimonial prohibitions extended to affines: if one married an adoptive daughter, her entire adoptive family was then forbidden, as it was for a biological family. As far as relatives by marriage were concerned, the restrictions were limited to the fourth degree Roman; they did not go as far as the seventh. In other words, a man could not marry his wife's adoptive first cousin's wife.

In the late Roman Empire, under Christianity's influence, concubinage — that is, sexual relations outside of marriage — was progressively forbidden. In 336 A.D., the Justinian Code forbade those who were married or single from concubinage with girls younger than twelve — prepubescent in all likelihood — and with relatives or relatives by marriage prohibited for marriage. It was not possible therefore to have as a concubine a woman who would be forbidden as a wife. In the ninth century, concubinage was totally forbidden in Byzantium under the reign of Basil I.

The Christian Tradition

This evolution, characterized by the progressive extension of matrimonial bans, goes hand in hand with the spread of Christianity. In the West, the church sought to moralize marriage by struggling against what it considered to be barbarous practices. It thus constructed its theory of indissoluble marriage, sanctified by the sacrament, in the twelfth century. In 1215, the Fourth Lateran Council reduced matrimonial bans to the fourth degree canon (eighth Roman), for consanguinity and affinity. During the Carolingian period, kings totally abandoned matrimonial questions, making them the responsibility of the church, whose tribunals judged all ruptures of the matrimonial bond. At the Council of Trent, between 1545 and 1563, marriage became a contract in addition to a sacrament, and both were indivisible. The state would continually seek to dissociate them and to secularize the contractual aspect. It met with some success, since an exclusively religious marriage was not possible, while an exclusively civil marriage was; in other words, one could not marry in the church unless one had already contracted a civil marriage.

Why consider marriage an irreversible union? Because of the principle set forth at the Council of Elvira: "the unity of flesh created between the wedded couple." This principle of *una caro*, which was the basis of the prohibition of incest of the second type and, by implication, of the first type, would later become the foundation of the theory of marriage itself. Polygamy, in the form of concubinage, was fought against, either as marriage condemned for reasons of social rank or incest of the first or second type, or as pure fornication. This indissolubility of marriage would go so far as to forbid remarriage: in the fifth century, those who were divorced could not remarry as long as the former spouse was alive; in the ninth century, widowers could not remarry. The Council of Meaux made the remarriage of widows licit, while that of Triburg made it illicit once again, but it was always a matter of leviratic remarriage, that is, marrying the deceased husband's relative.

Between the fifth and ninth centuries, situations authorizing remarriage were discussed — that of a woman who has left her impotent husband, a man who has repudiated his adulterous wife, a husband whose wife has taken religious vows, a divorced couple of different religions (Muslim and Christian, or Jewish and Christian in Spain, for example), as well as cases involving leprosy or incest. In these conciliar discussions, we see the appearance of incest of the second type, notably that of a woman with her brother-in-law or a husband with his stepdaughter. If a married man had a sexual liaison with the daughter born of his wife's previous marriage, the legitimate union was automatically broken off. Similarly, if a man committed adultery with his brother's wife, the brother's marriage was automatically broken off. In both cases, remarriage would not be possible for the two "culprits," but would be for the innocent person whose marriage was annulled, which presupposes, on the one hand, that these adulterers were not considered ordinary adulterers and, on the other, that what was incestuous was the relationship between the two blood relations. This suggests that incest was a contamination of the flesh of

94

two blood relations by a common partner, whether two brothers by the wife of one of them, or a mother and her daughter by the mother's husband.

Moreover, this would become a deliberate strategy to eliminate a cumbersome spouse or to change one's relations of alliance. Despite the indissoluble character of marriage, kings and lords had separations and divorces with the consent of the church, making use of their genealogical knowledge, which almost always allowed them to "discover" that their marriage transgressed some prohibition or another. A stepfather could violate his stepdaughter and then use this incest with his wife's daughter to have the ecclesiastical authorities annul the marriage he no longer wanted: "did not many of them [...], to get their marriages dissolved on grounds of incest, lure a sister-in-law or daughter-in-law into bed?"[11] Now, if the marriage is dissolved in this case instead of the sexual offenses being punished, it is so that the identity of substance implicit in all incest prohibitions will be dissolved. Indeed, the church recognizes only two cases of legal rupture of the matrimonial sacrament, the incest we have just mentioned and a wife's attempt to murder her husband (the reverse being inadmissible).

In terms of affinity, since two spouses are one flesh, according to the Council of Elvira and as elaborated by Saint Augustine, each communicates his kinship to his spouse to the sixth degree canon. No man can marry the woman one of his relatives has had as a wife, nor can he marry a relative of his first wife. In Rome, "affinity" was defined as all the spouse's blood relations; from now on, this affinity extends to the spouses of one's own relatives by blood or adoption and sometimes even to certain blood relations of one's blood relations' spouses. A woman cannot marry a man if one of her relatives has had him as a husband or if he is a relative of her first husband.

In the ninth century, according to Georges Duby, affinity resulted from simple *copula carnalis*, from simple sexual relations. If a man copulated with a woman, an affinity existed between them that prohibited each from marrying the partner's blood relative. The underlying reason for this affinity was not the sacrament, since there was none administered; this was fornication. Rather, the affinity derived from the idea that something had been established between the two partners, a community of flesh that was the result of simple sexual relations and not the sanctification of marriage, though marriage implied such relations. The ban was extended therefore to the relatives of those one had known carnally.

Burkhardt of Worms's *Decretum*, written between 1008 and 1012, advocated the *inquisitio*, that is, informing the bishop of the sexual transgressions of one's neighbors or close relatives, particularly women, who were considered easily swayed, deceitful, and weak. A list of questions distributed by the priest to the parishioners would allow one to determine whether adultery, incest, or any union existed within the prohibited degrees. Multiple punishments were set forth for each type of offense. For example, the guilty parties might be forced to eat dry bread, drink only water, and abstain from sex for ten days, or for a multiple of ten days up to a year, or only on holidays, or for periods of forty days for up to seven years. It was illicit to have sex with one's pregnant wife. Rape was also reported; like incest in other societies, it brought about climatological or biological catastrophes that endangered not only the guilty parties but the entire group. Its denouncement and punishment restored everything to order.

All the prohibitions we have enumerated since the Hittites are found in a series of conciliar or canonical texts: the two sisters, the mother and daughter, the brother's or son's wife, and so on. Certain famous unions were dissolved by the church for these reasons. For example, in 1092, Philip I wanted to marry Bertrade de Montfort, the widow of Foulque d'Anjou, but this marriage could not take place because Bertrade was a relative by marriage, the wife of a cousin to the ninth degree Roman, fifth degree canon. Similarly the marriage of Philip I to Berthe de Frise, born of the count of Flanders' wife's first marriage, could not take place since Philip and the count of Flanders were first cousins.

Before him, Robert the Pious had committed double incest. He had married a woman who was related to him by blood and who was also his godmother, thus someone with whom he had spiritual ties of affinity. Hugh Capet, Robert's son, complained loftily to the pope, "We cannot find a wife of equal rank because of the affinity between us and the neighboring kings."[12] He was indeed the cousin of Rozala, daughter of Béranger, the king of Italy, his cousin to the sixth degree; he was also Berthe's cousin to the third degree canon, as she was the daughter of Conrad of Burgundy but the granddaughter of Louis IV (Louis d'Outremer), who was Hugh Capet's paternal uncle. None of these girls was marriageable to the seventh degree canon. These difficulties, which prevented any alliance between royal houses, forced the church to go back to prohibiting marriage only to the fourth degree canon at the Fourth Lateran Council in 1215.

In the medieval imagination, consanguineous unions were feared for their teratological effects, since deformities were not genetic malformations but divine punishments. It was publicly rumored that the consanguineous marriage of Berthe and Robert the Pious had produced a child with a goose neck and head (it would be interesting to know why a goose and not, say, a snake or a cow). The incestuous marriage of the Count Geoffroy Martel d'Angers and Agnès, the widow of Guillaume, his cousin to the third degree canon (a second cousin), had calamitous effects: "the town of Angers was burned down in a horrible conflagration."[13]

In other words, since the risks of incest were perceived not as genetic but theological, they endangered not only the culprits and their offspring, but everyone around them.

Yves de Chartres wrote precisely — if not surprisingly, considering all that has preceded — that it is "by the mingling of bodies, the *commixtio carnis* [and therefore not the sacrament of marriage, except insofar as it implies the mingling of bodies], that a couple becomes one flesh in the mingling of sperm."[14] Thus, from a theologian's pen, the mingling of sperm (women were then thought to have sperm as well) is clearly said to create *una caro*.

With the Fourth Lateran Council, while the notion of marriage as sacrament and contract was being asserted, the obstacles leading to the annulment of marriages of a consanguineous and affinal type were established but reduced from the seventh degree to the third degree canon. The notion of agnatic kinship, *agnatio*, became a primary concern, referring to a line of men with a common forebear, the founding father of the house. It was impossible to trace every line back on both sides, male and female, since, at the seventh degree, every couple has 2^7 lines of ascendants, or 128 (unless, of course, certain ancestors are found to have had incestuous unions whose lines naturally merged). Duby justly remarks that the practice of handing down the paternal name and patrilocal residence made it much easier to trace the direct agnatic line than to track women's matrimonial peregrinations. The notion of lineage in the literal sense of Ourliac and Malafosse's definition — that is, a common trunk — now appears.

Duby has shown how, around the year 1000, the establishment of lineage, succession strategies, and women's matrimonial destiny within houses took shape. In order to survive and hand down their patrimony, while at the same time respecting the church's matrimonial prohibitions, the great families applied a matrimonial strategy founded on two rules: marry off all the girls, but let only one boy get married. Marrying off all the daughters, providing them with a dowry if possible, created lines of descent that, in case of sterility or a desired change in matrimonial alliance, would allow one to invoke an incestuous union in order to dissolve the marriage and contract another. It was a matter of using the law (the innumerable prohibitions on 128 lines) against the law (the indissolubility of marriage). Having only one boy married created only one line of descent through men and thus prevented conflicts between brothers and the scattering of the patrimony among their children. This is why Duby has counted only thirty-four aristocratic houses in the region of Cluny. These two rules allowed these great families to avoid the transfer of their property to the church as well as to avoid extinction or dispersion.

Duby provided a series of examples of men who accused themselves of committing incest with their wife's sister or mother before their marriage in order to obtain its dissolution, and who accused themselves with all the more impunity when the sister or mother were dead, unless incest was actually committed after the marriage.

It is striking to see these matrimonial prohibitions — which can be traced to earliest antiquity — also serve as a foundation for the sociopolitical system of the West during the Middle Ages. The logic of these prohibitions, based on the earliest systems of representation of physical intimacy and the body's interior, is tailored to the biological.

At the Council of Trent, canonical extensions were once again reduced, but priests were now obliged to record matrimonial alliances, that is, to keep marriage registers. This practice produced archival treasures that are the delight of historians — for example, the parish registers of Manduria, a small town in southern Italy, whose priest had attended the Council of Trent and, wishing to enforce its rulings to the letter, invented his own record-keeping method. He began by conducting a veritable ethnographic survey among his parishioners in order to reconstruct oral genealogies, which he managed to trace back to the middle of the fifteenth century. Then he established his method, numbering the families and the members within them in the order of birth; the individuals who contracted a union were identified by these two numbers. His method was applied by his successors until the beginning of the twentieth century. One can therefore systematically study the choice of spouse and the handing down of property over a very long period of time in these parish registers.[15]

A simple idea underlies the laws and representations of incest: if the same touches the same, it is incest. Therefore, there can be no marriage between those related by blood. That there is a ban between affines, and even certain blood relatives of affines (for example, a man's sister's husband's sister, which is to say, his sister's sister-in-law), follows logically. The body is implied in the most intimate way in the carnal union, the *commixtio carnalis*; so, too, is the commingling of bodily fluids. Though never explicitly stated, the meaning of these formulations can only be understood by applying the grid of this reading.

After the Fourth Lateran Council and Council of Trent, church doctrine was established and enforced as matrimonial law for the social body. Nothing new would appear until the twentieth century.

Modern French Law

Incest is only recognized and forbidden by French law in terms of marriage: the law forbids marriage between those who are related. But while French civil law punishes rape, it does not punish incest as a simple sexual relationship with a relative. Familial incest involving a minor is only punishable if it is comparable to rape. There must have been actual vaginal penetration, which makes the case of homosexual incest between a father and son, or fondling, unactionable. Between consenting adults, incest is not an offense. Here we discover a lacuna in French law: in the case of a daughter who is of age but mentally deficient, how does one establish consent?

In an article in *Le Monde* on September 15, 1978, entitled "Incest, or the Conspiracy of Silence," Josiane Cervoni wrote about a Bulgarian-born shopkeeper who set herself on fire after it was discovered that her husband was sleeping with her daughters; although she knew about it, she had done nothing: "According to the penal code, incest is only an aggravating circumstance in the case of rape or indecent assault on the person of a minor." Article 333 of the French civil code stipulates: "If the guilty parties are ascendants of the person who has been assaulted [...], punishment shall be temporary imprisonment, from ten to twenty years as provided in the first paragraph of article 331 [on indecent assault] and life imprisonment as provided in the preceding article [on rape]."

The civil code deals with incest in the section on marriage, as an obstacle to marriage. Title 5, section 1, pertains to the "necessary qualities and conditions for contracting marriage." Article 161 stipulates: "In direct line, marriage is prohibited between all legitimate or natural ascendants and descendants and relatives by marriage in the same line." In other words, heterosexual marriage being understood, a man cannot marry his mother or grandmother in ascending line, nor his daughter or granddaughter in descending line; a woman cannot marry her father or grandfather, nor her son or grandson. By extending the prohibition to natural descendants outside of marriage, the law signifies that marriage is forbidden between blood relations. As for relatives by marriage in the same line, a woman cannot marry her mother's or grandmother's second husband, nor her daughter's or granddaughter's husband, and, reciprocally, a man cannot marry his father's or grandfather's second wife, nor his son's or grandson's wife.

This article does not introduce restrictions related to whether earlier partners of the blood relation in direct line are or are not dead or divorced. Likewise, it does not specify whether the extension to relatives by marriage also applies to adoptive descendants. There are still other cases that the code does not address. For example, can the young widow of the father marry the older widower of the daughter from a first marriage? They are each relatives by marriage with regard to blood relations in direct line, but nothing precludes this marriage. The difference between legal and anthropological points of view truly comes to light here, the former stating general rules of filiation and alliance without too much concern about the ensuing consequences of these premises. Article 161 says no more about the blood relations of relatives by marriage; it does not say, for example, whether a woman, who cannot marry her mother's husband (the relative by marriage of a blood relation), can marry this man's brother (the blood relation of a relative by marriage). This is a matter for casuistic reflection. (See figure 8.)

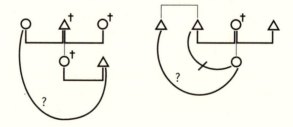

Figure 8.

Indeed, in the first case, the brother and the sister, the father and the daughter, possess a partially common identity, not as strong as that of a mother and her daughter or that of sisters. But there is something in common between the paternal aunt and her niece: can one marry the husband of the other? This type of incest would be deemed minor or nonexistent by most judges. In the second case, which involves the common sexual identities of a mother and her daughter and two brothers, the problem becomes more difficult to resolve.

Article 162, of July 17, 1975, stipulates that, "in collateral line, marriage is prohibited between the legitimate or natural brother and sister." The notion of natural filiation is thus reintroduced. But this text says nothing about what happens when the natural link of filiation or collaterality is recognized after marriage. In good faith, Ego marries Alter, who is found to be a consanguineous relative (father or mother, brother or sister), and this revelation is only made to them after the marriage has been consummated: must this marriage be dissolved? For the church, it must be annulled, as we have seen; the civil code, however, does not address the issue.

Adoption implies absolute legitimacy. Article 163, of January 3, 1972, states: "Marriage is prohibited between uncle and niece, aunt and nephew, whether kinship is legitimate or natural." Does legitimate or natural kinship include affinity and adoption, or is it limited to consanguinity? Can a woman marry her father's sister's husband, or her mother's sister's husband? This question is far from academic, since an uncle (or aunt) may well be in the same age group as his niece (or her nephew). And is natural kinship limited to common law spouses or does it extend to *copulatio carnalis*, to the furtive but fertile sexual relationship?

Article 164, of March 1938, outlines exceptions: "The president of the Republic is free to lift, for serious cause, prohibitions involving 1) article 161 on marriage between relatives by marriage in direct line when the person who has created the alliance is deceased; 2) article 162 on marriage between brother-in-law and sister-in-law; 3) article 163 on marriage between the uncle and niece, aunt and nephew."

The first two provisions of this article say more than they appear to say. By specifying that the person who has created the alliance is dead, the first implies that the ban cannot be lifted by the president of the Republic when this same person has divorced. Now, this was not the issue in article 161: in direct line, only the death of an ascending or descending relative through a very special dispensation, can allow marriage with his spouse. Thus, the legislature, by means of the exception, has introduced something not found in the principal article.

The second provision of article 164 is ambiguous: "Brother-in-law" and "sister-in-law" denote the husband's brother for a woman and the brother's wife for a man, but they may also denote the husband's sister's husband and this sister herself for a woman. In other words, if the husband has a sister who is married, the sister's husband is feminine Ego's brother-in-law and this sister her sister-in-law. Now, after being widowed or divorced, can feminine Ego marry this brother-in-law? Does the dispensation extend the notions of brother-in-law and sister-in-law to relatives by marriage of blood relations of relatives by marriage? This is the same problem that was raised earlier regarding a woman's mother's husband's brother, the woman born of her mother's first marriage, the brother a blood relation of a relative by marriage of a blood relation. (See figure 8.) In other words, the question is whether, in either case, the relatives by marriage of blood relations of relatives by marriage, as well as the blood relations of relatives by marriage of blood relations, are or are not relatives by marriage.

An earlier version of article 162, dating from 1802, added "and the relatives by marriage to the same degree"; in other words, "in collateral line, marriage is prohibited between the legitimate or natural brother and sister and relatives by marriage to the same degree." For example, a woman marries a man who has a brother; the two brothers are situated on the same line of filiation, since they have the same father or the same mother. Let us assume that it is the same father. If the two brothers are married, their wives are relatives by marriage in direct line in the same line of filiation and call each other "sister-in-law." Now, a girl has a brother born of the same father: they are also on the same line of filiation. Each of them marries; their spouses are thus relatives by marriage on the same line of filiation. Consequently, a man calls his wife's brother, as well as his sister's husband, "brother-in-law." A woman calls her husband's brother "brother-in-law" and her husband's sister or her brother's wife "sister-in-law." All are relatives by marriage to the same degree in relation to a same line of filiation, and the law forbids their union. (See figure 9.)

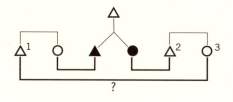

Figure 9.

The 1802 version of article 162 was first modified on July 1, 1914, when the following phrase was appended at the end: "when the marriage that produced the alliance was dissolved by divorce." Specifying that marriage becomes possible after divorce implies that it was not possible in the earlier version, but also, paraliptically, that it was already possible after the death of a spouse. This goes back to the age-old debate on whether a union was indissoluble even after the death of one of the spouses or if, on the contrary, it indeed dissolved upon this death.

Thus, prohibitions of alliance remain implicit and unexplained, although the ecclesiastical tradition proferred the notion of common flesh as an explanation. French civil law prohibits the union of relatives by marriage without asking why. From the viewpoint of Ego on a line of filiation — given the exclusively heterosexual nature of marriage, his relatives on the same line are necessarily male — prohibited alliances necessarily involve consanguinity between individuals of the same sex.

The daughter-in-law is forbidden to the father because he shares the same substance as his son, just as the mother's husband's brother is forbidden to the daughter because this would constitute a dual relationship of substantial identity, between the daughter and her mother, on the one hand, and between the two brothers, on the other. Again we find the figure of two sisters and their mother, prohibited since Hittite antiquity: a mother and her daughter cannot share the same man, two brothers cannot share the same woman. (See figure 10.) This is implicit in the law and provides a natural explanation for it.

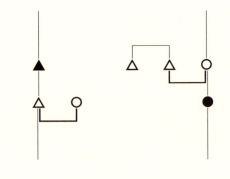

Figure 10.

This implicitness comes to the surface when the law is modified. The 1914 modification — allowing marriage between collateral relatives by marriage provided that the union that created the alliance had been dissolved by divorce — recognizes paraliptically that such marriages were possible after the death of a spouse, as traditionally has been the case in numerous societies, as we have seen. Canon law has evolved in the same direction; in 1983 it authorized alliance between brothers-in law and sisters-in-law if the marriage that created the alliance had been dissolved by death (the church does not allow divorce).

In her study of fifteen generations of the inhabitants of Lower Brittany, Martine Segalen often mentions cases of widowers remarrying their wife's sister in the late nineteenth and early twentieth centuries, when such unions were forbidden by both civil and canon law.[16] In Lower Brittany, an agricultural region, this type of marriage was perceived as the best solution to the problem of being a widower with children: the wife's sister was presumed to make a better mother for the children (since she was already their maternal aunt) than a stepmother brought into the family who would favor her own children. Such biases concerning the reciprocal sentiments of two sisters are somewhat perplexing. Strategies of inheritance were also a factor: if the two sisters had no brother, marrying one's sister-in-law allowed one to inherit from one's family-in-law without having to divide up the inheritance.

Two things are certain. First, individuals in different societies feel both repulsion toward and attraction to such unions. A single society, in the broad sense (in this case, French society), with disparate regional and cultural stocks, may offer different solutions to the same situation depending on the region. I say "situation" and not "problem," for, whatever the solution, it always seems to go without saying. The problem is never articulated.

Second, if these unions commonly occurred among the inhabitants of Lower Brittany and were legalized by the civil state and sanctified by the church, without prior request for dispensation, as Segalen's study demonstrates, then mayors as well as rectors in Lower Brittany must have shared the same general feeling as their flock and simply ignored both civil and religious law, which they had been entrusted to uphold.

In France, civil and religious law and the regional cultural conventions of choosing a second spouse among the blood relations of the first were applied (or ignored) in keeping with local practice, without controversy; however, in Great Britain, the question of marriage with two sisters was the subject of a long and ardent debate.[17]

English Law

In England, the debates on marriage prohibitions were extremely refined. Up until the nineteenth century, the degrees prohibited were those found in the *Book of Common Prayer*, which dates from the Reformation. But a series of acts of Parliament relaxed the bans concerning affinity, following the remarkably argued debates that took place between 1842 and 1907. The most debated issue concerned marriage between a brother-in-law and sister-in-law, particularly marriage of the deceased wife's sister.

The first act to emerge from these debates, the Deceased Wife's Sister's Marriage Act, dates from 1907. Yet it was not until 1921 that the symmetrical case (figure 11) — a woman marrying her deceased husband's brother — was allowed (the Deceased Brother's Widow's Act). Interestingly, one may note that both acts speak for a masculine Ego: the symmetrical counterpart of "the deceased wife's sister's marriage" should have been "the deceased husband's brother's marriage." That, however, would have required acknowledging that the law might as well speak from a woman's

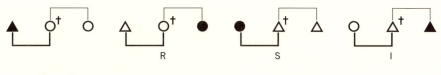

Figure 11.

point of view as a man's. The wordings encountered here are biased in the same way as the wordings of the Hittite laws.

Not until Parliament passed the Marriage Act of 1931 could a man lawfully wed his deceased wife's aunt or niece, that is, a person of third degree by affinity. This law expresses a subtlety that does not exist in French law. Take the case of the wife's niece: Ego's wife is indeed her maternal or paternal aunt, but Ego himself is not her uncle. The person she calls "uncle" is either her father's brother, or her mother's brother. Ego is only her aunt's husband, in other words, a relative by marriage of a blood relation. Reciprocally, for the wife's aunt, her niece's husband is not a nephew, but simply the spouse of a consanguineous relative. Through the Marriage Act of 1931, other possibilities arose: marrying an uncle's widow (the wife of a deceased brother of the father or mother), marrying the deceased wife's aunt (the deceased sister of the wife's mother or father), but not the deceased wife's mother; marrying the widow of a nephew (the son of one's brother or sister) but still not the widow of one's own son. (See figure 12.)

Beneath the seemingly disparate aspects of the prohibitions lifted in 1931 is a certain coherence. Only four cases are provided for, and they all speak from a man's point of view (since it was pointless to speak from a woman's). While the legislators may not have been aware of it, the feminine point of view is nonetheless implied, following from the reciprocity or symmetry of the masculine situations. It is thus naturally omitted, especially since it

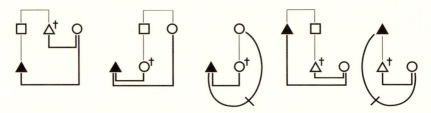

Figure 12.

corresponds to the social norm. The symmetrical case of each of the four masculine cases is always the reciprocal case of another of these same four cases. It is sufficient, therefore, to enumerate these four cases which automatically entail reciprocity; all symmetrical cases are provided for immediately.

As shown in figure 13:

1. A man can marry his deceased wife's niece. Reciprocally, therefore, a woman can marry her deceased (maternal or paternal) aunt's husband (case 5). Symmetrically to case 1, a woman can marry her deceased husband's nephew (case 6), which is the reciprocal of case 2.

2. A man can marry his uncle's widow. We have just seen that the reciprocal is case 6. Symmetrically to case 2, a woman can marry the husband of her deceased aunt (case 5), the reciprocal being that a man can marry the niece of his deceased wife (case 1).

3. A man can marry the aunt of his deceased wife. It follows that, reciprocally, a woman can marry the husband of her deceased niece (case 7). Symmetrically to case 3, a woman can marry her deceased husband's uncle (case 8), which is the reciprocal of case 4.

4. A man can marry the widow of his nephew; reciprocally, a woman can marry the uncle of her late husband (case 8).

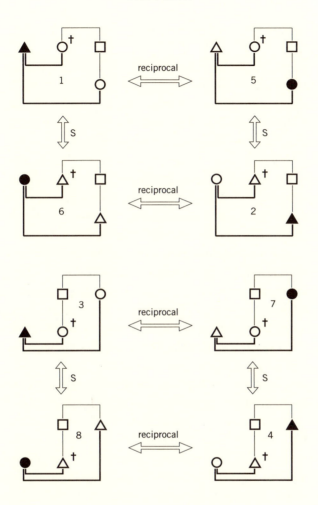

Figure 13.

Symmetrically to case 4, a woman can marry the husband of her deceased niece (case 7), which is simply the reciprocal of case 3: a man can marry an aunt of his deceased wife.

111

Not until 1960 did these unions become permissible in case of divorce.

All these marriages, now permitted, had previously been considered incestuous under civil law. However, incest was legally punishable only when it had taken place in direct line with the mother, the daughter, or the granddaughter, or collaterally with the sister, all cases of direct incest between blood relations.

The lifting of these restrictions concerning relatives by marriage by the legislative acts of 1907, 1921, 1931, and 1960, had first been brought up for discussion in 1842, and over the course of forty-six years was debated in detail in the House of Commons. The text of 1907 came up eighteen times for its second reading, which shows how closely fought the debates were. The 1921 law is a simple amendment to that of 1907, since its provisions are symmetrical to it: if a man can marry the sister of his deceased wife, symmetrically, a woman can marry the brother of a deceased husband, and, reciprocally, a man can marry the widow of a deceased brother. As for the amendments of 1931, they would require six sessions of debate.

In *African Systems of Kinship and Marriage*, the anthropologist A. R. Radcliffe-Brown commented on these parliamentary discussions.[18] He pertinently underscored that all the cases in question depended on the relations between a man and his sister-in-law, in other words, the incest of two sisters. Defenders of the 1907 law wanted to limit authorization to marriage with the deceased wife's sister. But their opponents rightly pointed out that the interplay of reciprocals and symmetricals opened a veritable Pandora's box. They were right, and perhaps showed more anthropological intuition than Radcliffe-Brown, who saw in the opposition to this law only the expression of conservative sentiments.

In the past, the break with Rome had been translated into important changes in matrimonial law. There could no longer be dispensations, but the number of prohibited relatives had been reduced in compensation. The bans concerning spiritual affinity had been suppressed and the method of calculating degrees modified. Henry VIII's edicts of 1533 and 1536 were purportedly based on "divine law," or "Levitical degrees." If a case was not provided for in Leviticus, the matter would now be referred to the common courts, not to the church tribunals.

In 1563, the *Tables of Archbishop Parker* prohibited any sexual relations between relatives and relatives by marriage mentioned by Leviticus, and it introduced "parity of reason," the logic of kinship based on reciprocals and symmetricals. Thus, a marriage was permissible either through conformity to divine laws or by parity of reason. In 1847, the common law courts adopted Parker's *Tables* and, with them, parity of reason. Now, the *Tables* prohibited to the third degree in consanguinity and in affinity, which implies, in this last direction, the ban on marrying blood relations of the spouse to the third degree and the spouses of blood relations prohibited by parity of reason. The wife's sister (second degree) was normally forbidden. Moreover, in the *Tables*, as in Henry VIII's edicts and in conformity to Roman canon law, affinity is created by a furtive liaison as well as by marriage.

Between 1842 and 1907, in the parliamentary debates on the possibility of marriage with the deceased wife's sister, the arguments advanced by both sides drew not only on law, but on theology, sociology, and anthropology.

There are three sociological arguments in favor of this type of marriage, and they are based on three distinct issues: the care of the children, the personal relations between sisters, and the social relations between a man and his sister-in-law.

The first of these arguments claims that the sister-in-law is by definition the best possible substitute mother. Consequently, if she comes to live with her brother-in-law in order to care for the children, sexual relations between them will be presumed, which will taint her honor. Marriage might as well be permitted. The adversaries of the law retorted that, if this union became legal, a sister-in-law who agreed to take care of the children would be obligated to marry her brother-in-law whether she wanted to or not. In other words, against the argument of convenience there was the counterargument of freedom of choice. But partisans of the law replied that if the marriage were made possible, the fact that it did not happen would, on the contrary, cement the honor of both the brother-in-law and sister-in-law, since it would mean they had no inclination for each other whatsoever, and it was hard to see why they would do in secret what they could do in public. This response also answered a further counterargument, namely, that if the sister of the mother became a wife and mother in turn, she would become an evil stepmother to her sister's children: "Maternity will have destroyed in her an aunt's tenderness." After presuming that the maternal aunt was the best replacement mother, it was now presumed that, when she became a mother, she would be the worst stepmother. That the paternal aunt might take care of her motherless nephews and nieces is never considered.

The second sociological argument, which was used by adversaries of the new law, concerned the law's effect on relations between two sisters and between a man and his sister-in-law: this corrupting law would immediately introduce suspicion between sisters, compelling the married one to see her sister as a potential — even mortal — rival from the first day of her marriage. Correlatively, the brother-in-law, seeing his sister-in-law as a potential wife, would feel an attraction to her from Day One.

Finally, the third sociological argument, advanced by partisans of the law, held that as a general rule a man does not consider his sister-in-law his wife, that inheritance laws in no way assimilate her to her sister, that she does not inherit from him if he is without child, that she must pay substantial inheritance dues if he leaves her an inheritance because she is not of his blood. In short, the laws point out everything that makes her a stranger. The laws of succession therefore do not cover matrimonial laws. From this point of view, *una caro* is not valid, as the two sisters no longer form one flesh. Or, more precisely, the identity of substance created by conjugal relations is ephemeral; it dissipates with death. Between a child and his mother's sister, on the contrary, there are almost maternal links, to the point that the son cannot marry her and can inherit from her, because the identity of substance is permanent in this case. Supporters of the law therefore invoked the laws of succession against the matrimonial laws: blood relations of the spouse must no longer be considered blood relations of Ego.

Biblical arguments for and against the law were also put forward. English matrimonial law was founded on Leviticus (through the adoption of Parker's *Tables*), and the law's advocates maintained that Leviticus permitted a man to marry his deceased wife's sister. In Leviticus, the ban was only valid during the wife's lifetime, and, as a result, the ban actually changed nothing fundamental. Their opponents objected that the famous verse of Leviticus had to be understood less as an interdiction bearing on the wife's sister than as the prohibition of polygamy. Since sororal polygamy was but a specific type of polygamy, they did not see any reason to formulate this prohibition bearing on the wife's sister, since it was symmetrical — they say "parallel" — to the ban on marrying one's brother's wife. They clearly saw that the ban drew its very principle from the consanguinity between brothers and sisters.

For them, the brother's wife and the wife's sister were in an "analogous" kinship relation with masculine Ego. The prohibitions in Leviticus addressed men but necessarily applied to women, too, who found themselves in a position of analogous kinship.

115

If the son cannot marry his mother, the daughter cannot marry her father. "Analogous" is not reciprocal (the reciprocal case here would be: "If a son cannot marry his mother, then a mother cannot marry her son") but symmetrical, so that the sexes are reversed: "the son" becomes "the daughter" and "the mother" becomes "the father." If a man cannot marry his father's sister or his mother's sister (his paternal or maternal aunt), this implies not that a woman cannot marry her nephew, by reciprocity, but that a woman cannot marry her uncle, by "analogy."

To support their interpretation of this verse in Leviticus as a general prohibition of polygamy, the opponents of the law pointed out that Leviticus contains as many bans on relatives by marriage as bans on blood relations. This is true, and it is explained immediately by the "one flesh" argument (Gen. 2:24, Matt. 19:6, Mark 10:8, Eph. 5:31). If a man cannot marry his blood relations and forms one flesh with his wife, then he cannot marry his wife's blood relations. We have a standard syllogism here. If one does not accept this reasoning, the opponents continued, a number of prohibitions not mentioned explicitly in Leviticus, but which are nonetheless observed, would be lifted. One could then marry the mother of one's father or mother, the daughter of one's brother or sister, or even one's own daughter; but in fact, the argument goes, they are prohibited "by analogy of kinship." Furthermore, if marrying the deceased wife's sister were to be legalized, then union with the deceased brother's or sister's daughter would have to be legalized as well. On this point, the adversaries of the law argued their position very well, but their "analogy of kinship" can only be based on the principle of the oneness of flesh as a principle of alliance and this principle itself has no meaning, other than metaphorical, unless it implies the exchange of substances.

The law's adversaries were influenced by the theory of imprinting, a medical theory that had currency in the nineteenth century.

A number of "scientific discoveries" supposedly established that, physiologically, a woman was an integral part of her husband, but not the reverse. They formed one flesh, not because each partner became the other's flesh but because the wife physiologically became her husband's flesh. The theory held that, if a man had children with different wives, each child would have only the attributes of his two parents, whereas if a woman had children with several husbands, the children she had with the second might have certain traits of the first. Without being too concerned about how such "discoveries" were supported, let us simply remark that a woman might well have been unknowingly pregnant by her first husband at the time she married her second. But more importantly, this theory of imprinting is based on the belief that, in the exchange of fluids, what is essential is what is transmitted by male semen. Hygienist doctors of the nineteenth century, such as Dr. Virey, maintained that male semen improved a woman, firming her flesh, giving her abundant periods, changing her character, making her independent, determined, and so on.[19] Ultimately, the woman who abused this beneficial contribution of virile semen turned into a virago, becoming male in both behavior and appearance. Thus a woman's flesh was dependent on an exogenous contribution of sperm. But if female flesh was transformed by male semen, this meant that female flesh was "imprinted" with it and transmitted its traits. In the case of remarriage, a woman retained the flesh of her preceding husband and was likely to produce children who resembled him.

For the adversaries of the law, the idea of the oneness of flesh was the cornerstone of all bans pertaining to affinity. Now, a law that does not proceed from a principle is devoid of all value. To change the existing law to allow a man to marry his deceased wife's sister was simultaneously to suppress all prohibitions concerning relatives by marriage. Having allowed the exception, all other bans on affinity would have to be lifted; one would have to allow divorce and even adultery, indeed, polygamy. It must be recognized that history has not proven them wrong.

Supporters of the law retaliated that they had absolutely no intention of going that far. They meant to preserve all the other prohibitions bearing on affinity, and they did not want to discuss divorce, adultery, or polygamy. At most eight deputies declared themselves in favor of the suppression of all bans on relatives by marriage. Challenging the principle of the oneness of flesh that was the cornerstone of these bans, they sought to limit incest to consanguinity. One of the more clever arguments against the principle of oneness suggested that if it applied to blood relations of relatives by marriage then it must also apply to blood relations of relatives by marriage on both sides. If a man cannot marry the sister of his defunct wife, and his wife cannot marry his brother in the case of his death, because they are one and the same flesh, then the wife's sister obviously cannot marry the husband's brother. This was meant to put the opponents of the law in an awkward spot, since they did not — and did not wish to — demand that two brothers be forbidden to marry two sisters. However, this argument was invalid, the law's opponents argued, because two husbands do not have the same flesh; only the wife becomes her husband's flesh.

In the end, the strongest counterargument of the proponents of the law was to contest the principle of the analogy of kinship — in particular, the analogy between a woman's husband's brother and a man's wife's sister. They rejected the argument that, through "parallelism," the law in Leviticus that prohibited uncovering the nakedness of the wife's sister was derived from the prohibition against a man's marrying his brother's wife. They noted a number of distinctions made under Hebraic law that tend to show that "parallelism" (in other words, the symmetrical) does not go with-

118

out saying. For example, Hebraic law forbids polyandry, but it authorizes polygamy; it punishes female adultery, but not necessarily male adultery; the woman is incorporated into her husband's family, although the man is not incorporated into his wife's. Therefore it is entirely possible that something be permitted to men and not to women; it is possible that a man would be allowed to marry his wife's sister and that a woman be forbidden to marry her husband's brother.

The great subtlety of these debates, which in fact lasted until 1940 — that is, for almost a century — is stupefying.[20] Many principles of anthropological analysis were more or less clearly perceived and expressed by the representatives of the people in these jousts: the interplay of reciprocities and symmetries through "parity of reason," for example, and the justification of bans bearing on relatives by marriage through the oneness of flesh, by means of sexual union but also through the substantial identity between blood relations, particularly those of the same sex, in filiation and in collaterality, as one clearly sees in the transitive example shown in figure 14. Additionally, these debates touched on all the psychological and sociological arguments concerning the necessity of maintaining harmony in families, how best to mitigate jealousy and rivalry among siblings, and the relative merits of a mother's sister as the stepmother of her nephews and

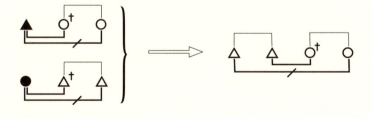

Figure 14.

nieces in comparison to any other woman, including the father's sister (outside of marriage, of course, in this case).

All these arguments are taken separately or grouped together in the anthropological literature on the subject. The anthropologists of the period who dealt with them were at times less discerning than some of the members of parliament. In 1940, Malinowski pronounced himself in favor of the ban on marrying one's defunct wife's sister; his argument did not rely on the consubstantial identity of blood relations of the same sex — a premise made suspect during the earlier political dispute — but on a supposed sexual jealousy between the sisters which would render the couple's life impossible, a minor psychological argument that would be difficult to apply universally.[21]

Just as stupefying is the relentlessness of both the proponents and opponents of the new law in defending their position and in countering each other's arguments. One might conclude that, without it being clearly perceived, the 1907 law offered a fleeting, furtive idea of incest of the second type, which exists between two blood relations of the same sex who, either simultaneously or after the divorce or death of one, take the spouse of the other (not to mention all the transitive consequences of similar impossibilities).

The Romanian Case

We will examine one last contemporary example from the sociocultural area formerly known as the Eastern bloc: Romania. A detailed study by Andreï Pandrea assembled a series of prohibitions expressed in proverbs.[22] "Lord, strike me dead for I have loved two sisters, and a sister-in-law and my mother-in-law at once." In other words, Ego accuses himself of the same offense as the Greek Callias, which we analyzed in chapter 2.

Let us consider a specific case, one that is problematic in both French and English law. In contrast, it is absolutely lawful in

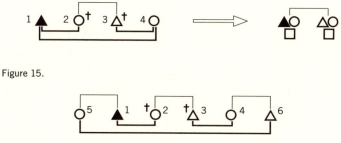

Figure 15.

Figure 16.

Romania for a man to marry his deceased wife's dead brother's wife.

French law sees (1) and (3) as brothers-in-law, but says nothing about the relationship between (1) and (4); on the other hand, popular tradition expresses itself clearly, referring to the woman's brother's wife as a sister-in-law to Ego. In Romania, a man can marry this sister-in-law. Yet, if the man forms one flesh with his wife, and his wife's brother (who is consubstantial to her) forms one flesh with his wife, as each of the spouses takes on the other's consanguinity, Ego therefore becomes a blood relation of his wife's brother's wife and should not be able to marry her. But Romanian law permits what English law forbade: although it recognizes the principle of *una caro*, Romanian law does not accord *una caro* the same extension. At some point in the chain (here horizontal) of alternate relations of alliance and consanguinity one has to stop: transitivity cannot be infinite.[23]

Yet, Romanian law is not particularly lax. On the contrary, in certain respects, its prohibitions are quite extensive. It is not possible to marry between "cross-brothers" or "cross-cousins," that is, between cousins of the sixth degree Roman (second cousins), which follows the common rule of the Catholic church. Nor is it possible to marry if one shares a relative by marriage up to the eighth degree. Underlying this prohibition is a notion that one finds in African societies, namely, the notion of rivalry: two individuals are rivals when they have both married a woman who belongs to the same lineage, in a society with unilineal filiation.

Two sisters of the same lineage *A* are going to marry into different lineages *B* and *C*. The men of lineages *B* and *C* who have married these two sisters will find themselves in a situation of rivalry because their children will have the same rights on the same maternal uncles; thus, the ban continues for three successive generations. The ban of rivalry would therefore seem more important than that of consanguinity, since it goes back to a higher degree, the eighth instead of the sixth. (See figure 17.)

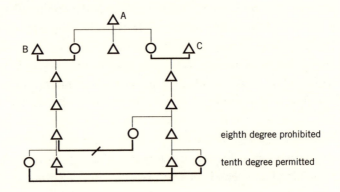

eighth degree prohibited

tenth degree permitted

Figure 17.

Now, in Romanian law, two brothers marrying two sisters happens to be prohibited. However, if these are not two parallel marriages but two crossed marriages, a brother and his sister with a sister and her brother, these marriages are permitted. This is because the parallel marriage adds rivalry to substantial identity, while the crossed marriage retains only substantial identity, since a brother and his sister cannot be rivals. In other words, crossed brothers-in-law and sisters-in-law can marry each other, the parallels cannot, because this introduces rivalry where solidarity should reign. Which shows once again that by "brother-in-law" and "sister-in-law" custom implies something quite different than law. (See figure 18.)

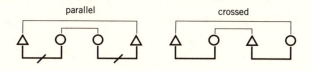

Figure 18.

Moreover, in Romania a man cannot marry a woman who bears the same family name, for reasons of preserving the diversity of patronyms. Nor can one marry when one is a parent of the spouses, for, if one accepts substantial identity between a father and his son as between a mother and her daughter, then, were a father able to marry his son's mother-in-law, this would, through transitivity, establish a liaison between him and his daughter-in-law, which falls under the ban against two men sharing the same woman. But history does not say whether the father of the wife can marry the mother of the husband: the situation is certainly different, for the mother-son and father-daughter pairs are not true identical pairs. Uncles and nieces or aunts and nephews cannot marry, but that is the common rule.

Romanians are also subject to prohibitions concerning spiritual kinship. Godfathers and goddaughters cannot marry, nor can the children of godparents and children of godchildren, and this can only be explained by the notion of rivalry. As everywhere in the Christian world, marriage between the male godparent and the female parent — that is, between the godfather and the mother of the child — is taboo, whereas it is not for the father and the godmother. A midwife cannot marry the child she has brought into the world, for she is equivalent to a godparent: she is a quasi mother and therefore cannot marry her quasi son. For the same reason, two children brought into the world by the same midwife cannot marry each other: they are quasi siblings. Her children cannot marry the children of children she brought into the world, by analogy to being a godparent and the alleged rivalry such a union would inspire. The prohibitions are fairly extensive, therefore, but they are always founded on the same principles.

The Romanian case is interesting in its completeness. The prohibitions bear on the four modes of consanguinity, affinity, spiritual affinity, and the very particular kinship that has to do with being brought into the world by the same woman.

Thus we have seen the growing complexity of a man's union with "two sisters," which the lengthy English debates recognized as a central question in the prohibition or authorization of marriage with relatives by marriage. Nevertheless, more profoundly, in the spirit of the church as well as civil law (Roman and French law), *copulatio carnalis* was sufficient to establish an essential relationship, equivalent in its effects to the bond established by marriage. This, in fact, is said, whether specifically or intricately and subtly, in the Koran, Leviticus, and the Assyrian and Hittite laws.

However, the *una caro* of the church ignores incest between consanguineous relatives who share the same partner and considers only the consubstantiality of spouses acquired by means of the carnal union, due to their natural consubstantiality, which creates an identity between them. This is an essential point, which was

perfectly expressed by Hittite law, where the ban on a man touching two sisters and their mother (at the same time) pertained to
women who were related to each other but not related to the
man either by blood or marriage, the sole relationship between
them being the carnal, sexual relationship, the mingling of bodies
and fluids.

It is based on this configuration, whose symmetrical equivalent would be the impossibility for a woman to have relations with
two brothers and their father at once (that is, reciprocally and
expressed from the male perspective, the impossibility for two
brothers or for a man and his son to share the same woman), that
the transitive series of reciprocity and symmetry of bans on relatives by marriage are constructed. We have seen this configuration, inexpressible in any other way due to the differential
valence of the sexes, in both the scope and casuistry of the various
codes that have expressed it in history.

PART TWO

Incest of the Second Type and Semicomplex Systems

Introduction

Between the historical societies we have just examined and the exotic societies anthropologists study, there is no rupture: the same phenomenon calls for the same sort of consideration. Studying "primitive" societies allows us to understand customs that are deeply rooted in our own cultures. A solution is not diffused from a common source; rather, humanity always and everywhere arrives at similar solutions to similar problems.

In the following chapters, we will consider the relationship between incest of the second type and what I have called "semi-complex systems of alliance." It will then be possible to understand why the prohibition against this form of incest is not universal, unlike that concerning consanguinity. We will also establish the relationship among the matrimonial rules of these systems of alliance, the prohibition of two sisters, and overall systems of representation of bodily fluids.

CHAPTER FOUR

Two Sisters in African Societies

My fieldwork among the Samo revealed a society in which the two sisters taboo was essential to the functioning of the system of kinship and alliance.[1] In *L'Exercice de la parenté*, I analyzed this semicomplex system of kinship and alliance of the patrilineal Omaha type at length.[2] Claude Lévi-Strauss was the first to have envisaged such a system in his famous Huxley Memorial Lectures, though he did not actually give it a name.[3] I have defined it as an intermediary system between elementary systems, where the choice of spouse is oriented toward groups and sometimes even prescribed, and complex systems (such as our own), which do not determine the choice of spouse but forbid access to certain people based on relationships of consanguinity or alliance between them.

Located between the two, semicomplex systems entail a series of prohibitions on individuals who are consanguineous cognates or related to Ego by marriage, as complex systems do. But these prohibitions also target persons who are distantly or uncertainly related to Ego and who belong to the same social group of prohibited filiation. This feature situates semicomplex systems in an intermediary position in relation to elementary systems of alliance, which sometimes direct future marriages toward specific individuals (the maternal uncle's daughter, for example), but more generally toward social groups as a whole, particularly groups of unifiliation.

Semicomplex Systems

In societies with patrilineal filiation, a semicomplex structure of alliance, and a complete Omaha terminological system, a man cannot choose a wife (or, rather, is not given a wife) who belongs to certain lineages designated before birth: often four (his own, his mother's, and his two grandmothers', though sometimes only discrete lines in this last case), sometimes two (his own and his mother's), more rarely eight if the great-grandmothers' four lineages (or discrete lines) are added to the first four. Demographically, when these lineages have many daughters, a significant number of potential wives are prohibited *a priori*.

"Lineage" means all relatives through masculine chains who are alive when one chooses one's spouse. For example, Ego's mother's mother's father's father's brother's son's son's son's daughter would be forbidden to him, because from his mother's mother down to the daughter in question, there are only men, and therefore this girl belongs to Ego's maternal grandmother's agnatic lineage. This girl is thus forbidden, although she is only a cousin to Ego to the tenth degree Roman. (See figure 19.)

There is a whole series of prohibitions on the sharing in common of the same maternal or grand-maternal lineages: if Ego's mother's lineage is the same as his intended bride's grandmother's, he will not be able to marry her. (See figure 20.)

Also forbidden to him in the previous generation are all his mother's co-wives, all his father's brother's wives (and the women born in the same lineage), those of his father's patrilateral parallel cousins, i.e., all the men he calls "father." In his generation, all lineages where his brothers, agnatic brothers, agnatic parallel

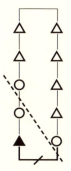

Figure 19.

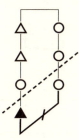

Figure 20.

cousins, and all men he calls "brothers" have previously married are forbidden. Again we find prohibitions between brothers-in-law in the broad sense, as in England or Romania, and for the same reason: namely, the suspicion that ties existed prior to the death of the intermediary persons, or even that a series of crimes made the matrimonial union possible.

All these marriages are impossible in Samo country. One might conclude that it is difficult, if not impossible, for a Samo man to find a spouse in his area who does not fall under one prohibition or another. And yet it becomes clear that the very proliferation of prohibitions allows one to choose one's spouse from among one's closest relatives, without breaking any taboo. Let us see how.

To account for all these bans, Lévi-Strauss explained the system's mode of functioning by the fact that when a given marriage had taken place between two lineages, a second marriage had to be impossible for several generations (two, three, or four, depending on the number of prohibited uterine lineages) in the same or the opposite direction. (See figure 21.)

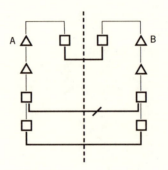

Figure 21.

Now there were certain problems which the genealogical data made plain. First of all, it was evident that one did not necessarily marry far away; in fact, most people married in their own village. Then, while it was forbidden to marry into one's mother's lineage, one's mother's co-wives' or paternal uncles' wives' lineage, and one's paternal grandmother's lineage, it was not forbidden to choose a wife in lineages from which the grandfather had taken other wives. It goes without saying that the grandfather's other wives' lineages could not be the same as the grandmother's, strictly speaking, since a man cannot take a wife in the lineages of his previous wives and his brothers' wives (one therefore cannot marry two sisters). As a result, these lineages almost seem to constitute favored areas of choice. In other words, polygamy and sibling groups with many males can play an important role in the regulation of alliances. In figure 22, although Ego, who belongs to lineage *A*, cannot marry daughter *B* who comes from his paternal grandmother's lineage, he can easily marry daughter *C* (from the lineage of another of his grandfather's wives) or daughter *D*, from the lineage of a paternal great uncle's wife.

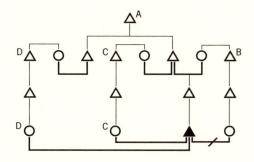

Figure 22.

Given the various bans and the fact that rules are stated in the masculine, it seems renewal of alliance was only prohibited for individuals of the same sex in the lineage from which a relative of a previous or the same generation had already taken a spouse. A man cannot marry a woman in the lineage from which his brother has already married. But while true for a brother, it was not for a sister. Clearly, what was not possible for parallel blood relations became possible for crossed blood relations, or cross-siblings, in keeping with the transitivity of all the rules of prohibition. If masculine Ego cannot redouble his brother's alliance in the same lineage, then, symmetrically, feminine Ego cannot redouble her sister's; but it does not follow that a brother and a sister cannot redouble their alliances.

If two brothers cannot marry two sisters, and if a man cannot marry two sisters, then, it follows, reciprocally, that a woman cannot marry her sister's husband, nor can a woman marry her sister's husband's brother. Symmetrically, two sisters cannot marry two brothers, nor can a woman have sexual relations with one of her husband's brothers during the husband's lifetime (this is an incestuous act, a "doglike act"), though leviratically she may marry the husband's younger brothers.[4] This does not in any way imply, either reciprocally or symmetrically, that a woman could not marry the brother of her brother's wife. (See figure 23.)

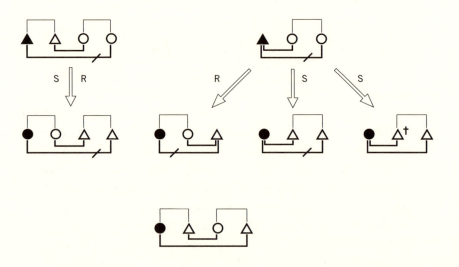

Figure 23.

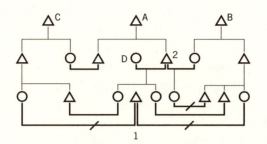

Figure 24.

Similarly, masculine Ego (represented as [1] in figure 24) cannot take a spouse in the lineage from which his father has already taken his spouse ("father" in the real and classificatory sense, that is, all the men his real father calls "brothers" in his lineage), whereas his sisters may. A father (represented as [2] in figure 24) cannot give his daughter to the lineage that has given him the mother of this daughter (for then she would marry in her mother's lineage), but he can give her to a lineage that has given him another wife or has given his brother a wife.[5]

Symmetrically, it is not possible for a woman to marry in the same lineage as her sister, her mother, or her father's sister. Therefore, in determining the choice of spouse, there is a clearly formulated prohibition against pairing identicals: two brothers, father and son, two sisters, mother and daughter, and also the father's sister (the paternal aunt) and her brother's daughter (the niece).[6]

Lévi-Strauss's reasoning was certainly correct, except that what prevents the renewal of exchange between two lineages over several generations is not *any* marriage, but the previous marriage of an agnatic blood relation of the same sex. The marriage of a blood relation of the same lineage but of a different sex,

137

on the contrary, which renews the earlier alliance, is highly desirable — with the exception of the daughter married in the mother's lineage. The prototype of such a union realized by the Samo is the sister exchange represented at the bottom of figure 23.

One might imagine complex strategies being carried out based on the multiplicity of bans and their subtractive effect. In fact, due to polygamy and the presence of several brothers or several different lines in a single lineage, and to this particularity of symmetry,[7] it suffices to change lines alternately or even simultaneously at each generation to create a new alliance, for crossed alliances to be woven regularly between two lineages.[8]

Consequently, there is a close correlation between matrimonial rule and incest of the second type. The latter is essential to the functioning of the semicomplex system of alliance. Pierre Etienne, an ethnologist who introduced the notion of rivalry, analyzed the semicomplex system of the Baoulé and made similar observations.[9] There are still other African examples, such as the Ashanti, the Tallensi, and the Nuer.

A Few Words on the Samo and Ethnological Method

The Samo are a population of the former Upper Volta, now called Burkina Faso, with several village communities in Mali. They are agriculturists who mostly cultivate millet and sorghum. They have developed ingenious processes for conserving grain for several years, but remain quite poor. Their country is subject to extreme climatic hazards, so many young men leave to work on plantations on the Ivory Coast during the dry season and return to cultivate their own lands during the rainy season. This creates an alternation of conjugal absence and presence.

Numbering 120,000 to 130,000, the Samo do not form a large ethnic group like the Mossi, who are several million, but they are not a small tribe. They are divided into three prefectorial subdivisions, once called "circles" in colonial times: Tougan, Toma, and Kiembara. These subdivisions correspond to distinct linguistic areas, as the Samo language comprises three dialects that are not necessarily mutually understood. Those who speak Tougan and Toma understand each other to some extent, but those who speak Toma and Kiembara have a much harder time. Dialects are distinguished by the term that begins each sentence, attracting the interlocutor's attention, a sort of interpellation: *matya* in Tougan, *maya* in Toma, *maka* in Kiembara. The differences affect vocabulary, grammar, and the tone system. Moreover, there are local variations within each dialect, so that, judging from a person's vocabulary and way of speaking, others can easily identify the village he comes from, or at least the region.

Despite these linguistic divisions, the Samo share the same social institutions found in the Toma region, with a few variations. The village communities are totally autonomous; they are not subjected to an organized central power, to a chiefdom. From the once-frequent intervillage wars, Samo villagers have retained a frank hostility toward one another. Each village owns its land and is divided into two moieties, one governed by an earth master, the other by a rain master. A moiety is composed of a number of lineages with one name and a chief whose religious role is to assure the well-being of the collectivity. In this segmentary system of lineages, all members of the same lineage form one body and must support each other in case of disputes with outsiders. All conflict between individuals of the same lineage is managed by the lineage; conflict between individuals of two lineages of the same moiety is managed by the moiety or the blacksmiths; conflict between individuals of two lineages belonging to each of the moieties is managed by the blacksmiths; conflict between individuals of two villages, each wedded to the cause of his own people, degenerates into war. The control of the bush returns to village associations governed by a bush master who officiates at certain rituals (the opening of the hunt, bush fires, and so on). In principle, war is not waged and captives are not taken from within the same bush mastery.[10]

In the heart of *matya* country, in the administrative district of Kouy, under one bush master, I took the set of villages (*gana*) constituted by Dalo, Gono, and Twãre as a base of reference. These villages are associated by *kudiena* alliance, a matrimonial alliance that also includes mutual help or collective activities of all sorts, such as drinking millet beer or hunting as a group, so many signs of peace. A *gana* is a sort of matrimonial isolate and zone of peace, where there is preferential choice of spouse.

Lineage (*sõ*) is the unit of reference in the villages, their two moieties governed by a *tudana*, an earth master, and a *lamutyri*, a rain master. There are no clans, that is, no association that goes beyond the scope of the village, uniting lineages that have the same origin and the same name. Nevertheless, there have been schisms, a branch of a lineage deciding to establish itself elsewhere. The matrimonial prohibitions and civil relations diminish over several generations, until the memory of common origin fades and disappears, leaving no trace. Each lineage also constitutes a residential unity, a "neighborhood" in village language, so that all men from the same neighborhood are related by blood. A lineage consists of an ensemble of discrete lines, *gulè*, meaning "tree branch," the same metaphor used in English.

I conducted a genealogical survey in each lineage in the presence of the assembled lineage and several old women who were descended from it and had married in the vicinity. Women were generally more interested in these questions of kinship and consanguinity; they remembered, quite impressively, not only their own history, but also that of other members of their family. I started with the doyen — the oldest member of the oldest generation, not necessarily the oldest person — in order to go back in direct line to the apical ancestor, then descend again from generation to generation through lineal brothers or sisters[11] to the current generation, the exchange of women between lineages allowing information to be cross-checked. By going from the giver lineage to the receiver lineage and vice versa, information concerning the women was gathered twice, as daughters in one lineage and as wives in one or several others. (See figure 25.)

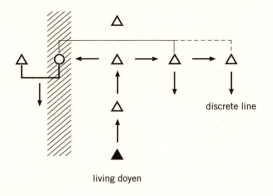

discrete line

living doyen

Figure 25.

When my interlocutors could not tell me whether several individuals were brothers with the same father (in other words, when they could not give me the name of a common father), I considered them heads of *discrete* lines. This proved to be of particular importance since the prohibition on the grandmothers' lineage of origin concerns only these discrete lines and not the lineage as a whole. The ban of the lineage as a whole bears on the parents' generation, the father, the mother, the father's brothers. As we have just seen, while one cannot marry in one's grandmother's lineage, one can in lineages from which the grandfather has taken other wives and in lineages from which his brothers have married.

When the lineage reaches its optimum population, around twenty-four people, discrete lines sometimes secede and settle elsewhere, if necessary in a new village that they set up. They bring some of their lineal altars with them, and make sacrifices to the ancestors; they retain the same origin with the matrimonial prohibitions that this imposes, until, with time, they eventually constitute an autonomous lineage. These schisms play an essential role in regulating matrimonial exchanges, since they create new partners for other lineages.

Lineage is thus an exogamous residential unity; it has a name and its own supply of first names, so that on meeting someone named Nyisa Drabo, one immediately knows this person is a first-born child (Nyisa) in a lineage of earth masters and gravediggers (Drabo). The first name corresponds to the order of birth and the lineal name to attributions that are more ritual in nature than professional, each lineage contributing its share to the common good. There are lineages of earth masters, rain masters, black-smiths, hunt masters, war masters, market masters, and so on.

Mastery is achieved on an altar on which the doyen of the lineage makes propitiatory sacrifices. When a line secedes and settles in another village, its altars may compete with altars already being used by a lineage. The line can then either specialize, in a certain type of hunting, for example, or take new attributions. Thus when French colonial leaders asked the villages to designate administrative officials, a mastery of whites was created and attributed to newly formed lines. This caused serious problems, for the mastery soon found itself enjoying considerable power, such as policing conflicts and collecting taxes, roles incompatible with its status as a new line.

Descent is patrilineal: all men and daughters of the lineage are therefore related through the chain of men. Residence is patrivirilocal: that is, men live with their fathers (patrilocality) and wives join their husbands (virilocality). If a woman abandons her husband for a man of another lineage, a whole series of procedures is set in motion to retrieve her, particularly the erection of revenge altars. These are so feared that if a piece of one is brought to the place where the woman has taken refuge, the villagers will urge her lover to send her away. But the attempt to retrieve children is most ardent, for they belong to the father's lineage and not to the mother's.

A man is never without descendants. If a woman realizes that neither she nor her co-wives are able to conceive a child with him, they arrange to come back from a trip pregnant. As sterility is never male, these children will belong to her husband: the social takes precedence over the biological. If a woman has children before her marriage, or during it but by another man, they also belong to the husband's lineage, if only because they share his life, his residence, and his food. And even if a man chooses celibacy, which is extremely rare, he is not without descendants since he is the "father" of his brother's children.

Sterility is always considered female. A woman is symmetrically called "mother" by the children of her real or lineal "sisters," though by birth the children belong to lineages other than her lineage of origin and her host lineage(s) by marriage. A woman who does not have her own descendants is more easily forgotten than other women, as no one offers sacrifices to her memory after two or three generations.

A daughter is promised in marriage as a very young child, but an institution called *sandana* accords her a prenuptial lover. Her legal husband cannot touch her before she reaches puberty; once she has, and her father has made the puberty sacrifice that allows

143

her to have sexual relations, three years must pass before she joins her husband. During this time, the husband works in his father-in-law's fields, with the help of friends in his age group. Meanwhile, the young girl takes a lover, whom she often chooses in accord with her mother, respecting alliance prohibitions. As a rule, she will not join her legal husband before three years unless her lover gets her pregnant; the baby will be the first born child of her legal marriage. Her lover visits her each night in her hut. Until then, she shared her mother's hut, the father having his own and his various wives having their own. When her father makes the puberty sacrifice, he constructs a hut for his daughter, who then receives her lover openly and publicly.

This institution echoes the notion of "first fruits," the opening of the female body. The child born of these prenuptial relations has particular characteristics: he belongs to the lineage of his social father, he will constitute the same lineal blood through food and word, and he will be given the lineal name. But biologically he comes from two other lineages that cannot claim him. He is attributed particular powers because he does not truly belong to anyone; he belongs to the earth (in fact, the term that refers to him, and that he bears as one of his first names, means "child of the earth"). He is considered slow-witted, somewhat doltish, but he is seen as having divinatory gifts. If this prenuptial child is a girl, she is thought to be more fertile than others.

Women may have children outside of *sandana* or marriage; women who do so are called *gagaré,* "free" or "wild." A woman who is not under a husband's authority is said to be *gagaré.* Generally, this is a woman who was married and does not wish to be subjected to a spouse's authority again. Those women who remain in their husband's lineage, or return to their lineage of origin but have no sexual dealings with anyone, are considered mistress women. Particularly respected, they provide for themselves and raise their children alone (if they have remained in their husband's lineage) by cultivating the land or making small artisanal handiworks. Those who leave the village go to the capital, Tougan, where they make a living brewing and selling millet beer. They run taverns and are reputed to be of easy virtue. If they are pregnant, they must designate a father, to whom the child will be returned when it has been weaned, if it is a boy; if it is a girl, she will be returned to her father when she is between seven and twelve years of age. No child can be attached to its mother's lineage.

There are two matrimonial statutes. First marriage, called *woso* or *furu*, which also means "hot," "dangerous," and "in danger," is indissoluble and involves the lineage as a whole. If a woman refuses the husband to whom she was given at birth and flees with her lover, her entire lineage will try to find her. These flights are not uncommon, for a little girl is often given in marriage by her father and the doyens of the lineage in order to repay a matrimonial debt; consequently, her husband may be forty-five years old at her birth and sixty when she must join him.

These age differences have two consequences. First, they affect genealogies, for men may have children with all their wives, from their first wife at twenty-five to their last after sixty-five. Thus, there may be a forty-year gap between two brothers with the same father, accumulated over generations. Genealogical levels therefore do not involve age groups. For women, on the contrary, genealogical levels may be extremely close; uterine lines secede every fifteen years provided the first-born child is a girl each time, whereas strictly agnatic lines will be much longer. This is characteristic of Samo memory and of all polygamous societies that extend over twelve generations at the most through women and five at the most through men.[12]

The second consequence is that women are often young widows. As they belong to the lineage they have been given to, they often remarry their deceased husband's younger brother leviratically. A woman may therefore marry her husband's brother, but only after his death, not after divorce.[13] Because the dead return to visit the living, the brother will have his new wife's door walled up and have another door made. The deceased brother will be unable to enter his widow's hut and will collide against the blocked door, because the dead recognize only what they have known. Here again, symbolically, we find the ban on two brothers living with the same woman. If the second husband did not block the old door of her hut, the children born of this second marriage would belong to the first husband beyond death. The younger brother would father children in the name of and on behalf of his dead older brother, who would be present during lovemaking.

There are also secondary marriages called *sana*, which only involve individuals, not their lineages. If a woman does not wish to remarry leviratically but wishes to reunite with her prenuptial lover, for example, this marriage is considered secondary; it can be broken off without a conciliation procedure. There are other cases of legitimate separation, such as a sterile first union. Divination is then used, for instance, to establish incompatibility between ancestors who once detested each other and now refuse to meet again to produce a child together; or it will detect an incestuous relationship that went unnoticed. Finally, if a man's legitimate wife has repeatedly run away, he may, out of weariness, renounce her. But he will never renounce the children she may have from other secondary marriages, who consequently will return to him. Thus there are children who are born in one lineage and then, at seven or ten, live in another lineage, their legitimate father's, whose matrimonial prohibitions they will respect. But if someone, out of hatred, anger, or jealousy, publicly tells a child he is a bastard and was not born in the lineage, this child is obliged to return to his lineage of origin, which will inscribe him in his place

146

in order of birth, following a ceremony. These cases are very rare and underscore the primordial importance of the spoken word and recognition.

Matrimonial debts between lineages condemn women to a predestined fate. When a woman is pregnant, the recipient of the child, if it is a girl, is already known. The number of potential recipients is not unlimited; unions in both directions made by this lineage are considered. Close watch is kept over the pregnancies of women of lineages from which a wife is expected for certain adult men or their sons. The woman is therefore a good of exchange; she does not exercise her own will, except in secondary marriage and in the *gagaré* ("free" or "wild") state, and even then, only after fulfilling her matrimonial contract.

Secondary marriages do not necessarily occur in the village the woman comes from or the village of her first marriage. Generally, they take place in a third village, at the market place. If a woman has wed a second time in a lineage of a matrimonial area other than her own, her sisters or daughters will eventually do the same, not in the same lineage, since that is forbidden, but in a nearby lineage within the same zone of familiarity created by the sister's or mother's remarriage. In fact, in societies of patrilineal descent, where a woman is a circulating commodity, she often suffers a deep emotional lack. In her host lineage, she has a relationship with a husband she has generally not chosen, whose relatives may mistreat her. A woman's only solid emotional bond is with her children. Consequently, these zones of familiarity in secondary marriage constitute places of friendship and solidarity between women of the same origin, while respecting matrimonial rules.

While conducting these genealogical surveys, I identified the kinship system as Omaha type, for which there had been no African example until then. It was one of the first systematic investigations of kinship in an African population, conducted in

147

several villages with different dialects, after a list had been compiled of all the possible positions of kinship over four generations.[14] Beyond the multitude of possibilities, a difficulty arose in
that the Samo, like most populations, do not describe their kinship relations beginning with Alter, as the French do, but with
Ego. The question "What do you call the wife of the brother of
the wife of the son of the brother of your father?" (the sister-in-
law of a parallel cousin) makes no sense; it must be asked another
way, starting with the informant himself: "What do you call your
father's brother's son's wife's brother's wife?' And if the individuals in question do not exist in Ego's personal genealogy, one cannot obtain an answer.

A method was worked out, which turned out to be wonder-
fully effective not only among the Samo, but also among the
Dogon, the Mossi, and the Bobo.

With cowries[15] representing the female sex, pebbles representing the male sex, and twigs representing filiation, collaterality, or alliance, I diagrammed and explained the terminology of
multiple relationships in schemas involving only elementary relationships (father, mother/son, daughter; brother/sister; husband/
wife). When the informants were familiar with the procedure, I
constructed more complex schemas (which had appeared on the
preestablished list) or they themselves constructed the chains of
kinship they wished to comment on.

Let's suppose the following schema, in which the lineage of
Ego's maternal grandmother is also that of Alter's mother, which
thus represents a shared uterine stock, making marriage between
them impossible (in France, this would be a female cousin in the
general, indeterminate framework of female first cousins). (See
figure 26.)

The question was, how does Ego refer to this cousin and can
he marry her? A digression allowed me to see how kinship termi-

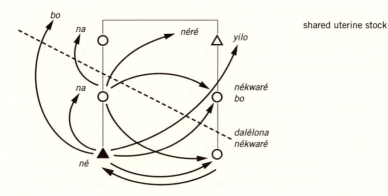

Figure 26.

nology is learned: by reference to appellations used by one of the two relatives who appears on the chain, with a deductive code for the terminology that Ego must use. In the case of this figure:

"I call my mother 'mother' [*na*].

"My mother calls her mother '*na.*' A mother for my mother is a grandmother for me [*bo*].

"My mother calls her mother's brother 'maternal uncle' [*néré*] [which is at the core of the logic of Omaha kinship systems]. A *néré* for my mother is a grandfather for me [*yilo*].

"My mother calls her maternal uncle's daughter 'little mother' [*nékwaré*]. A mother for my mother is a grandmother for me [*bo*].

"My mother calls her little mother's daughter 'younger sister' [*dalélona*]. A sister for my mother is a little mother for me [*nékwaré*], and she calls me 'child' [*né*].

"I cannot marry my little mother."

As we have seen, in an Omaha terminological system, Ego calls his father's brother "father" and his mother's sister "mother" or "little mother" — these are parallel siblings — while the mother's brother and the father's sister go by specific kinship terms. The children of those Ego calls "father" or "mother" are necessarily called "brother" or "sister," which then leads to particular appellations for these children based on whether Ego is male or female (a man calls his "brother's" child "my child" and a "sister's" child "nephew" or "niece"; a woman calls a "sister's" child "my child" and a "brother's" child "my sibling").

There is a remarkable transitive and deductive logic in learning a system of appellation, which, at the very least, is difficult to accept for those used to another internal logic of kinship. It is nevertheless a remarkably precise system with a strongly patrilineal ideology.

To pick up where we left off, consider figure 26, in which Ego and Alter cannot marry each other.

This female cousin whom Ego cannot marry does not in fact belong to any of the four lineages prohibited to him; nor does he belong to any of the four lineages prohibited to Alter. The fact that he calls her "mother" does not justify the ban. The deductive logic itself of the system of appellation causes appellations of close kinship to be given to distant and marriageable relatives. What unites Ego to Alter in a kinship relation that prohibits marriage between them is that they are of the same uterine stock (*to goro*), from the maternal grandmother for the one, from the mother for the other: they reunite, as they say in Samo language, of the same maternal lineages. To share a lineage is to not belong to a forbidden lineage. Alter's mother belongs to the lineage of Ego's grandmother through agnatic descent, but her daughter belongs to her father's lineage, which cannot be Ego's lineage (by reciprocity, since Ego cannot marry Alter's mother, who belongs by birth to his grandmother's lineage).

If this female cousin is forbidden to him, through the notion of shared uterine stock, understood as sharing the same uterine lineages, one must certainly assume an awareness of incest of the second type: that a mother and her daughter, and two sisters, share the same substantial identity, that they are, essentially, the same person.

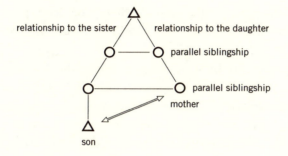

Figure 27.

This can be illustrated by figure 27, placing relations of siblingship on the same level, as they are expressed by the appellations in figure 26. This provides a clearer view of the foundation of Omaha systems, namely, that a brother's relationship with his sister is equivalent in its terminological consequences to a man's relationship with his daughter.[16]

Yet even if this terminology is automatically deduced, kinship eventually comes undone. At a certain degree (beyond common descent from the grandparents), the system picks up again for all speakers and develops horizontally: every man whom the purely deductive and transitive logic of appellation would consider a "maternal uncle" becomes a "little father" who will engender children Ego may call "brothers" but more generally will call by their first name or another close appellation of kinship.

Thus we see the core of the system developed over three or four generations, then some ambiguity where, for certain distant cousins, terminology hesitates between crossed appellation (which would be correct) and parallel appellation (which reestablishes the horizontality of the appellations), and finally an area in which certain kinship relations are no longer designated according to the rule of deductibility, although the kinship relations are known. The choice of spouse will be made in these zones of familiarity.

Starting with these genealogies, which attested to actual marriages, revealed Samo laws, and concretely illustrated abstract kinship schemas ("I cannot marry this relative, I can marry that one"), I was able to verify that the bans were indeed respected. Creating a computer model based on this data, I determined the kinship zones in which the choice of spouse was made preferentially. I then tested a number of hypotheses in order to understand how exchanges were possible between the same lineages on a regular basis and how it had come to be that each of the three villages in this survey constituted its own principal zone of endogamy, while the multiplicity of the prohibitions would have led one to postulate both lineal exogamy and residential village exogamy.

Above we noted that the accumulation of rules had a subtractive rather than additive effect.[17] The main hypotheses had to do with the symmetry of parallel blood relations and the nonsymmetry of crossed blood relations with regard to whether an earlier alliance between two lineages could be renewed, a man's sister being allowed what his brother was not, and, reciprocally, a woman's brother being allowed what her sister was not.

Numerous calculations using this data made clear the complex adaptation between lineages prohibited because of common patrilineal descent or because of the implicit rule against sharing in common the same uterine stock. "Implicit" is not really the right word, since the Samo call these partners "unmarryable" (and, in fact, they are, genealogically), but this is not an explicitly formulated law, as the others are.

There is a close correlation therefore between the exogamic rule that governs the functioning of semicomplex Crow and Omaha systems of alliance and the repugnance for incest of the second type founded on the sensed identity of same sex blood relations, an identity that will be encountered through a common sexual partner.

In fact, several stocks of identity coexist, and we should distinguish between that which involves common descent (the other's lineal origin) and that which involves sharing in common. The exogamic rule justifies the first case but says nothing of the second, which alone explains the notion of differential identity and the prohibition pertaining to incest of the second type, because the two individuals are of common uterine stock and are of the same maternal or grandmaternal lineage.

As we have seen, two "sisters" cannot have relations with the same man. If a man commits adultery with his wife's "sister," the marriage is automatically broken off and the husband's lineage may ask for nothing, except, perhaps, forgiveness. Similarly, two sisters cannot marry two brothers, nor can a mother and daughter marry the same man, or marry in the same lineage (a second marriage for one of them). The two sisters may be full siblings of the same paternal and maternal stock, with common stock of physical matter and symbolic virtue; agnatic half-sisters who share only the father's matter and the symbolic nature of his lineage; uterine sisters who, like the daughter and mother, share only the matter that comes to them from a maternal grandfather (or, for the mother, from her father) and the symbolic virtue of this lineage; or, finally, parallel cousins, whether patrilateral (who there-

fore belong to the same lineage as Ego) or matrilateral, who share
the same uterine lineages with Ego. Moreover, there is the particular female substantial identity that unites the father's sister to
the brother's daughter: both are born in the same lineage, and, as
we saw in figure 27, the slant of the system of appellation places
them in a relationship equivalent to that of two sisters in following generations. (See figure 28.)

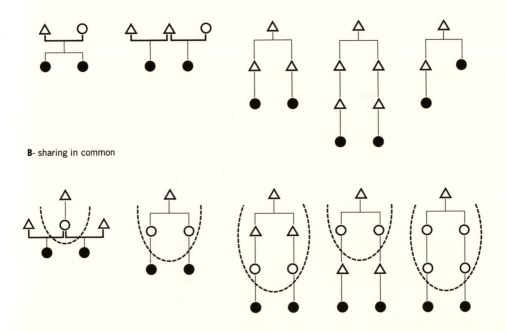

A- patrilineal descent

B- sharing in common

Figure 28.

Incest of the second type is also present — overpresent, one might say — in the exogamic rule. Due to the principle of not redoubling an alliance made by a relative of the same sex, incest of the second type does not have to be formulated explicitly; it is contained in a more encompassing prohibition. But the fact that the rule on sharing in common (recognized and clearly expressed: "we are of the same stock") is not cited as an exogamic matrimonial rule suggests that it is only stated this way to convey the impossibility of incest of the second type.

The Baoulé

Pierre Etienne studied a population on the Ivory Coast, the Baoulé, who also have a semicomplex system of alliance and who are of particular interest to us because they observe the same prohibitions as the Samo, accompanied by unique rituals, notably one of atonement for breaking the prohibition of two sisters, which they call *plo-plo*. The Samo have a ritual to undo incest between blood relations or affines who live sufficiently far away from one another for it to have been committed unknowingly. If one discovers by chance, divination, or denouncement that spouses are related, there is a ritual to undo their distant consanguinity, after which they wear a special wire bracelet of twisted copper and iron, signaling to the world that their consanguineous relationship has been broken.

The *plo-plo* ritual that puts an end to the kinship relationship is much more elaborate and explicit. "Culprits of this sort of incest are subject to a somewhat mortifying ritual of atonement and ceremonial purification. Entirely naked, they are forced to hit one another with two halves of a kid goat or a sheep split lengthwise. [...] This act atones for the crime symbolically. What should have remained separate was mixed; therefore, what is naturally united is separated. Let us add that the sacrificed kid goat or

155

sheep is cut lengthwise while still alive. The purpose of this ritual is to obliterate kinship relations symbolically between the two guilty parties."[18]

This *plo-plo* incest does not occur between a man and a woman, but between two blood relations, men or women, through the intermediary of a common partner. The ritual takes place not between the individuals who have had the culpable relations but between blood relations who have found themselves in a situation of incest due to this fact. "They have mixed themselves," the Baoulé say. "They have entered into an incestuous relationship." This incest is similar to marriage between parallel uterine cousins, also punishable by a *plo-plo* ritual. But whereas sexual relations between uterine cousins oblige the offenders to marry in the event of pregnancy, marriage with two sisters remains absolutely impossible: a man may, in certain circumstances, marry his cousin, but he cannot touch two sisters, because two sisters cannot touch each other. And yet a man's uterine female cousins are considered his sisters. Every society defines its threshold of tolerance. Still, the sacrificed animal, cut in two while still alive, certainly connotes a radical break of identity. What is more identical than one body?

Etienne concluded that the Baoulé were more tolerant toward eliminating a prohibition of matrimonial alliance than toward redoubling it (marrying one's cousin but not marrying two sisters). I see things differently: the redoubling of the matrimonial alliance is absolutely possible between blood relations of the opposite sex, whereas it is impossible between siblings of the same sex. It is true that Etienne was not asking the same question as I am; he was not interested in the problem of symmetry in alliance but in completely different questions of a psychological order.

Baoulé explanation for the prohibition concerning two agnatic sisters is the same as that of certain English members of parliament. One cannot marry a woman and her sister at the same time, because they cannot be rivals. But this justification is secondary; the essential lies elsewhere, in the logic of identity and difference.

Etienne saw this in another case. The Baoulé do not practice sister exchange,[19] unlike the Samo, who authorize it: "When we asked why I could not marry my sister's husband's sister, they clearly found the question absurd; they looked as though they felt sorry for us": "'You're already *sia* [related by marriage] to the man who married your sister. What's the use in being *sia* to him a second time by marrying his sister?'" In other words, since this man and his sister's husband are already relatives by marriage — they work, hunt, and drink together — the man gains nothing by redoubling this alliance; whereas by marrying a woman who introduces him into a new relationship of alliance, he makes new partners. Etienne justly comments: "This is no doubt a naïve way to express the principle of not redoubling matrimonial alliance but, in the last analysis, we find it the most pertinent." The reason used to justify the prohibition of two sisters — they could not be sisters and rivals at the same time — is perhaps accurate on the psychological level of sexual fantasy, but it masks another, deeper one that supposes the meeting of identical flesh through a common partner. One must keep in mind that the *plo-plo* ritual concerns only these two sisters who are "mixed" and not the man who made them mixed.

The prohibition against a man marrying his wife's sister and the one against marrying his sister's husband's sister are different. In the first case, alliance is redoubled by two female blood relations in the same lineage; in the second, alliance is redoubled between two lineages, which is possible for two blood relations of opposite sex. The Baoulé do not confuse relations of parallel symmetry (that is, between two brothers, two sisters, and so on) and the crossed relationship between a brother and a sister, which is possible, though of little social use, as the Baoulé wisely pointed out. Marrying the sister's husband's sister is possible, but it seems senseless.

The Samo and Baoulé have different viewpoints on the social utility of this type of marriage, which is the sort of variation allowed for by coherent semicomplex Crow-Omaha systems of alliance. For the Samo, simultaneous or close sister exchange immediately confirms a relationship of alliance between two lineages by inaugurating a succession of debts in both directions and simultaneous or deferred reimbursements. The sisters, moreover, are rarely actual sisters, but rather classificatory lineal "sisters." The Baoulé clearly prefer deferred return and the possibility of opening the field of alliances as widely as possible at each generation.

Among the Antaimoro of Madagascar's low valley of Faraony, a similar ritual, called *fafy*, sanctions cases of incest: its goal is either to erase the kinship in order to yield to the sexual relationship, or, on the contrary, to obliterate traces of the sexual relationship in order to yield entirely to the kinship.[20] In this example, kinship and identity first and foremost are a matter of engendering (father/son, mother/daughter) rather than siblingship.

"If a man sleeps with his wife's daughter, the daughter by this act 'destroys what made her mother a mother and places her in a situation of impurity.' The goal of *fafy*, the daughter's purifying sprinkling of blood onto the mother's body, is to renew the mother/daughter relationship by eliminating the effect of the sexual relations. But the incestuous relationship that must be eliminated in order to reestablish former ties is *between the mother and daughter*, not between the daughter and the mother's husband."[21]

Among the Samo, there is a ritual similar to the *plo-plo* ritual, but for incest of the first type between close blood relations. The guilty parties are taken to the marketplace and stripped, a chicken is sacrificed over their genitals, and they are sent through the bush, naked and covered with blood. It is, as Etienne would have said, a "somewhat mortifying" ritual.

Other African Examples

Among the African systems with this particular semicomplex matrimonial structure associated with unilineal rules of filiation and Crow-Omaha kinship terminology are the Mkako of Cameroon,[22] the Minyanka of Mali,[23] the Mouktele and the Mofu of Cameroon,[24] and numerous others,[25] each with particular variations that denote these systems' suppleness and adaptability to the social system as a whole and to various representations.

Particularly interesting is the early research by the great English scholars who attempted to explain incest as it was encountered in the field: Robert Rattray among the Ashanti,[26] Meyer Fortes among the Tallensi,[27] and E.E. Evans-Pritchard among the Nuer.[28] These examples are taken up in Jack Goody's famous 1956 article, "A Comparative Approach to Incest and Adultery."[29]

With the title, the stakes are set. Goody notes that certain societies make no distinction between incest (which we are calling "incest of the first type") and other forms of sexual offenses. To clarify this, he makes a distinction between incest and intralineal adultery, extralineal adultery, and incomprehensible matrimonial situations that represent neither incest nor adultery, such as a liaison with two sisters. Why "incomprehensible"? Because he assumes that if a man were able to have a liaison with a woman — to sleep with her (simple fornication) — she would not belong to the categories forbidden to him. If she were "allowed," her sister and the women of the same lineage would be, too.

A man's relationship with his brother's wife, in societies of patrilineal law, would come under intralineal adultery, whereas a man's relationship with his wife's mother or sister would come under extralineal adultery. One can see the suggested gradations: fornication, extralineal adultery, intralineal adultery, incest (to which one may add relations with a menstruating woman).

The Ashanti form a matrilineal society. They have two terms to refer to incest, *mogyadie* and *atwebenefie*. The term *mogyadie* ("eating up of one's own blood") denotes consanguineous incest: sexual relations between siblings (since they cannot marry), between those who call each other "brother" and "sister," and between uterine half-siblings exclusively. A sexual relationship between a father and his daughter does not come under the *mogyadie* category, for they are not of the same matriclan: the daughter belongs to her mother's, the father to his own mother's. But while this is not an offense in the matriclan, it is one in the allied group, the father's matriclan, and thus another term is used to denote it : *atwebenefie* ("vagina near to the dwelling-house").

A second type of incest, which does not involve blood relations but the wives of male members of the matriclan and the mother and sister of one's own wife, is also referred to as *atwebenefie*. A third term — *baratwe* — designates relations with an "unclean" woman, which may mean a woman who is having her period. Now, this term is linked to the preceding one because the offenses have the same consequence: sterility. Rattray has translated *mogyadie* as "incest" and *atwebenefie* as "adultery," though the first type of *atwebenefie* relationship is not adultery at all but indeed incest between father and daughter. While the Christian principle of one flesh causes us to assimilate spouses' kinship groups, the Ashanti, according to Rattray, distinguish clearly between a man's descent group and those of his different wives', since the Ashanti do not consider affines to be relatives. But this does not solve the problem of how to refer to father-daughter incest.

In my opinion, it is not *mogyadie*, for two reasons: the identity of the bodily substances of father and daughter is weakened, as is the symbolic idea of common descent, because they are not the same sex and do not come from the same lineage.

Rattray establishes a link with the Trobrianders, of whom Malinowksi wrote: "It must be clearly understood that, although father to daughter incest is regarded as bad, it is not described by the word *suvasova* (clan exogamy or incest), nor does any disease follow upon it; and as we know, the whole ideology underlying this taboo is different from that of *suvasova*."[30] Unfortunately, Malinowski does not elaborate on this ideology. The *suvasova* of the Trobrianders corresponds exactly to the *mogyadie* of the Ashanti; it is incest within a clan which provokes a certain disorder, and father-daughter incest is not thought to have disastrous consequences in either of these matrilineal societies, for it does not take place within the matrilineal clan. Malinowski does not mention the other two types of sexual offenses described by the Ashanti as *atwebenefie*: relations with the wives of clan members and with the wife's mother or sister.

If we look at what Ashanti informants place in the same category of *atwebenefie* — adultery with the brother's wife, the son's wife, the wife's mother, the uncle's wife, the wife of a fellow member of an age group or association, the wife of one's own slave, the father's wife other than the adulterer's own mother, the wife's sister whether single or married[31] — we could effectively say that these are adulterous acts with the wives of members of the group (matriclan as well as patriclan) in the broad and even metonymic sense; the others take place outside the group (with the wife's mother or sister). But from my point of view, the Ashanti informants quite logically call them the same thing without bothering to differentiate between intra- and extra-group adultery because these incestuous "adulterous acts" lead back implicitly to the same formal situation, that of incest of the second type. On the one hand, incest exists between two real or assimilated (classificatory) male blood relations (father/son, brother/brother, uncle/nephew; the master/slave relationship is one of paternity, the co-workers' relationship, one of fraternity) who share the same sexual partner; on the other hand, incest of the second type exists between two female blood relations (mother/daughter, sister/sister) sharing the same sexual partner.

Seen this way, the father/daughter relationship would also come under the *atwebenefie* category. As I have said, there is a dual weakening of the identity between a father and daughter, through gender difference and the fact that they belong to different matriclans. On the other hand, the maternal substance is fully present in the daughter: this is *atwebenefie* incest of the second type, between the mother and the daughter, and not *mogyadie*, direct incest between opposite sex blood relations of the same lineage. (See figure 29.)

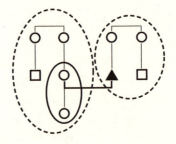

Figure 29.

Meyer Fortes claims that the (patrilineal) Tallensi have no word to designate incest, which is not to say they have no concept of it, since they talk about it, albeit obliquely. One reason might be that the passage from a circumlocution to a word is the passage from the thing to the concept, which is not immediate. Another reason has to do with the ethnologist's craft itself: our interlocutors only answer the questions we ask them; they have no way of knowing *a priori* what we are getting at, especially since we ourselves only later discover the meaning of our questions (and therefore the pertinence of the answers). Each human group inhabits a world of obvious givens which are never explicated but which gradually reveal themselves to whomever has penetrated this group. Consequently, it could very well be that the Tallensi have a word to designate incest, but that Meyer Fortes simply never heard it.[32]

This incest that has no name consists of sexual relations in the extended family, not only with blood relations of the kindred core — with the father's sister, the daughter, or the sister — but also with all the wives of the men of the group: the father's, brother's, or son's wives. As the system of filiation is patrilineal, all kinship relations are naturally defined from the male point of view. While incest in the extended family with a distant cousin or great-niece is considered somewhat scandalous, incest in one's core group with the wives of men in the group is horrifying. Meyer Fortes thus restricts incest to these two last cases and considers every liaison with the wives of men of the lineage outside the extended family as falling within the province of adultery. The first case (incest of the first type but in the extended family), which is still a matter of sexual relations between blood relations, seems to elude him. This confusion stems quite simply from pinning onto the indigenous reality Western categories that boil down to the incest/adultery pair.

Using these two examples, the matrilineal Ashanti and the patrilineal Tallensi, Goody proposed dividing sexual offenses into three categories: First, offenses that have taken place within the group of filiation, which includes those we call blood relations, since only those who belong to the group of unifiliation are involved. Second, offenses that are committed with the wife of a member of the descent group: the wife of the father, brother, son, uncle, nephew, and so on. Third, sexual liaisons with any married women. Since this third category is adultery, the question is, which of the two preceding categories actually represented incest: the sexual offense in the descent group or with the wife of a male member of this descent group?

Now, Meyer Fortes clearly indicated that the second category constituted incest for the Tallensi, not the first, as Goody suggested. Goody sees the importance of patrivirilocality here; because the men of the small group of residence are distinct from the other men of the lineage, adultery with their wives would be horrifying. There is a strong patrilineal emphasis; indeed, all the men in a lineage live together, so that if adultery was not rigorously sanctioned within this group, there would be no end to the disputes. This standard sociological explanation — preserving peace in the group rather than sowing confusion — would be convincing if only the wives of men who lived together were prohibited; but this is not the case, since the wife's mother and sister, whom Ego does not live with, are also prohibited. (See figure 30.)

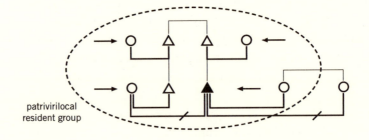

patrivirilocal
resident group

Figure 30.

The reason lies elsewhere. If the Tallensi consider incest of the first type with a fairly distant relative merely shocking, while sexual relations with the wives of the brother or the father compel horror, it is because identity of gender is more important than identity of cross-sex kinship. When a man sleeps with his father's sister, his own daughter, or his sister, there is identity of blood but gender difference; thus identity is not total. Whereas incest is horrifying with the brother's, father's, or son's wife because subjacent to it is a certain representation of consanguineous homosexuality, an intensification of identity through gender and blood. While the matrilineal Baoulé are most concerned by cases of two women — two sisters or a mother and daughter — united by the same partner, the patrilineal Tallensi are most concerned with cases of two men — two brothers or a father and son.

This objection to Goody's argument might also be made: there can be no adultery unless the women are married. The prohibition of two sisters or a daughter and her mother does not imply that they are. In other words, a man's wife's sister may be single and her mother a widow. In this case, is it adultery or something else that would come under a fourth category, fornication, for instance? According to Goody, the explanation lies here: these women are not prohibited since one is descended from the same lineage as this man's wife and the other from a third lineage. They are nevertheless forbidden in order to avoid confusion of status. Indeed, if a man sleeps with his sister-in-law or his mother-in-law, whether they are married or single, he is making them equivalent to his legitimate wife and therefore cannot really consider them simply a sister-in-law or mother-in-law.

Goody also uses patrilineality to explain the Tallensi's horror of sexual relations with wives of group members, since among the matrilineal Ashanti, these relations are criticized merely as improprieties. For societies with patrilineal filiation, he says, women who enter the group are essential to its survival since they ensure descendants; therefore the legal relationship that assures the group's perpetuation cannot be disturbed. This explanation is rather surprising since, as we have seen, children belong to the legitimate father, no matter what. Moreover, men of the same generation call each other "brothers" and are considered "fathers" by individuals of the following generation; consequently, a man is never without descendants. This rule alone renders the lineal group robust and capable of resisting the perturbations of adultery.

From this point of view, patrilineality constitutes a factor of tolerance. A man unable to impregnate his wife would, on the contrary, be interested in having recourse to the services of another man of his lineage. Moreover, certain societies, like the Mossi, recognize the right to flirt with the brother's wife, which can lead to a passing fling (*rakirolle*).[33]

Despite being horrified by sexual commerce with wives of members of the group, the Tallensi will allow a younger twin brother access to the older brother's wife (though the reverse would constitute a major offense). The asymmetry in the twins' order of birth introduces a slight difference between them, as if the older twin belonged to the preceding generation. That only the younger can enjoy his twin brother's wife and not the reverse is a subtle adaptation of various rules: the twins are perfect identicals, the same body in two envelopes. But only the younger one has access to the father's wife, for as a general rule among the Tallensi and in western African societies, a relationship with the son's wife has more formidable consequences than one with the father's wife. It is a kind of excess of power.

As one can see, these prohibitions are not solely explained by rules of filiation or sexual appropriation in marriage, or even by status distinctions, but by something that has to do with the symbolic. While the encounter of two identicals is feared in the case of a father and son or two brothers, identity is absolute in the case of twin brothers; they are the same, indeed, one and the same if they are identical twins. They have gestated in the same womb for nine months, bathed in the same amniotic fluid, and been nourished by the same blood and paternal sperm: therefore they can meet again in another womb without endangering anyone. In a way, they are immune to the excess of the identical. Similarly, two twin sisters may share the same sexual partner, and among the Mossi, it is even an obligation, as we have seen.

We do not know and probably never will know (because what goes without saying remains unsaid) why a given society selects one particular system of alliance rather than another from among the several systems that would be equally compatible with its social rules, or why another similar society will select a different system.

Having thus classified sexual offenses in three categories, Goody sought verification among the Nuer, a population of cattle breeders who are well known thanks to Evans-Pritchard's studies. The Nuer as a whole present a series of traits found almost nowhere else. They believe that at menopause a sterile woman must be treated like a man. She returns to her group of origin, becomes an uncle to her brothers' daughters, and as such receives her share of the bride-prices. Having acquired a herd of animals, she can in turn pay a bride-price to procure a wife herself, indeed, several wives, who give her descendants through the intermediary of a servant who acts as a genitor (recruited from another ethnic group, the Dinka) and who receives a share of the bride-prices for the daughters that he sires.

The Nuer also practice phantom marriage, that is, bearing children on behalf of a dead person. Indeed, to pay the bride-price, men must acquire a large herd of animals and often do not manage to do so until late in life. Sometimes they die first, without descendants. A younger brother or nephew (the son of

167

a brother) may procure a wife with the dead man's livestock, but the children engendered will be the children of the deceased older brother or uncle. If the younger brother in turn dies before having procured a wife of his own, and therefore is without descendants, his nephew will take over, using the deceased's herd to acquire a wife and engender children in the deceased uncle's name. Now, in reality, one of his social nephews would be his own biological son. But among the Nuer, social genealogy takes precedence over biological genealogy.

The Nuer have a word to designate incest: *rual*. It denotes the two categories that we have already encountered, consanguineous incest and the sexual relationship with wives of men belonging to one's own clan. Evans-Pritchard also offered an explanation of this second category of incest. According to Evans-Pritchard, one cannot have relations with male blood relations' wives, for they are perceived as potential if not actual mothers of future blood relations. Nevertheless, *rual* very explicitly concerns relations with the father's, son's, and brother's wives, to the exclusion of relations with the wives of agnatic half-brothers, paternal uncles and patrilineal parallel cousins, which is simply considered bad form. In the first group, there is only one vertical or horizontal mediation in the father-son, brother-brother chain, whereas in the second there are two or more. With the wife of a paternal uncle, there is a double mediation, collateral between brothers and vertical between father and son; with the wife of a patrilineal parallel cousin, there is a triple mediation, vertical from the cousin to his father, collateral from the uncle to the father, and vertical from the father to the son.

Rual incest brings supernatural sanction — disease, drought, epidemic — not only against the protagonists, but also their entourage and the entire group. Another ethnologist, P.P. Howell, writes, "It is not considered correct [among the Nuer] that two kinsmen should have sexual relations with the same woman at the same period."[34] He thus broadens the domain of prohibitions to cases where there is neither consanguinity nor alliance between the two partners, which goes back to what Goody called "fornication." In "at the same period," we find an equivalent of the Hittite distinction "in the same place."

Howell continues: "[...] sexual relations with the legal wife of another man create an impurity [and Howell does not specify whether this man is a blood relation], and [...] there is greater impurity if two men of the same kinship group have sexual relations with the same woman."[35] In the first case, the two men sharing the same woman are not related, whereas in the second they are; the woman is the wife of one in the first case, and the wife of neither in the second. While one can see that the adultery of the first case is reprehensible, it is harder to see what is reprehensible in the second case, unless it is this incest of the second type between blood relations of the same sex who encounter each other again in the same womb. There is yet a third case. Howell adds: "[...] adultery is an offence which brings greater spiritual dangers when the husband and the adulterer are kinsmen."[36] This time, the two men are blood relations and the woman is the wife of one.

Goody interprets the differences between the Nuer and the Tallensi, both patrilineal, in terms of conflict between the individual and collective aspects of law, between exclusive rights over one's wife and the appurtenance of her offspring to the entire lineage. "This interpretation receives support from the Nuer version of the common African prohibition on two members of a descent group having intercourse with the same woman."[37] But he does not specify the status of this woman. Among the Tallensi and the LoDagaa, whom he has personally studied, this prohibition concerns full siblings. But he omits the case of Tallensi twins. According to Goody, the corporate character of the lineage is stronger among the Nuer, who say it is wrong for two kinsmen to court the same girl. He places this offense under the category of fornication. But he introduces a moral connotation here that is totally extraneous to the Nuer. He does not see the essential thing — namely, that the two men are related and therefore have the same substance, and that through this sort of "fornication" they will encounter each other in the same womb, a source of great danger. He is blinkered by a legal consideration that leads him to seek the rule's justification in a desire to avoid the conflict inevitable when two blood relations become rivals. In other words, Goody offers endless ad hoc arguments to explain this sexual prohibition, when there is essentially only one: the recognition and prohibition of incest of the second type.

Even this brief look at African societies with semicomplex systems of alliance allows us to note the presence of a common ideological substratum (which takes various forms due to each society's own definition of the identical): the awareness and refusal of incest of the second type. This association is characteristic of but not exclusive to this structural type of marriage system, since the ban concerns not only the redoubling of an alliance contracted by a blood relation of the same sex, but also simple sexual relations with a common partner not involving prior marriage. In a complete reversal, one sometimes finds that pure identicals, such as twins, must not or cannot be dissociated (the case of twin sisters or the *rakirolle* law among the Mossi); ultimately, this is less a matter of reversal than a consequence of the extreme logic of the notion of the identical. There are other possible variants: the ban may apply to full siblings but not to half-siblings with the same father, or it may proscribe redoubling in a first marriage but not in a second, and so on. These variations do not seriously affect the structure of the whole but adjust it slightly, for there is no society that does not anticipate and tolerate certain compromises of its rules. These adjustments do not damage the common ideological substratum.

We will establish the viability of these systems and whether they are securely built on an ideological foundation using Malinowski's representations.

CHAPTER FIVE

From Matrimonial Logic

to Human Representation

From the outset, we have spoken of substance, substantial identity, corporality, carnal union, and the exchange of fluids. Now, moving forward in the same line, I wish to demonstrate that the hypothesis concerning fear of incest of the second type, unformulated as such but conveyed by other rules and behaviors, is confirmed by the existence, among various African groups, of complete conceptual sets of representations involving identity and the body.

The Rules Underlying the Practice

The exogamic rule alone cannot explain the prohibition of incest of the second type, the rigor of which we have just seen in various exotic populations. Indeed, the obligation to marry a foreigner and not a blood relation makes this foreigner's blood relations foreigners as well, *a priori*. The wife's sister might have been chosen in place of the wife; she becomes forbidden because her sister was chosen. Nevertheless, the fact remains that these bans of the second type have something to do with the identical structure of these semicomplex systems of alliance, which are found in almost all parts of the world, particularly North America and Africa.

The systems of alliance subject to patrilineal (Omaha) or matrilineal (Crow) rule, examples of which we have seen, are not preferential or prescriptive: they prohibit. Unlike elementary systems of generalized exchange, they do not assign a wife such as a "mother's brother's daughter," who might be a distant cousin but of the same lineage. Nor do they assign choice to a particular kinship group, as do elementary systems with moieties (or sections), where individuals born in one moiety must choose their spouse from the other (the prototypical union under such a system being the marriage of double cross cousins). (See figure 31.)

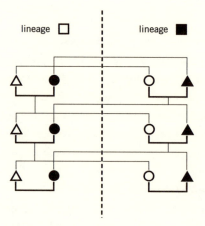

Figure 31.

Semicomplex systems function as elementary systems do, in that they concern groups, not just individuals in genealogical chains. But they differ in that they prohibit rather than prescribe. Our European complex systems of alliance also prohibit marriage between individuals based on the degrees of kinship uniting them; semicomplex systems, additionally, forbid alliance within entire groups to which an individual may have no direct link of consanguinity at all. In fact, the same lineage may include distinct lines that go back to apical ancestors who were parallel cousins, though the collateral relationship between the two brothers at the origin of these two lines cannot be established. (See figure 32.)

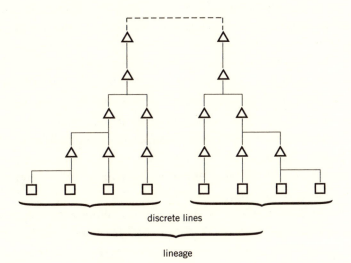

discrete lines

lineage

Figure 32.

The prohibitions are often numerous. Among the Samo, for example, it is forbidden to take a wife in one's own lineage (a woman called "sister," "paternal aunt," or "daughter"), in one's mother's lineage, and in those of both grandmothers. Some societies do not go so far back, the bans ending at the mother's lineage; but others go back even further, like the Amba described by E.H. Winter,[1] to the lineages of all four great-grandmothers. Moreover, the Samo prohibit taking a wife in the four primary lineages of any previous wife (that is, in her parents' and her grandmothers' lines). It is also forbidden for a man to marry in a lineage in which either his father or classificatory brothers, including patrilineal parallel cousins, already married.

There is a subtle yet essential clarification to be made. When a lineage is considered forbidden for a given male, every female born in this lineage is forbidden to him, however many generations separate the blood relations involved. It is impossible to take a wife in the grandmother's lineage, even if the woman, biologically speaking, is only a very distant cousin of the grandmother in question; this cousinhood passes through men *ad infinitum*. On the other hand, bans pertaining to these lineages are only valid for the individual in question — or rather, him and his full siblings — and for genealogical positions that represent only three generations (his own, his mother's, and his grandmothers'). But a man does not transmit to his children, born in his lineage, the ban relative to his own grandmothers' lineages. And that is where subsequent unions will be made preferentially. We will see the conceptual importance of this simple observation.

In addition to these bans concerning blood relations (four lines), the blood relations of affines (the wives' lineages), and the affines of blood relations (the lineages of wives of certain blood relations), there are still others that concern the sharing in common of the same maternal or grandmaternal lineage, as we have seen, even if neither potential spouse was born in either of them. Therefore, one cannot marry if lineages are related over three generations, whether through men or women. For example, a man cannot marry the daughter of his maternal grandmother's brother's son; on the other hand, his son can, since this is his great-grandmother's line. If this girl married elsewhere and had a daughter in turn, this daughter would also be forbidden to Ego although she belongs to her father's lineage. But the fact remains that her mother's lineage is the same as that of Ego's maternal grandmother. This is what I call "sharing in common." The bans, therefore, are even more extensive than the rules explicitly state, since ultimately one cannot marry any cognate relative — that is, through

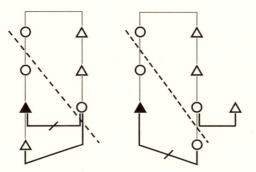

Figure 33.

men or women — over several generations. (See figure 33.)

Added to this is a prohibition "of propriety" against marriage between a brother-in-law and sister-in-law. A man may not marry his wife's brother's wife, after the death of his wife and brother. Her lineage is not forbidden to him *a priori*, but the suspicion of previous adultery and murder is cast on this union.

The bans are so numerous it would seem practically impossible to marry in a neighboring area (both in terms of kinship and residence). And yet, one can and does. A marriage at the last level forbidden to Ego will be allowed his son, and that is where he will marry. To understand this, two ideas must be kept in mind. First, the accumulation of rules does not work through addition but through subtraction. (See figure 34.) Second, matrimonial rules are always decreed in the masculine: it is not a matter of *homo* but *vir*. This has been cause for extreme confusion. Lévi-Strauss writes: "The most suitable manner of defining a Crow-Omaha system is to say that each time Ego chooses a line from which to obtain a wife, *all* [emphasis added] its members are automatically excluded for several generations from among the spouses available to Ego's line." The plural implies both sexes. Elsewhere in the text, Lévi-

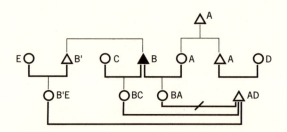

Figure 34.

Strauss writes, "the rule holds for both sexes...," which is certainly true in reciprocity and in parallel symmetry for both sexes, but false in positions of crossed symmetry.[2] We have shown above that a man could give a daughter to the lineage that gave him a wife, on the condition that she not be a daughter born of that union, whereas none of his sons could marry into this wife's lineage. Lévi-Strauss speaks of several generations: the number in fact varies for each society, based on the canonical relationship between the number of lineages of ascendants prohibited and the number of generations. If two lineages are prohibited, they will be for two generations, if four lineages are prohibited (up to the grandmothers), they will be for three generations, if eight lineages are prohibited, they will be for four generations.

What parallel symmetry makes impossible, crossed symmetry allows. While two brothers or a son and his father cannot duplicate their alliances, nothing forbids a father and his daughter, or a brother and his sister, from doing so. The key to semicomplex systems of alliance is the possibility for opposite sex blood relations to redouble their alliances and the impossibility for same sex blood relations to do so. Therefore, there can be complete cycles of consanguinity, and regular sister exchanges, generation after generation, simply by changing collateral line each time.[3]

Here again we find incest of the second type. Relatives of the same sex (a father and son, two brothers, two sisters, a father's sister and his brother's daughter) born in the same lineage cannot marry in the same lineage. This is also true for a mother and daughter, though not born in the same lineage, and for two uterine sisters (born of their common mother's two successive husbands, neither of whom is related to the other) or for two parallel female cousins, that is, in this case, born of two sisters.

Therefore, the need to marry out (the exogamic law) does not explain all of these bans; it accounts only for some of them. We must look to another logic, that of incest of the second type, namely, the impossibility of "making what already touches naturally touch carnally."[4] Substances considered identical in nature cannot meet through members of a given society, although there are other societies that in fact oblige identical things to meet.

Extreme forms of the matrimonial functioning may follow in which appellations of kinship (as in Omaha systems, where the father's brothers are called "father" and the mother's sisters "mother"), the line of unifiliation, and matrimonial rules work together toward completely preestablishing an individual's range of choice, by forcing him to respect the essential (here, the prohibition of incest of the second type), without, however, forcing him to take his spouse in foreign territory.

How do we reconcile polygyny, unifiliation, the multiple prohibitions of the matrimonial system, and the hypothesis that duplication of a previously contracted alliance is only possible between crossed blood relations, not between parallel blood relations (that is, the prohibition of incest of the second type, recognized in terms of pure sexual activity as well as matrimony)?

Say man B has received woman A, and then another, C; his brother B' could therefore not marry in either A or C, due to the rule that two brothers cannot marry in the same lineage: he will therefore marry in E. The wife A of B has a brother who married in another lineage D, and he had a son AD (his father comes from A and his mother from D). Now, B could not give his daughter BA to lineage A, from which he took a wife, due to the rule that a daughter cannot be married in her mother's lineage; on the other hand, nothing forbids him from giving the daughter that he has had with his wife C (BC) or the one his brother has had with his wife E ($B'E$): BC or $B'E$ do not in fact have any lineage in common with AD. If B had been able to take another wife in A or if his brother had been able to marry there, he would never have been able to give a daughter to A. This is what I call the prohibitions' "subtraction effect." (See figure 34.)

By including the grandparents' lines, one can show over three generations, in an even more subtle and refined manner, that the combination of all the prohibitions of various generations are precisely what allows one to marry without a problem.[5] Polygyny and the multiplication of lines of descent induced by the ban on renewing previous alliances of blood relations of the same sex allow matrimonial debts to be repaid easily.

We shall see that marriages are made with the closest possible kin. There are several ways to go about this, coming within a hair's breadth of incest of both types. One consists of open repayment of the contracted debt, due to an individual's redoubling of the alliance concluded previously by a blood relation from the same lineage but of the opposite sex, either in the same generation — a man may marry his sister's husband's "sister" — or the following generation: a man may marry a daughter of one of his paternal aunts, in the broad sense, or a daughter may be given in marriage to the lineage that gave the father a wife who is not her mother. We have seen that crossed symmetry is logically possible and deductible from prohibitive rules decreed in the masculine, if parallel symmetry (between brothers, between sisters, and so on) is not. Here we are closest to incest of the second type.

If daughter *BA* married man *A* in return for her mother's marriage (man *A* belonging to the same lineage as the mother, of whom *BA* is the identical), this would be a form of substantial incest. By marrying daughter *BC*, *BA*'s half-sister (by the father), the meeting of almost identical substances does not occur, even though there is an alliance in both directions between the two lineages, even though the daughters are actually half-sisters. This shows that the issue here is neither lineal exogamy with no return nor the simple relationship of collateral kinship between sisters, but rather the particular relationship that involves the sharing of substances. (See figure 35.)

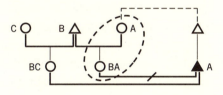

Figure 35.

The second way to marry the closest possible kin is to come full circle in consanguinity, that is, closest to direct consanguineous incest of the first type, by marrying someone who belongs by birth to a lineage forbidden to one of Ego's parents. Among the Samo there is an explicit order of proximity that states that one is closer to a relative born of a daughter from one's mother's lineage than to a relative born of a daughter from one's paternal grandmother's lineage, which is a little bit closer than a relative from the maternal grandmother's lineage, and all these relatives are closer to Ego than those linked to him by the sharing in common of the same maternal and grandmaternal lineages. (See figure 36.)

181

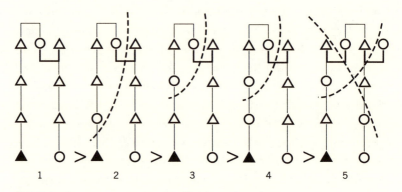

N.B. This represents only one of several possible configurations.

Figure 36.

Finally, there may be systems of redoubling ties of alliance which involve several lineages intermarrying. In fact, we know that it is impossible to marry someone who has the same maternal uncle as oneself, or the same maternal great uncle: "rivals," that is, co-takers of wives in the same lineage (all sons-in-law, in a way), cannot independently take a spouse in the lineages or lines of this mother or these grandmothers; this also holds true for their descendants for some time, but additionally they cannot marry one another. This ban applies to them and their full siblings but not to agnatic half-siblings or patrilateral parallel cousins. One can consequently establish elaborate strategies in which three or four lineages will be in continual matrimonial partnership, by organizing cycles or circuits.

Thus, members of the lineages *B* and *C*, issued from marriages represented in figure 37, cannot intermarry (they share in common the same maternal lineage) nor marry a member of lineage *A*, which is by definition the lineage of their respective mothers. It is also true for the members of lineage *D*, who cannot marry either in *A* (the lineage of a maternal grandmother), or in *C*,

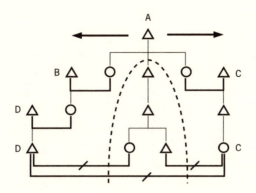

Figure 37.

which shares with *D* a grandmaternal lineage, that of a father's mother.

Clearly, the trick is to make the best use of the mechanisms established by the social rule in order to avoid incest of both types while remaining among each other as much as possible. Tinkering with the rules of the game presupposes perfect knowledge and mastery of them.

In *L'Exercice de la parenté*, using a computer to process marriages over *n* generations in three villages that formed an area of endogamy and peace, I was able to show that endogamy was stronger within each village than in the three villages as a whole (there were twenty-six lineages and thirty-four discrete lines in total). This endogamy is not the result of indifference toward or utter disregard of the prohibitions: indeed they are respected 98 percent of the time.

But overall, in marriages where at least three great-grand-mothers and great-great-grandmothers were known for each spouse, 40 percent of the marriages "came full circle," (as defined above), a number lower than we might have gotten had all these grandmothers been identified. I classified these marriages that came full circle in consanguinity by number according to the hierarchy indicated in figure 36; case 5, which is cognate, represents the greatest number of possibilities (twenty) while corresponding to the least restricting definition. As I wrote in *L'Exercice de la parenté*: "Since the greatest number of cases appear where constraint is strongest, it seems possible to speak of preferentially contracted unions among nonprohibited blood relations closest to Ego, the criterion of proximity being a function of lineal appurtenance and the hierarchical order of the lineages such as it is demonstrated by the Samo."[6] Let us hasten to add that this type of choice, which I have qualified as preferential, statistically speaking, is not constrained by questions of vicinity or cousinhood (since the closest female cousin could be the one "next door") or by the scarcity of potential wives unrelated to a man. For the young men who participated in my inquiry, I compiled a list of all the girls they could marry: that is, girls who fell under no prohibition. One young man, whose case is detailed in my book on kinship, had a range of forty-four to fifty-seven potential wives to choose from and chose a close, but not prohibited cousin who was related to him in two different ways.

As far as regular exchanges between lineages, of the 997 marriages used as a basis for this study, 32 percent were followed by reciprocity, with series involving several lines of descent in the same lineage (discrete lines, or lines descended from brothers or co-wives of the same man), from three to ten exchanges, at the same time or in succession, alternated generation after generation.

I concluded that the members of the lineages, men and women both, led by the doyen, knew how to play the matrimonial game.

Two remarks must be made regarding the supposedly unconscious character of matrimonial functioning. The first is that the locals — in this case, the Samo — are perfectly conscious of the obligation to exchange between lineages, which is logically implied, or, if one prefers, induced, by all of their rules. During the Samo's annual festivals, I attended several village meetings where doyens of each lineage gathered to deliver a speech based on a recognized hierarchy, the audience arranged behind its leader, listening but having no say in anything. Various matters of importance for village life were discussed — the sacrifices to be made, the capacity of calabash scales for selling honey and beer (and the annual establishment of a standard measure) — and then matrimonial accounts were settled between villages. I clearly recall the indignation of a blacksmith-lineage doyen who listed all the daughters the lineage had given over the past thirty years (three or four — he could not recall the fourth, who probably did not exist, according to my genealogies) and those received in exchange: only one. Payment was clearly due![7]

In addition to this awareness of the rules' implications, there is also a much more abstract and formal awareness of possibilities offered by a combination of different factors: polygyny, multiple sibling groups, the remarriage of widows, patrifiliation, and prohibitive rules of alliance. These can be cleverly manipulated to construct theoretical models in a purely gratuitous game. The Samo told me that in addition to prohibitions they also have preferential marriage. It is as follows:

A man has two wives, one of whom was previously married and had a daughter. The man has a son with this woman and a daughter with his second wife. The two daughters have been given in marriage to different lineages (because parallel symmetry would be impossible), and they each give birth, one to a boy, the other to a girl: the union of this boy and girl represents the ideal marriage for the Samo, because they have the same maternal uncle, who is one of their mothers' uterine brothers and the agnatic brother of the other's mother, yet they transgress no prohibition, that is, neither belongs to a lineage prohibited to the other or has a lineage in common on the mother's or grandmothers' side. (See figure 38.)

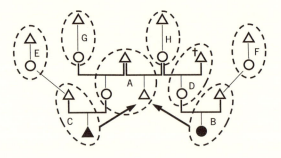

Figure 38.

Figure 38 shows that man *B* has successively first married woman *H*—the widow of man *D*, with whom she had daughter *D* —and then woman *G*. From wife *H*, he has a son, and from his wife *G* a daughter, both belonging to lineage *A* by birth. A transitive relationship exists between these children which somewhat recalls the subtle delights of Talmudic exegesis: daughter *D* is the half-sister, through the mother, of her brother *A*, who is in turn the half-brother, through the father, of his sister *A*, who has no kinship relation with daughter *D*.

The circles surround the four lineages in consanguinity prohibited for boy *C* and girl *B*, who are born of the marriages of these two daughters. Now, while the agnatic lineage in circle *A* is indeed the lineage of the mother of boy *C*, it is not the lineage of the mother of daughter *B*, who is in *D*, nor that of either of her two grandmothers, who are in *F* and in *H*.

186

Nonetheless, daughter *B* calls man *A* (to whom the arrows in the figure 38 are pointing) "my maternal uncle," because he is a uterine brother of her mother (he and his full brothers, if he has any). My Dalo informants laughed as they outlined and explained this magnificent example of the subtle manipulation of their own rules. Nothing, they say, prohibits this marriage: neither partner belongs to a lineage prohibited to the other, and they have no maternal lineage in common, although they actually have the same maternal uncle. They claimed that this marriage was the preferred one. However, in all of the genealogies I had drawn up (each of which covers five to nine generations on average, twelve in some cases, totaling 2,450 marriages), I found no marriage of this type corresponding exactly or even approximately to this "preferred" matrimonial schema, even by extending two sides or a single one from one generation, or by reversing the order of the sex of the series of half-brothers and sisters (which would make it a matter of a paternal aunt instead of a maternal uncle).

Therefore this is a purely intellectual exercise, in which a series of descriptive kinship traits are juggled to reveal potential flaws in the system. It may be very entertaining to come up with the possibility, but it is never realized because it comes too close to incest of the second type. Naturally, daughters *D* and *A* are not sisters, but they have a common brother, and according to custom, *D* followed her mother to her mother's second husband's house, where she remained until she reached the age suitable for marriage. Daughters *D* and *A* lived in the same courtyard. The marriage of boy *C* with girl *B* would be a short-circuit of quasi identicals, through the intermediary of their two mothers, quasi sisters.

I view these refinements, which were not invented for the sake of the ethnologist, as casuistry to help young people understand their own laws, and as a display of the teachers' intimate knowledge of the connections between the rules, a web so intricately interwoven that it is impossible to extract one strand without destroying the whole.

It becomes patently clear that a close relationship exists between the functioning of semicomplex systems of alliance and the prohibition of "two sisters," since the impossibility of parallel symmetry exchanges is one *sine qua non* of the proper functioning of these systems. The refusal of incest of the second type in its various forms is absolute.

The question is how this relationship pertains to the idea of common substances traveling from one body to another, through generation (insemination and generation) and copulation, of course, but also breast-feeding and affiliation of another nature — food, daily life, language, and recognition.

As I researched Samo kinship terms, it seemed that the words used — to be "on" a common maternal uncle, to have "common stock" or "same stock" or "one stock" (from *to*, "stock," *goro*, "one") — suggested a materiality behind the abstraction of the terms, and, further, that this materiality was not simply the expression of the physical character of kinship relations expressed concretely through given individuals. This was a materiality in the representation of the body, in the representation of the human being. Along with the other surveys, therefore, I conducted a long study on the representations of the person and the genesis and transmission of fluids.[8]

Where Do Bodily Fluids Come From?

The representation of the genesis of blood is joined to restrictions concerning choice of spouse and corresponds to an overall ideological system that, in this case, "cultivates difference," since the combination of identical characteristics is thought to have harmful effects on individuals and the social body.

188

In the Samo model, the human being is a composite of multiple sanguinary substances, each characteristic of an agnatic stock (the mother's lineage is that of her father and his brothers), with varying importance in the body. Now, the essential point is that the dominant marks must not be doubly present in an individual, that is, they cannot be transmitted to the same child by both of his parents.[9]

The mechanisms of the genesis of blood were explained to me in detail using schemas of transmission that must be represented by eight agnatic stocks. (See figure 39.)

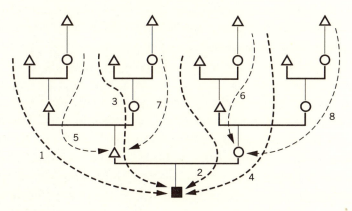

Figure 39.

In Samo thought, each parent cooperates in the construction of certain attributes and components of the person, when they do not come from divinity, ancestors, or an overall immaterial stock: the father gives blood and its attendant breath and spirit; the mother gives the body, shadow, heat, and destiny; the ancestors contribute their trace; the double is taken from the immaterial stock of what might be called "souls in suspension"; divinity gives the life borne by breath and blood.

Blood comes from the father, who received it from his father and his paternal ancestors. It is the blood of the lineage, which comes first. The mother gives the body, with its shadow, warmth, and sweat, but above all flesh and bone, which contains bone marrow. No distinction is made between the bone marrow and spinal cord, both thought to be made of blood; the spinal cord is also made of sperm.[10]

A child comes into the world with an initial allocation of blood that comes from its father, via semen, but every individual also will produce it for the rest of his life from bone marrow, by ingesting and digesting food. An adult has more blood than an infant; he must therefore produce it. But the child obtained its bones and marrow from its mother, who fabricated them from her own blood (which, during pregnancy, she no longer lost); this is blood she received from her own father as well as blood she herself produced from the marrow of her bones, which came to her from her mother and therefore from the blood of her maternal grandfather. Based on these observations, it is clear that the blood a human being receives from its father at birth is also a composite, since the father's blood is in part the product emitted regularly by his bone marrow and therefore derives partially from the stock of his maternal grandfather, and so on.

This composite product is not homogeneous, an emulsified mixture. The marks of various agnatic stocks are distinct from each other and associated in the living body according to a balancing process whose order and value are always the same.

At the forefront is the clearly visible mark of the lineal sanguine stock transmitted from father to son; then, on the side of paternal contributions, we find the less obvious stock of the father's mother, who has fabricated the bones of her child from her blood, and, in residual fashion, the sanguine marks of the lineages of the two great-grandmothers on the father's side. The bones that produce blood during the individual's life are also the product of mixed blood, in which the contributions of four distinct agnatic stocks are similarly juxtaposed, with different values: a major expression, the sanguine mark of the mother's lineage; a minor expression, that of the mother's mother's lineage, then, in residual fashion, that of the lineages of the two great-grandmothers on the mother's side. We see that the human being carries eight different sanguine stocks classified within him, only four of which does he transmit to his children, while his spouse provides these children with the other four stocks. In the form of blood, borne by semen, or bone and marrow, which produces blood, a man or woman consequently transmits the dominant 1 and 3 of the paternal and maternal series, then the minor (or recessive) 2 and 4, residual stocks present only as tiny traces in the newborn's body. (See figure 40.)

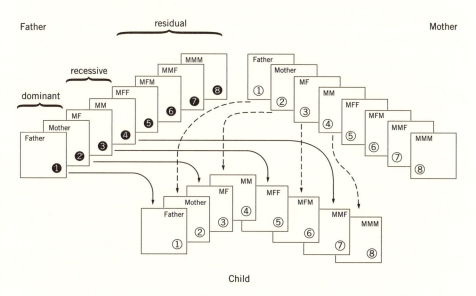

Figure 40.

Thanks to the artifice of this hierarchically ordered classification of bloods that associate, then dissociate, in the human being without ever creating a homogeneous mixture, a figure is outlined wherein blood is only identifiable through the relationship to a multiplicity of lines of patrilineal filiation (the lineages) and not as a substance *sui generis*. Moreover, the blood of the paternal lineage is always highlighted. This scholarly construct, with the rigor of a Mendelian model, reinforces the patrilineal ideology of filiation. It is in relation to these patrilineal lineages, to which individuals are genealogically and socially tied, that the multiple prohibitions that organize alliance are stated.

As we have seen, careful arrangement of these rules — particularly rules against taking two sisters, or against two "brothers" marrying two "sisters," or against a "father" and his "sons" taking a wife in the same lineage — rather than limiting the possibilities for a potential spouse in a man's zone of familiarity, in fact narrowed this choice to blood relations located just beyond the area of the prohibitions' scope.

It then becomes clear — and this is the essential thing — that the two series constituted by social rules of alliance, on the one hand, and by so-called genetic representations of the transmission of blood and the fabrication of the body, on the other, converge, though the Samo do not consider the latter the ultimate reason for the former.

Conveyed in terms of sanguine marks, unions that join two people with at least one major or minor mark in common in either register (paternal contributions of blood, maternal contributions of marrow) are forbidden as incestuous; if entered into, they would dry the body of its fluids and lead to sterility in the most serious cases. Here, three generations suffice for the residual traces of both parents' great-grandmothers to disappear in a child, as we have just seen. On the other hand, it is possible for Ego to marry someone with one of Ego's major or minor marks as a residual mark (and vice versa), particularly if these marks correspond to branches that are clearly distinct from the same stock, that is, different lines of the same lineage. But it is good to marry bearers of the same residual marks, those from great-grandmothers which are not transmitted to the following generation.

While excessive identity is harmful, and while two similar dominant marks work against each other and dry up the possibility of descendants, it is nevertheless good for different bloods to be somewhat familiar to each other. The search for the perfect balance between the close environment and the distant world, between incest and union with a foreigner, is also the search for the perfect harmony of bloods.

The underlying idea is this: putting identical things together is damaging. This central idea motivates both the prohibitions concerning an individual's component lineages (his lineage, his mother's, and his two grandmothers') as well as those concerning the impossibility of two members of the same sex and lineage redoubling their alliances over two generations (two "brothers," a "father" and his "son," a man marrying two sisters, two "sisters," a paternal aunt and her niece, and a woman having relations with her husband's younger brothers during his lifetime).

Yet, when one considers all its implications, this remarkable intellectual construction, which closely unites alliance and filiation, does not exhaust all representations: it says nothing of the mechanisms of the father's transmission of blood to his child, for one thing; furthermore, if blood is indeed transmitted by the father, this would mean that a woman's first-born child, engendered by a man other than the mother's husband (its social father), would bring foreign blood into this man's lineage.

These concerns require an extended response. According to the Samo, sperm carries the blood from one body to another. It is

193

transformed into blood in women's bodies. The repeated infusions of paternal semen during part of the pregnancy molds the baby and gives it its initial allocation of blood. A child born after its father's death bears the first name Pako, which immediately identifies the conditions of its birth, and is considered a fragile being because it is unfinished.

From this perspective, therefore, it would seem that each woman's first-born child would be an intruder in its paternal lineage (that of his mother's husband) because it would bear the blood of someone other than this socially affirmed father. This is not the case at all. While sperm is certainly considered the means by which a man transmits lineal blood, still in the forefront as the dominant mark, the blood itself is not considered a perfectly identical liquid for all men, even for all men of the same lineage, who are the products of different uterine sanguinary stocks; nor is dominant mark lineal blood considered an invariable substance, but an easily influenced and evolving substance whose distinctive qualities and properties, specific to each lineage, are constructed collectively through foods, based on various prohibitions. A young girl promised in marriage begins in childhood to observe the alimentary prohibitions of her husband's lineage as well as her own. The children she will bear, or nurse, must not have substances in their bones or absorb substances incompatible with the mark of the lineage of common descent. Thus, even if the child is sired by someone other than his *pater* or social father, it is "nourished" by foods of the lineage when it is still in its mother's stomach, its blood becoming that of the lineage.

Added to this purely material process is the ideal process of the spoken word and recognition. As a Samo saying goes: "The word creates filiation, the word takes it away."

The passage of fluids from one body to another, specific food taboos, and social recognition are the essence of belonging to a lineage. Filiation is therefore partly seen as the result of a mechanics of fluids, with transmissions, developments, transformations, and differentiations. Paternal blood itself is developed through the marrow of various grandmothers and the food specific to the lineage, maternal marrow transforming this alimentation into lineal blood, itself nourished and fortified from within by regular contributions of semen.

Clearly this model corresponds to observations that are no doubt naive but also scientific in nature, resulting in the elaboration of a theory that engenders a series of transformations. Blood comes from the father, which implies that the father nourishes the child during gestation, which he does with his sperm. Paternal sperm is then transformed into blood in the maternal womb. The interruption of the menstrual cycle during pregnancy proves this. During their menstrual cycles, women discharge the surplus semen they have transformed into blood, but when they are pregnant this semen transformed into blood goes directly to the allocation of blood in the child's body. After giving birth, sexual relations are totally prohibited, yet for some time the mother still does not lose blood, because it is transformed into the milk with which she feeds her child.

The Samo model of the circulation of bodily fluids takes into account at once the functioning of the rules of alliance and the substantial constitution of a human being, his somatic identity. These are not faulty reflections based on conflicting observations, but a rigorous logic that draws all its conclusions from that which can be known, given the Samo's empirical knowledge of the body and their possibilities of observation. Attested principles can be found here, such as hematopoiesis and a Mendelian model that includes the successive erasure of certain transmitted characteristics, and also their resurgence, generation after generation. If a man marries a woman who has the same recessive stocks as he does, this will reinforce, rather than make disappear, the residual traces in their children.

Perhaps most surprising is that this model, which appears so abstract to us, is very concrete for the Samo: it is discussed over a drink rather than in a classroom.

Alliance should not be considered a solely social choice. By creating favored alliances, one of course seeks to renew relations with other lineages for political, economic, or geographical reasons, and so forth, but one also seeks to recombine, in a way, the somatic characteristics of the individual, so that the very definition of the person's identity is at stake.

Whether of the first or second type, incest in general (and not only in the Bible) has consequences that affect not only rules of alliance but also this circulation of bodily fluids; it has legal consequences as well as more profound consequences on the human body, the social body, and the very makeup of the world.

The legal consequences — that is, punishments — vary from one society to another. They range from simple mockery to abuse of the guilty parties to ostracism to death, particularly by fire. This last punishment is specifically motivated since incest is considered a combination of the identical, and therefore of heat; the effect of this combination of heat is annihilated by even more intense burning.

The more interesting consequences affect individuals' daily lives. There are three principal calamities associated with incest, but they are actually the same consequence, which has two sides: drought or flood. Drought is female infertility, the barrenness of the herds, the drying of the earth when the rains stop or ground water is depleted. Flooding is rivers overflowing, tidal waves, downpours, but also hemoptysis and hemorrhages. When two men's semen meet in the same womb, the semen of the weaker surges back into his own body and comes out in the form of blood (spat up or bled out). Otherwise, it accumulates and becomes ele-phantiasis, particularly of the genitals. These maladies affect the culprits, but sometimes also their brothers, their sisters, or mem-bers of their lineage.

Drought brings on plagues of all sorts, such as invasions of harmful insects, grasshoppers, locusts, fleas, or rats that devour the grain supply. While flooding also brings plagues, such as frog or toad infestations, drought is clearly more dreadful. Earthquakes may destroy towns or villages; incest may provoke volcanic erup-tions or make the sun fall from the sky.[11]

The social consequences are riots, insurrection, and war, as well as fraternal battles that manifest the identicals' hatred of each other.

In this regard, the story of Callias told by Andocides is para-digmatic. Between the time Callias committed his successive incestuous acts of the second type — mother-daughter, then grand-mother-granddaughter — and the time he became a tyrant, Athens experienced a dramatic period of uprisings and wars. Though nothing happened to him personally, there were grave conse-quences for the city.

Incestuous relations of the first or second type may be sought out in certain societies or on certain occasions (before war or large hunts, for example). In other societies, incest appears to be inscribed either positively or negatively in sets of meaning that go beyond it, challenging the world's equilibrium and the hidden or manifest order of things.

PART THREE

The Rules of the Game

CHAPTER SIX

The Identical and the Different

In the last chapter, we saw how the matrimonial prohibitions of a particular system, the semicomplex Crow or Omaha system, were linked to representations of the body's formation through maternal and paternal contributions of various bodily fluids (blood, semen, milk). Ethnologists have long been interested in these questions, though our reference, the Samo, no longer constitutes an isolated case, a *hapax*. Once one examines these questions, in fact, elaborate representations can be found in all societies, simply because it is impossible for an individual, a social and sexual being, not to ask questions about the body.

The very notion of identity involves a representation of the body and its place in the world. A human being's first topic of reflection is the body's integration into the animal or plant species surrounding him, the world around him. There is a sort of pressure gradient of interpretation that starts from the subject's body and moves concentrically further and further into the world. The first irreducible and incontestable given, at once anatomical and physiological, is the difference between the sexes.

Hermaphrodite species without sexual differentiation exist in nature, but they are not immediately observable; in reality, their identification is a discovery of modern science. What is immediately observable without the use of an instrument is animal sexual reproduction and the capacity of male and female sex organs to fit together anatomically. This essential observation is at the origin of our most profound mental categories, those of the identical and the different. A person is identical because he bears the same sexual apparatus, or different because he bears a different sexual apparatus.

The identical and the different appear for this reason to be the principal categories of thought, anchored in primordial observations of the human body. Gerald Holton's themata— one/various, continuous/discontinuous, and so on — all refer, ultimately, to the identical and the different.[1] Indeed, these are not the abstract categories of modern scientific thought, but the categories of thought in general. All human societies function on the basis of these implicit categories, even if they have not developed "scientific" discourses.

To a certain extent, systems of representations shared by all individuals in a society may also be considered scientific discourses, insofar as they are coherent and structured wholes that aim to express a reality, with the intellectual and technical means of observation available at the time. But while observational techniques in the West in our era certainly differ from those used in other periods in Western history (or in other histories during different periods), the intellectual tools hardly differ at all: observation, comparison, experimentation, generalization. Even more, a grammar is founded on the opposition between the identical and the different, on the classification of objects in one or the other category, and on the movements that affect these objects because of their attributed character in a classificatory category.

These are presuppositions, but they are based on detailed observation of sets of representations of human societies, always founded on a primacy, a consubstantial identity, whose nature varies depending on the culture. Consubstantial identity generates various sorts of social organization: filiation, alliance, appellations, and behaviors, groupings, rules of etiquette, and global systems of representations.

We saw how the Samo's system was linked to their system of representation of the makeup of children's bodies, and was thus articulated, as it were, term by term, justifying the three prohibited generations for matrimonial alliance between blood relations. The Samo themselves explain that the same stocks cannot be combined through alliance because this would be "putting the same on the same," which is bad. This explanation, thus, raises a whole series of anthropological questions.

Indeed, one cannot be satisfied with the allegation that the combination of identical things brings misfortune. The first question is how this identity is established, why that which is defined as "identical stock" never falls off in the direct agnatic line in the same lineage (that of one's birth), while it ceases to exist in a few generations in cognate line (that is, between individuals of the same stock). In fact, there is not only common descent, but also sharing in common. Masculine Ego cannot marry a woman of his mother's lineage, because the kinship between these women is traceable exclusively through men. This is the very definition of agnation. But neither can he have relations with someone who is not of his mother's lineage but shares it in common with him, as maternal lineage, for example (that is, a daughter whose mother also belongs to this man's mother's lineage). Ego and this daughter are considered to be of the same stock. The sharing in common of the same stock defines "cognates," that is, relatives whose chain from one to the other is interrupted at least once by a woman. And while the identity of the stock exists *ad infinitum* in the lineage of common descent, the one in which a man (or woman) is born (the agnatic lineage, consequently), identity ceases to exist in the cognate ensemble once one goes beyond the mother's and grandmothers' genealogical levels.

One answer to this question, necessary if insufficient, involves the conception of the person, the representation of reproduction and relations between the male and female in the constitution of a new being. We have seen how the Samo envisioned this constitution through the combined contributions of the father and mother. They came upon the rather scholarly idea of an infinite regression of all contributions of fluids that come from founding stocks through women, while the constant allotment by paternal ancestors in agnatic line remains unaltered. In fact, comparison of this idiosyncratic theory of the child's constitution with the rules of alliance, which permit marriages between cognates at the fourth generation after a female link, suggests that three intermediary generations are in fact required for the physical contributions from a child's maternal ancestors to fade, though they never completely disappear.

In other populations with the same type of system of alliance, two to four intermediary generations are required, but there is always a canonical link between the number of prohibited lineages and the number of generations it takes for the ancestors' blood through women to fade. In each new alliance, each individual enters as the bearer of eight stocks, only four of which are transmitted to his offspring, so that the actual contributions fade from generation to generation in a well-established order from the closest to the most distant. The closest, the most identical consequently, are all the members of an individual's paternal lineage, then those of the paternal grandmother's lineage, finally those of the maternal grandmother's lineage, and so on, theoretically without end.

Cognate prohibitions (and those preventing agnates from taking spouses of the same lineage or the same maternal or grandma-

ternal stock over two consecutive generations) prevent the dominant lines of the same blood, or a dominant line in the bearer and
a recessive line in the spouse, or even two identical recessive lines
in the two bearers (which would become the dominant line in
their offspring), from being reinforced through agglutination, that
is, through union of that which was separate. This is the result of
cognate prohibitions and not their goal, for "goal" would imply
that the system of representation precedes and organizes the system of alliance, whereas the two are born together and are in-
extricably linked. This is indeed what the Samo say: "Identical
stocks cannot be put together."

This is basically the same idea as the "scent of kinship" conceived by Peter Damian in the twelfth century to justify marriage
between cognates and not only between agnates, between persons
who can recognize a common stock beyond the seventh degree
canon (that is, over fourteen generations, which, as one might suspect, is difficult to establish).[2] Let's take just one example: a man's
son's daughter's son's daughter's daughter's daughter, and then,
on the other side, this same man's son's daughter's daughter's
son's daughter's son have a scent of kinship in common that prohibits marriage between them. This scent of kinship is the "certain something" or the "almost-nothing," to use the philosopher
Vladimir Jankélévitch's expression, that signals common descent
in the same lineage. Peter Damian, in his *De parentelae gradibus*,
explains that this scent of kinship translates the affinity between
different branches issued from a common ancestor at different
levels. He wrote, "Nature itself ensures that fraternal love is recognized until the sixth degree of kinship in the human entrails
and exudes a sort of odor of natural community that exists between relatives." He says "six degrees," but as he does not take
into account the apical ancestor, this in fact makes it seven degrees
for marriage to become possible. Beyond that, "when the family

205

founded on kinship comes to be lacking, at the same time as the words to designate this" — one may assume they were lacking much earlier — "the law of marriage is presented immediately and reestablishes the rights of the ancient love between the new men." Peter Damian thus establishes a homology between the scent and terminology of kinship. Beyond the seventh degree canon or the fourteenth degree roman, the scent of kinship lingers in spite of everything, so that alliance can throw out its net and bring what is dissolving on the fringes back to the center.

Peter Damian sees alliance in semicomplex systems as alternating chronological series with expansions and contractions. The series begins with a union between two persons who come from two different lines, which subsequently entails the nonrenewal of marriage between these two lines, and thus the expansion of alliance through the scattering of members of the lineage in outside unions, but eventually, after a certain amount of time — three generations among the Samo, six in the canon law of the twelfth century — that "certain something," which Peter Damian calls the "scent of kinship" and which the Samo believe is transmitted in the fabrication of blood, becomes an "almost-nothing," which can only be saved from eradication by urging the following generation to renew the alliance. New kinship is reestablished with kinship on the verge of disappearing. This is not an obligation but a matrimonial preference.

The Samo are more realistic; they are content with three intermediary generations. They do not speak of scents of kinship but traces in blood. Blood is a sort of composite substance that can be dissociated and reassociated differently, the way simple diagrams can be placed on top of each other to produce a complex image, or the way photographic plates, each establishing only one part of a total image, might be combined in various ways to produce a different image each time.

In a way, what we have here is the notion of paternal and maternal chromosomes, which combine and transmit their hereditary characteristics, except that the Samo conceive of it very pragmatically: given the proper means, they feel it would be possible to extract the paternal and maternal elements from clotted blood, and undo, so to speak, what is done at conception. Blood is different in each person, not only because it is transmitted to him by his parents, but also because the food he eats affects the composition of his blood.

Identity by community of substance can be endowed at birth or constructed in two ways. First, by attribution of the name, which constitutes public recognition of the social link based on the analogy between common descent in the paternal lineage and the semen that transmits the paternal blood to the child's body, between the word, a vehicle of filiation, and semen, a vehicle of blood. Secondly, by food: one peculiarity of the Samo system is that the first-born child of each legitimate union is necessarily born of a genitor other than the mother's husband, the social father who gives it its name; the common food, that of the lineage, also enters into the composition of the child's blood and gives it its lineal identity.

A concise but particularly pertinent Samo saying concerns individuals born of the wife's prenuptial liaison: "What the word has done, only the word can undo." Language binds not only individuals but lineages: filiation is recognized by doyens of the lineage well before the legitimate union is actually realized, and the promise is made to welcome the child in his future lineage of origin by sharing common food. The "word" implies the commitment of the lineages and individuals directly concerned, but also the tacit commitment of others.

In certain cases — if there is a conflict between agnates or two moieties of a village, for example — someone may call the first

THE RULES OF THE GAME

born a bastard (these cases are very rare, and malicious, because everyone knows the status of the first-born). The lineage must then sever itself from the accursed person and he must go join his genitor's lineage. Complex sacrificial procedures are required to cut the link of filiation created by common foods and to gain the acceptance of the ancestors of the new lineage. Moreover, the individual will never be anything but an outsider there, since the food he has eaten most of his life has given him the blood of his previous lineage. If he has already had children, they must leave with him. Therefore, this is a serious matter, serious enough that I have encountered only two such cases in the course of a genealogical survey conducted over twelve to fourteen generations in three villages, involving several thousand individuals.

The question remains why the putting into contact of two identicals, of two persons having an even partially common substance, is prohibited not only among the Samo but also in populations where the choice of spouse involves a wide spectrum of prohibitions. The answer is this: there are only two possible structural arrangements based on the good or bad effects that the combining of the identical may produce in various domains. If "combination of the identical" is thought to produce harmful results, it will be prohibited, and the juxtaposition or combination of different elements will be sought. Inversely, if combination of the identical is thought to produce good effects, it will be sought out and the combining of different things will be avoided. A society may advocate combination of the identical or reject it in all areas, or, alternatively, combination of the identical may be avoided in marriage, say, but sought in medicine, or, as in Greek and Arab medicine, such combinations may be sought to treat certain pathologies and avoided in the treatment of others. Many combinations are possible.

208

The Grammar of the Psyche

The logic of fluids, elements repelled or attracted by each other, can only be understood by constantly working to order the mass of observations that can be made on the world. Theoretically, I have claimed that the primordial observation is that of sexual difference, which cannot be broken down into parts. Subsequently, other elements are classified and objects endowed with particular characteristics based on that primordial distinction.

A second fundamental observation of the functioning of the animal kingdom is the awareness of the fact that intimate bodily contact is necessary in order to procreate, that the sexual relation is essential for breeding, that men are born neither through parthenogenesis nor cloning. Certain anthropologists have, indeed, denied such an awareness to certain groups, observing that these people believe children to be born through the intermediary of ancestral spirits who lodged themselves in the female's stomach.[3] Since then, Torben Monberg and others after him have shown that, when the question was put to them plainly, the Trobrianders laughed at the thought of being unaware that a man and woman had to have sex in order to have a child.[4]

The idea that intimate bodily contact causes the circulation, indeed, the exchange of humoral substances was added to this primordial awareness. This is obvious for male ejaculation; but most societies also believe there is an ejaculation of a female fluid, so that copulation results in a mixture of liquids.

The discourse on bodily humors is always inscribed in the complex of representations specific to a society, which varies from one society to another based on the means of observation at its disposal, but which never ceases to be rational. An ideological complex of meaningful relations always underlies social relations. A relationship is thus necessarily established between the logic of bodily humors and systems of alliance, even if the individuals in a given society are not aware of it. No informant, whether from an exotic society or from our own, has the capacity to reconstruct all the mediations that incorporate his system of representations in a system of alliance and vice versa. It is up to the anthropologist to do so.

In fact, the logic of bodily fluids is only partially, and indirectly, expressed in a prereflexive mode of "knowing without knowing," as Sartre would say. For example, in France it was once thought that girls having their period were not supposed to bathe or walk in the rain. Personal hygiene was allowed at the end of the period, but during menstruation, prolonged contact with water was not advised. To use my grandmother's Burgundian expression: "You don't 'paddle around' in water when you have your period," not even to do the wash. Why? No one ever bothered to explain. The mother or grandmother setting out this prohibition for a girl is just passing on what she has been told herself. This prohibition can only be explained if one admits of an unconscious notion that the association of the flow of blood and the flow of water, a combination of wet on wet, may bring about a dual negative effect, either amenorrhea, one (water) suppressing the other (blood), or, on the contrary, constant hemorrhage, one (water) attracting the other (blood), both condemning the young girl to infertility. It is still said that women having their periods (women whose blood is flowing) prevent emulsions from setting (mayonnaise, custard, blood stew, and so on) or make them turn sour, as though pickled.

If this prohibition, like the others, is not questioned, it is because it is part of a system of implicit representations that make sense as a whole. It is up to the anthropologist to expose the prohibitions' raison d'être by explicating the system of representations that justifies and legitimizes them. It is not enough to postulate that each society has a system of representations that possesses an inner coherence; nor is it enough to postulate the existence of structural variations within broader cultural ensembles. It seems to me, based on African data as well as data from more diverse cultural areas, that one can reduce all these systems of representations to a few invariant broad themes that form a base logic, which is also invariant. That in certain societies the combination of identicals causes drought while in others it causes flooding is a difference of content. Beyond content, the same structure is at work, and it is this structure's articulations that must be brought to light. I have identified five essential ones.[5]

The first is the natural homology, indeed, the absence of a break between the body in its socialized vital functions (reproduction and digestion), its natural, meteorological environment, and its social environment. Transfers are conceivable from one register to the other: social transgression has effects on the body and on the natural environment; reciprocally, changes in climate have effects on the body and the social environment. Thus, the young girl from Burgundy who walks in the rain during her period runs the risk of infertility. In Samo country, the young girls' puberty sacrifice cannot be made during the rainy season because the girls would risk infertility by hemorrhage. This is a perfect example of the absence of a break between the social (the puberty sacrifice), the natural (the rainy season), and the bodily (menstruation).

The second is the expression of this homology in symbolic content, which certainly varies by society, but is everywhere governed by the same formal law. This law is based on the idea that the equilibrium of the world — understood as the ensemble formed by the natural, the social, and the bodily — is a whole composed of elements linked by a sort of Le Chatelier principle,[6] so that any imbalance in one register, whether a surplus or lack, is immediately compensated for by an imbalance in another or the same register. Any disruption of the world's balance must be compensated for in one way or another. For example, among the Samo, it is forbidden to consume lamb that has not been slaughtered at home, so that when one is invited for a meal in another lineage, there are certain words to utter and rituals to perform in order to permit the incorporation of meat whose blood has flowed on other altars.

The third is the circulation of substances in a world that must be kept in balance. It is an obvious fact that liquids flow more easily than solids. The world is thus traversed by an ensemble of flows — the flow of money, words, rains, rivers, and bodily fluids — which are indispensable for the production and maintenance of life. Without rain a region dies; without bodily fluids an individual dies; without dialogue a social group dies. The circulation of flows must therefore be properly regulated. In Christian societies, rogations, a ritual involving processions around the church and through the parish, was meant to regulate rainfall. This mechanics of drainage and retention, of loss and accumulation, functions on the basis of several analogical series in which certain elements — considered identical or different in various places — are thought to draw each other out or push each other back. This mechanics allows one to predict the consequences of certain actions. The consumption of lamb (a physiological act) not slaughtered at home and not subjected to a certain ritual (a social act) has harmful, entirely foreseeable consequences (children's digestive illnesses) which the Samo ritual obviates.

The fourth is that this mechanics of attraction and repulsion of fluids is thought of in terms of pairs of opposites: hot/cold, dry/wet, light/dark, high/low, superior/inferior, inside/outside, heavy/light, and so on. All these binary oppositions are engendered by and articulated by way of the fundamental opposition of the identical and the different. If a man is the point of reference

212

and he is considered hot, then all men are considered hot, since all men are identical; because women are different, they are considered cold, except at certain times in their life. The first opposition in categories of the identical and the different is male/female, a paradigm for all other conceptual oppositions: Sun and Moon, superior and inferior, exterior and interior, high and low, right and left, light and dark, hard and soft, heavy and light, mobile and immobile, and so on. Each term in these oppositions can be associated spontaneously with either the masculine or the feminine, based on shared culture. Right is male, left is female; brightness male, darkness female; the high is male, the low is female; the hard, hot, heavy, external, and mobile are male, while the soft, lightweight, internal, and immobile are perceived as designating the female in a somewhat natural way. The dry and the wet are more ambivalent, as are other oppositions.[7]

The fifth is that these dualistic oppositions also involve order and hierarchy: one term is always preferable to the other, the hot to the cold, the dry to the wet (or the wet to the dry, depending on the society, time of year, and medical system), the high to the low, the superior to the inferior, the heavy to the light, the light to the dark, and so on.

These five rules — the natural homology between body, natural environment, and social environment; the required equilibrium among these three elements; the circulation of flows; the binary oppositions that qualify the world; and the hierarchical relationship of preference between the opposed terms — constitute the logical substratum on which ritualizations, prescriptions, prohibitions, and reparations are established in all societies. Still, it must be assumed that actions have an effect as well as a meaning.[8] Every action is efficacious, none is gratuitous. Judicious attempts can then be made to anticipate or cancel out the effects of an action. A priest or a seer with intimate and practical knowledge of this logic can provoke or prevent certain consequences. This means mitigating the foreseeable effects by a ceremonial action, anticipating rather than waiting for divine sanction. Of course, these consequences have to be foreseen, which is not always possible, since misdeeds may be committed without individuals knowing it.

Illnesses may be triggered by trivial acts that go unnoticed but which subsequent divination will detect as being at the source of the illness. Prolonged drought or lack of rain (when rain is to be expected) are attributed to unknown incestuous relationships; if the problem persists, all the potential authors of such offenses and other sexual offenses, such as copulation in the bush or on the ground (hot acts committed in hot places), will be ardently sought out.

It is also possible to indulge in forbidden things and to cancel out their effects by performing rituals beforehand that would normally be done afterward. While the mechanics of fluids is a rigorous system, it never functions as absolute determinism in any society. There is no social act whose effects cannot conceivably be warded off.

Among the Agni of the Ivory Coast, for example, the sovereign's remains, a concentrate of heat, must be buried in a riverbed in order to be permanently cooled. But to do this the river must be temporarily diverted. A diversion canal is therefore dug and the king's body buried in the drained riverbed. The water is then allowed to resume its normal course so as to permanently cool the soil, which has been subjected to the excess heat transmitted to it by the king's body. If he were put into the ground without this precaution, he would dry out the entire country. This is a social and religious rite that temporarily alters the natural environment in order to avoid more serious and longer-lasting alterations that would result from the bringing together of two identical forms of heat: the heat of the land and the heat of the sovereign's body. Balance is threatened; it is restored by a preventive act.[9]

Behaviors of this sort, which combine the three elements, are frequent in many African, American Indian, and Melanesian societies, among others. These behaviors find perhaps their fullest expression on the occasion of a death and the concommitant treatment of the corpse, again because of necessary beliefs concerning the localization of certain essential fluids in the body. If vital humors such as semen are concentrated in the head, bones, and bone marrow, these remains will receive particular treatment: enemies to whom an afterlife must be forbidden will be dismembered or thrown to the animals; burial of kinsmen will guarantee the stock's continuation; cremation will reestablish meteorological order by restarting the rain cycle; bones will be collected in an enclosed area or ancestors left to the water's current to be cooled and born again elsewhere. In *First Contact*, a documentary film by Bob Connolly and Robin Anderson, the Melanesians think the Belgian merchants approaching them for the first time are ancestors brought back to life, since they have come up the river and are white as the ancestor's bones.[10] In China, ancestors' bones, bearers of blessings and protection, were buried at the top of hillsides so that in time they would descend softly in the wind toward their relatives.

Comprehension of this ordered whole, this interaction of forces, is situated at the mechanical level of cause and effect. Religious and moral rationalizations in terms of misdeed, sin, or defilement are often superimposed where it is only a question of a mechanics of fluids with its underlying logic and objective, concrete, relative notions (insofar as they cannot be conceived of independently of each other) that entail no value judgment in and of themselves. The issue is the danger run by one or several individuals or by the entire community, a multifaceted danger that can strike violently or insidiously: illness, epidemic, drought, infertility, floods, quarrels, wars, events that signal an upset in the balance. One may question the explicative value of frequent notions of defilement, sin, purity, and impurity in anthropological or philosophical literature. These notions exist, of course — this is not being denied — but they add a moral connotation to the primary notion of balance, danger, and rectification. Defilement may be grafted onto the notion of balance, but cannot be substituted for it.

The notion of defilement is unknown to the Samo. Misdeeds are considered to be social and often occur without the culprit's knowledge. Thus a Samo woman may step on an insect in the bush, crushing it without realizing it or knowing that its death may have harmful consequences for her health or fertility. Her misdeed is not intentional, and any harmful consequences occur mechanically, without reference to the idea of expiation. We have seen that it is always possible (though not always done) to anticipate the effects of acts yet to be committed; but not carrying out a ritual by a certain date may also be the cause of sanctions, which will be remedied by other rituals. The gods and ancestors are often intent on their laws and demand their due. It must never be assumed that they will close their eyes to repeated offenses against them. Rituals of rectification can be anticipated: for example, among the Samo, if one knows that kinship exists between a man and woman who plan to be married (kinship lost from sight but that comes under the prohibited categories of marriage in stocks of dominant or recessive blood), the marriage may take place after a ritual that solemnly presents the two candidates to the ancestors, appeasing them. The ritual is accompanied by the wearing of a special bracelet that marks the kinship broken between them.

To understand these chains of cause and effect, as well as the effectiveness of acts and rites, a set of unusual notions should be examined: accumulation, contagion, and short-circuit.

This logic of primordial categories forms a structural framework of specific images, which each society supplies based on their own inclinations. I say inclinations, and not choices, for choice implies the awareness of choosing, while inclinations result from relationships that necessarily exist between various levels of social and symbolic activity. In the same way, a river's course may be inflected by the presence of a rocky platform, which it will not penetrate if clayey ground stretches beside it. A river is only hemmed in by rock if there is nowhere else to flow. The sinuous course of representation is also a function of the inflections which impose the world's elements upon it to preserve the coherence of the whole. It is not possible to study one isolated element without ruining the perception of the whole.

Therefore, as we study incest of the second type, we are gradually led toward other areas of reflection, toward a comparative method.

As discussed earlier, the prohibition of incest of the second type (the prohibition of two sisters in particular) is not universal. It is a type of union that may even be sought out. Everything depends on the way identical or different things must be paired or separated in a given society. The basic reasoning remains the same: it is dangerous to do one or another of two acts. Social rules therefore accompany these concerns, advocating or preventing union between persons who, to varying degrees, share a substantial identity.

Prohibition of incest of the second type is, as we have already analyzed, a typical feature of semicomplex Crow or Omaha systems of alliance. Matrimonial prohibitions correspond to a certain idea of the progression of substances (blood, marrow) that travel along genealogical lines and result in the creation of the child, who is endowed with a plurality of identities arising from the "dominant," "recessive," and "residual" stocks of ancestral blood in him. By marrying one's closest possible kin, a union is made in difference (that is, dominant and recessive blood cannot meet). But this difference is agreeably and usefully amended by bringing together residual stocks of blood. Difference, yes, but with a touch of identity. Inversely, some systems advocate unions between first cousins. In the typical example of Arab marriage between patrilateral parallel cousins, a combination of the identical is clearly sought after. Nevertheless, through nursing, some children incorporate a substance which is that of their wet nurse's husband, conforming to the belief that milk is derived from the husband's spermatic contribution to the woman breast-feeding. Since milk brothers and sisters cannot marry, two cousins who marry will have had different wet nurses. Identity, yes, but with a touch of difference.

In societies with an elementary structure of alliance, marriage is advocated between certain types of cousins. A man marries his mother's brother's daughter; for her, this man is her father's sister's son. In this case, what changes is the very notion of substantial consanguinity: it is total between same sex blood relations, two brothers, two sisters; it is incomplete between blood relations of the opposite sex, brother and sister, uncle and niece, and cross-cousins. At each stage a new rift occurs, such that only the rift of gender difference occurs between parallel first cousins, while cross-cousins (matrilateral for a man) have three broken links between them. (See figure 41.)

While cross-cousins can marry, parallel cousins cannot, no matter what the length of the genealogical chains uniting them, as long as they are still forged by persons of the same sex. Given this, those whom we consider — through the grid of our own kin-

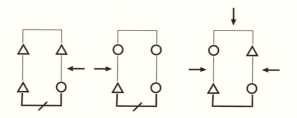

Figure 41.

ship system — blood relations at the same degree as the others are not considered blood relations but potential affines in societies that practice this type of preferential marriage. The boundaries do not occur in the same places. Often, language closely follows this ideal distinction, which shifts the line of identity and difference to places other than those marked out in the Arab or Crow-Omaha systems. Thus, the maternal uncle is referred to as a "father-in-law" and his daughter as a "wife," even if the marriage does not take place with her. She may marry her cousin, and kinship terminology reflects this possibility.

This brief sketch of the various systems of alliance suggests that the criteria used to identify them must incorporate a specific representation of the identical/different classification. Biologically speaking, the status of blood relations varies in relation to Ego as a function of kinship degrees. Socially speaking, the lack of differentiation does not exist. These distinctions must be noted for what they tell us about the identical, the different, and the combination of the two.

Besides the overall social rules governing the functioning of society, incidental rules exist that also correspond to a shared ideology and tell us something about identity, the importance of the social relationship as opposed to the genetic relationship in this area, and thus the fairly rigid limits of categories of the identical and the different. They tell us something about boundaries.

A Samo woman's firstborn child is not the child of the legitimate husband, as we have seen. A distinction exists between the *pater*, the one who creates the social inscription in a lineage, and the genitor, in this case the *sandana*. Lineal identity is constructed later, by respecting the food taboos of the lineage in which one is socially inscribed; the baby's body is accustomed to the food of his social lineage since his mother respected not only the food taboos of her own lineage but those of her future husband's, from the moment she was promised in marriage as a child. This firstborn, who is rarely the son of his *pater*, must always remain unaware of his genitor's identity. The marriage bans to which he must later submit come from his mother and his social father, with whom he has no genetic identity and only a consubstantial identity through food. The repression of incest presupposes kinship relations recognized and organized by society itself. Similarly, in our society, if a couple fully and legally adopts two children born of different parents, these two children become full-fledged brothers and sisters from a legal point of view and will never be able to marry each other. A Samo man is unaware of his genitor's name by definition; if he is chosen as a *sandana* by a girl who is not forbidden by a marriage ban but who happens to be his agnatic half-sister by blood, then he is informed of the biological link between them; this is done confidentially and in a roundabout way. He is not told "You cannot be this young girl's *sandana* because you have the same father." Rather, he is told, "This girl is not for you, because there is something between you." The "something between you" is an established expression, equivalent to "the scent of kinship." Now, if the social link prevails in matrimonial exclusion and is the only link that counts in recognizing kinship, why would one prevent this biologically consanguineous union? It can only be because of the famous "some-thing" passed between individuals through simple engendering, which establishes a touch of identity between them.

We are certainly on the outskirts of identity. There is no straightforward, solid definition that could be used in all situations made possible by the inventiveness of the human race. Here, something comes from paternal blood at birth, and then is obliterated in the long run by lineal communal consumption; what should have been the child's dominant mark of blood had his genitor been his *pater* is reduced to only a touch of blood, which is residual but cannot be paired with its identical, dominant in the young woman who chose him as *sandana*. All this is conveyed quietly in the half-light of evening around a vat of millet beer.

Another example of the importance of socially recognized status is the fictional sale of a child, a symbolic, thus ritualized, sale of legitimate infants, born after a succession of miscarriages or inviable births. The reasoning of the local system of interpretation through divination is analogous to the system of the biological compatibility of the parents' Rhesus factors. In this case, the question is the incompatibility between the father's and mother's blood; for each spouse at least one trace of blood comes from ancestors who were antagonistic during their lifetime and continue to find each other unbearable in the afterlife. They refuse to be reunited in the same child, and are thought to cause the death of children systematically. The only way to mollify them is to prove to them that the child is not or is no longer the property of their stock, so the child is sold as a slave to someone else. This transaction was proposed to me several times for a few CFA (African Financial Community) francs. The mother said publicly, "This child is being sold as a slave! He will render you great service! Do you want him? Will you integrate him into your family?" The ritual response is, "Yes, I want him! I'll buy him! How

221

much are you asking?" The amount is ridiculously low, around five CFA francs, or a few cents. "I want five francs." "Here you are!" The exchange is made publicly before witnesses. The mother gives me the child, whom I take in my arms. I keep him for several minutes to an hour, after which I bring him back to his mother, telling her publicly, loudly enough for the ancestors to hear, "I am giving him to you to nurse, for I do not have the time to do it! Take good care of him! Do not forget that this is my child and my slave. I need him to work in my house later! If anything happens to him, you will be responsible!" This lets the ancestors know that they can no longer attack the child, because his social affiliation has changed by this act of symbolic transfer, which would normally be accompanied by a transfer of food. To a certain extent, ancestors may be duped and deceived. This example involves the "something" that creates identity between individuals and that the ancestors are able to recognize.

The jealousy of co-wives may also prompt the symbolic sale of a child. By complimenting the child of a wife whose fertility they envy, they draw down on him the malevolence of the divinities and genies of the bush, and may provoke his death. The best way to protect the child is to sell him to someone of another lineage. He is then sheltered from the co-wives' malice. Symbolic transfer always plays on the fringes of social identity versus biological identity.

Certainly, there are other important themes around which symbolic thought is articulated, but they all refer in some way to the opposition between the identical and the different. Such is the case of the opposition between the living and the dead, between the human and the infrahuman (the animal and the vegetable, the entire world of living things other than man), between the human and the superhuman (gods, the dead, powers, forces, and so on). But we will not deal with that here.[11]

222

The Genesis of Identity

This section is based on my 1979 article "Symbolique de l'inceste et de sa prohibition" in which I first advanced the idea of a second form of incest, marking the entrance of this notion into anthropological literature.[12]

Two identical things have the same definition and the same characteristics. In the domain of kinship, in an Omaha system, two matrilateral parallel cousins have the common characteristic of being in the same situation in relation to their maternal lineage, because they are born of two sisters who married differently. These cousins therefore differ through agnatic lineage but have a common identity in terms of uterine lineage. The identical and different cannot be absolutes, but relative notions that depend on the observer's point of view: from their father's point of view, these two cousins are different and have nothing identical about them; from the point of view of their maternal lineage, they are, on the contrary, identicals.

Nevertheless, there is an irreducible characteristic in kinship: a child is born of his mother and shares this characteristic with his brothers and sisters. The irreducible is female engendering, uterine descent, and fraternity. This is a banal observation, but banality is sometimes difficult to observe.

Identity and difference between the sexes articulates all symbolic thought and provides the basis for all rules of filiation and alliance. In collaterality, for example, this is a general law which Lévi-Strauss formulated well before me: "it is the idea that the *brother-sister* relationship is identical with the *sister-brother* relationship, but that these both differ from the brother-brother and the sister-sister relationships, which are identical with one another."[13] Since then, the identity of same-sex siblings has become a widely used principle in ethnology. As far as I am concerned, on the basis of an analysis of semicomplex systems, and not elementary kinship systems, I would counter that the brother-sister relationship is not identical to its reciprocal, sister-brother. This relationship, on the contrary, is the basis of nonidentity since it originates in sexual difference. A brother and sister and a sister and brother are not two identical relationships the way the relationships between two brothers and two sisters are to each other. The first case involves gender difference, the second, identity.

We have seen that difference is transcribed in opposition. Binary categories are subjected to a hierarchical type of classification in which male is superior to female, or "better" than female, as high is superior to low, full superior to empty. This asymmetrical relationship is also the unequal relationship that is "the basic element of all structures of kinship, for everything is included in it: necessary alliance with other similar units, the engendering it is issued from and engenderings to come, the choice between two principles of filiation, the crossing of collateral lines that emerge from it, the relative relationship of birthright."[14] It is the conceptualization of a biased relationship of sexual dominance that is deduced from observations made on the body. From these observations concepts are derived that allow one to consider the world theoretically, as well as value-coded categories that allow one to organize the world concretely and live in it.

The Effects of Sexual Difference
What can be built on the notion of the identical and the identical/different pair?

The absolute identical is Ego, identical to himself: a series of interesting representations shows the monstrous effects of procreation in various places, starting with masturbation, the prime example of excess of the identical. Then comes a same-sex twin, then, siblings born of the same parents, same-sex siblings; then among cousins, parallel cousins of the same sex. Let us recall that parallel cousins are those born either of two brothers or two sisters, in contrast to cross-cousins who are born of a brother and a sister. Consequently, the first are considered more identical to each other because they share the same paternal or maternal substance, or both at once. The impossible negation of sexual difference is the inviolable mark of otherness.

Let's consider a few curious gaps in the spectrum of logical possibilities in kinship systems. This systematics is based on terms that denote brothers and sisters and cousins of the same generation, and those that denote the brothers and sisters of parents and their cousins. These terms can be associated or dissociated. Now, among all the possible combinations, only one possibility is missing. In our own kinship system, we call the father's sister, the mother's sister, the father's brother's wife, and the mother's brother's wife "aunt." Nothing in the nature itself of these positions implies that they must be designated by the same term. Nomenclature is not biologically founded in any system; it is always a social construct based on a certain distribution of identities and differences.

On examination, one can see that only four out of five possibilities of association are realized. In the first, the same term designates all siblings and cousins, whether they are parallel (offspring of the father's brother or the mother's sister) or cross (offspring of the father's sister or the mother's brother). Within this system, known as "Hawaiian," Ego uses "brother" and "sister" to refer to siblings in the strict sense but also to parallel and cross-cousins. In contrast, in the second system, known as "Sudanese," there is a different term for each of these categories, a particular term that designates all of Ego's parallel cousins, whether from his father's or his mother's side, and another that designates his cross-cousins on both sides, and a third that designates his brothers and sisters. In the third system, the "Eskimo" system, which is

225

our own, the same term refers to siblings according to sex while a single term designates all "cousins," parallel and cross alike. The fourth possibility describes the Iroquois, Crow, and Omaha systems, where the same term designates both siblings and parallel cousins, a term completely different from the one designating cross-cousins. No known society has ever opted for the fifth possibility wherein a single term denotes siblings and cross-cousins, while another term denotes parallel cousins. This implies that awareness of identity cannot involve changing sex, that is, the collateral relationship of a brother and sister, which infers the relationship known as "crossed." The notion of identity is based on commonality of sex, which entails situations of parallel kinship in subsequent generations, and these two traits are universally perceived as being of the same nature.

Therefore, in some systems, all cousins may be called the same thing: "brother," "sister," or "cousin." Only parallel cousins may be called "brother" or "sister" by Ego in the Crow, Omaha, and Iroquois systems. But while cross-cousins, like parallel cousins, may be referred to as "brothers" or "cousins," cross-cousins are never called "brothers" like siblings, when parallel cousins would be called something else by Ego. Thus, the concrete reality of historical and ethnographic data denotes a logical gap that is explained by what I call "the differential valence of the sexes."[15] (See figure 42.)

The differential valence of the sexes, which implies the different place the two sexes occupy in a table of values and, more generally, the dominance of the male over the female, follows from the observed difference of the sexes and their powers and makes it impossible for the brother/sister relationship to be at the basis of a perfect identity.

Therefore we can assert that the notion of the identical, as an overall ideological category, was never built on the absolute

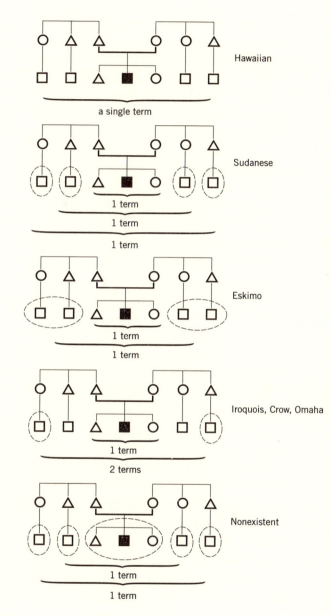

Figure 42.

227

primacy of Ego's similarity with his cross-cousins alone among all cousins.

This criterion allows us to explain the absence of the fifth possibility, which assumes the unthinkable, namely that the female could dominate the male. In this regard, in the logical relationship established in kinship systems between male and female, there are, again, only three possibilities. Our system realizes one of them: namely, the (terminological) equality between the sexes. The second possibility, which occurs more freqently, holds the male superior to the female. An extreme representation of this is found in the Omaha system, wherein a sister is the terminological equivalent of a daughter: she is therefore not even of the same generation as her brother, but of an inferior generation. The third possibility, symmetrical to the preceding one, is found in the Crow system, a matrilineal semicomplex system whose basic principle implies the preeminence of the female over the male in terminological construction, but not necessarily in social reality. This preeminence, moreover, is so unthinkable that there is always a place in the construction of the terminological whole where the male reasserts his superiority or at least his equality.[16]

If we consider the terminology of procreation rather than siblingship, we see that gender similarity is also the fundamental criterion of the identical. These father/son or mother/daughter relationships are the favored vectors of identity in the most diverse societies. Here again, one may note the absence of certain elementary possibilities in the construction of systems of filiation.

Rodney Needham has enumerated the six modes of descent that are logically possible, only four of which have actually been realized.[17] The first is patrilineal filiation through men, which passes from a male to a male. The second is matrilineal filiation, where filiation is only recognized through consecutive female links. The third is mixed; it is a dual patri- and matrilineal filia-

228

tion, where only two lines are recognized among all possible lines (eight on the level of grandparents): the totally agnatic line, which passes through successions of men (Ego's father, his father's father, his father's father's father, and so on) and the line that only passes through women (Ego's mother, his mother's mother, his mother's mother's mother, and so on). These rather complex systems are called "bilineal systems." Only two lines establish Ego's identity. Finally, there is our own system, which recognizes the pertinence of all lines of descent, whether composed exclusively of men, exclusively of women, or alternately of men and women. Thus one can inherit from one's maternal grandmother as well as from one's maternal grandfather, from one's great-great-uncle through one's father's mother, and so on. Although the Western system has a patrilineal inflection (everyone bears his or her father's name), filiation here is cognate; it can be recognized through any line.

Two other possibilities remain. First, the alternate system, in which filiation would pass from father to daughter and from mother to son. But the father would take his filiation from his mother and the mother from her father. Every individual therefore would belong to the descent group of his opposite sex parent, so that a granddaughter and her paternal grandmother would be from the same descent group, just as a grandson and his maternal grandfather would be. Finally, in the parallel system men would transmit filiation exclusively to their sons and not to their daughters, while women would convey filiation only to their daughters and not to their sons. A daughter would therefore never belong to her father's descent group, nor a son to his mother's.

To Needham, these last two systems, alternating and parallel, "probably could not be employed socially as regular and exclusive principles of transmission and incorporation, though certain rare and uncertain approximations to them have been reported."[18] For example, the system of the ancient Incas was a parallel system, if we can rely on the chroniclers of the Discovery who were blinded by their own system.[19] Examples of alternating systems may have been encountered in Indonesia.

All these gaps have the same explanation, namely that the category of the identical as a primordial ideological category cannot be built on the similarity of crossed relatives, who, in filiation or collaterality, present a sexual difference. Certainly, in the Hawaiian case, siblings, parallel cousins, and cross-cousins are referred to in the same way. Yet no figure exists wherein parallel cousins would be put aside and cross-cousins identified with siblings. A dominant crossed system would imply the preeminence of the female over the male, since the mother's brother, and not the father's, would be identified with the father.

A whole inventory could be made of ethnologists' accounts that point out, often parenthetically, the relationship between the prohibition of incest of the second type and the notion of the identical, by describing the system of kinship and alliance and the correlative system of representation of a given society. The notion of the identical is explicitly related to the incest prohibition, and it is seen in relation to representations of a person's constitution, starting with paternal and maternal contributions.

Richard Huntington observed that the most abhorred, most odious incest in the system of representation of the Bara of Madagascar is not that committed between siblings in the broad sense (between brothers and sisters with a common father, or the children of two brothers) nor between primary relatives (father/daughter, mother/son), but between the children of sisters.[20] For example, a sexual relationship with Ego's mother's mother's mother's sister's daughter's daughter's daughter, who is a second cousin to the eighth degree, seems rather distant, since it involves a boy and girl whose great-grandmothers are sisters. (See figure 43.)

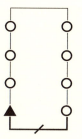

Figure 43.

To the Bara, this incest is abhorred because they come "from the same heart," "from the same womb," like a brother and sister born of the same parents. This union would be a combination of the identical, a return to the source. On the other hand, agnatic half-siblings, those who share the same father but have different mothers, belong to the same lineage but are considered quasi, not absolute brothers, blood relations born of the same parents. While children of the same father cannot marry each other, those of two brothers can, after a ritual. Consequently, patrilateral parallel cousins may marry each other, but matrilateral parallel cousins may never marry, because they come from the same womb, from the same grandmother, which is obviously not the case for the former. This situation is found in numerous societies, among the Greeks, for example, where the agnatic half-brother is not considered *adelphos* but *frater*. *Adelphos* is someone who has the same mother as oneself (possibly the same father, but the same mother suffices). Sharing the same womb creates the strongest identity.

A relationship between two cousins with a common great-great-grandmother causes the female partner's fluids to encounter the man's mother's fluids, similar since they come from the same woman and are transmitted through women. This is not the

231

case of agnatic parallel cousins. In the Bara system of representation, which Huntington describes, the fluids and substance that make up the child come essentially from the mother and not the father. Such a society, which absolutely prohibits matrilateral parallel marriage but accepts patrilateral parallel unions, shows a preference for cross-cousin marriage, because there is no actual common substance between them. A man can marry his mother's brother's daughter, for though he shares some of the same substance as his mother and her brother, transmitted by his maternal grandmother, he has nothing substantial in common with his mother's brother's daughter, who obtains her substance from her own mother, to whom he is not at all related. (See figure 44.)

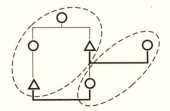

Figure 44.

Yet, since something is also transmitted by men, this marriage of close kin — where closing the circle occurs in the first generation, not the fourth, as among the Samo — combines an exclusively dominant stock in one with a recessive stock in the other. Absolute lack must be avoided as much as combination of the identical.

Every society constructs its own gradations of the identical. Among the Bara, it is the parallel identity of the female sex that takes precedence over that based on the male sex, but it may be the reverse in other societies. Nevertheless, this construction goes hand in hand with the basic features of social organization, filiation, alliance, power, and so on, since one is always dealing with co-structured conceptual sets.

In their description of life on the island of Tokelau in 1975, Judith Huntsman and Antony Hooper reported that full siblings are considered identicals there; they are called *tutuha*, which means, precisely, "the same."[21] This identity prompts different attitudes depending on whether the siblings are of the same or opposite sex. In the latter case, avoidance is standard starting in early childhood; brothers and sisters must avoid each other, not only sexually, which goes without saying, but also in everyday life, and cannot eat or live together. Not only can they never touch each other, they cannot even see each other face to face.

Generally, the incest prohibition needs to be stated as a social rule only when the principle of the identical is not so strongly structured, that is, when blood relations of different sexes come into contact, since the strongest structuring of the identical is the fact of the commonality of sex. Incest is forbidden between brother and sister, but not between two brothers or between two sisters; between father and daughter and mother and son, but not between father and son and mother and daughter. These prohibitions are so profound they do not need to be stated. Of course, these are infertile relations, but the risk of fertilization is not, in my opinion, the only reason for the prohibition of incest of the first type between blood relations and relatives by marriage. The relationship itself is challenged, whether fertile or not, because it puts identical substances in restricted circulation.

In our societies, incest is only punished legally if it is heterosexual and vaginal, that is, if it entails the risk of impregnation and only as an aggravating circumstance of rape. Thus, incestuous fondling, stroking, and even fellatio and sodomy are generally ignored by the law, as is homosexual incest. Reo Fortune saw this

233

clearly, as I noted in the introduction to this volume, and he wrote: "The prevailing emphasis on incest taboos as they are related to the regulation of marriage has resulted in an almost total neglect of homosexual incest."[22] He did not accord it much attention either. This is a passing remark, where homosexual incest is understood not as incest of the second type as I have defined it (indirect homosexual incest through the intermediary of the same sexual partner) but in the strict sense of the term — sexual relations between same sex blood relations or affines.

Other authors have elaborated on this. For example, Maurice Barry and Adélaïde Johnson address mother/daughter and grandmother/granddaughter incest, which violates the principle of identity in the most profound way.[23] The sociologist Herbert Maisch wrote in 1970 that he had encountered father/son and grandfather/grandson incest.[24] Consequently, one may conclude that actual homosexual incest exists; doctors, psychiatrists, and criminologists acknowledge it. Moreover, in some societies, consanguineous homosexual practice between certain relatives is not only licit but encouraged. Lévi-Strauss reports that among the Nambikwara a young man's potential brother-in-law is his cross-cousin, "with whom, as an adolescent, [he] indulges in homosexual activities which will always leave their mark." And he comments, "Brothers are closely related to each other, but they are so in terms of their similarities [...]. By contrast, brothers-in-law are solidary because they complement each another and have a functional efficacy for one another, [...] they play the role of the opposite sex in the erotic games of childhood."[25] It is therefore possible, and even recommended, to have homosexual relations with the cross-cousin whose sister one will marry; they prefigure the relations with the sister and are never in competition with them. Lévi-Strauss says nothing about what happens between parallel cousins, but when asked, he confirmed that their status was identical to that of siblings who were "close in their similarities," and therefore that these homosexual activities were absolutely prohibited between them. In this society, the essential criterion of identity is not gender but the parallel, as opposed to crossed, character of kinship relations.

In his conclusion Lévi-Strauss quotes Balzac's remark on the subject of "that artificial and temporary 'conjugality' between young people of the same sex in some schools," a conjugality expressed by the term Activists. Balzac writes, "It is strange, but never in my time did I know brothers who were 'Activists.'"[26] Homosexuality, certainly, but not concrete incest, which would be the most profound form of incest of the first type.

A number of societies in New Guinea — the Etoro (studied by Raymond C. Kelly), the Kaluli (by Edward L. Schieffelin), and the Baruya (by Maurice Godelier) — practice the same types of incestuous homosexual relations.[27] In 1976, David M. Schneider wrote: "[...] the Etoro of New Guinea believe that semen is necessary to the proper growth and maturation of boys and so they are fed semen direct from its source, by mouth, as often as is deemed necessary. The ideal inseminator is the boy's father's sister's husband, but other older men may perform this function as well." The Etoro think that young boys come into the world with empty testicles and that it is therefore necessary to fill them. This gives a particular connotation to the transmissions of fluids. In effect, a man exhausts his allotment of semen; he may renew it by consuming certain vegetable substances, but it will be of lesser quality. It is therefore necessary for a married man both to control his sexuality in order to economize his semen and to prove himself generous by making a gift of it to young boys. In a male household, a man is obliged to nourish a relative with his substance, at times a relative by marriage, at times a blood relation, sometimes by fellatio, sometimes by sodomy. In a way he is repaying his debt:

235

the father's sister's husband pays his debt by giving the ability to procreate to the son of the man who has given him a wife.

Kelly has shown that the definition of incest and matrimonial prohibitions are isomorphic to prohibitions pertaining to the insemination of boys, except that, in the one case, it is a couple of relatives of both sexes and, in the other, a pair of the same sex. In other words, the alliance prohibitions will bear on sexual relations with the wife of the inseminator, for he and the inseminated will encounter each other in the same womb. Schieffelin reports the same belief among the Kaluli of New Guinea. A father cannot inseminate his son nor a brother his brother for they are already of the same substance. The father's sister's husband, who will be the inseminator, may be the father's cross-cousin: thus one sees the structural isomorphism between bans concerning homosexual insemination and those concerning heterosexual marriage. There are, then, in various societies, licit homosexual relations between men (and sometimes between related women) wherein the strongest criterion of the identical shifts from the commonality of sex to the parallel nature of the kinship relation, in filiation as in collaterality. This does not mean that these societies have not considered the question of sexual difference, since sexual difference determines the parallel or crossed character of lines of descent.

At issue here and in all societies is establishing what is propitious socially and biologically, and whether it is preferable to associate identical things or different things. While certain societies make a single choice and combine the identical or the different in all areas, others vary their choices depending on the area, or even within the same area. Furthermore, what is lucky for one individual may be unlucky for another, just as what is favorable for one community may be unfavorable for another.

As a paradigm, the identical and the different serve to polarize all other conceptual pairs, although some may include a middle term — the lukewarm between the hot and the cold, for example, or the midway between the high and the low. But this is not always the case, so conceptual polarity remains prevalent. The polarity induced by the opposition of the identical and the different is also organized into a hierarchy through the opposition of the male and the female. These two fundamental conceptual pairs underlie the two rules for manipulating all other conceptual pairs: the first is that things that are different attract each other under certain conditions and repel each other under others; or, inversely, things that are identical attract each other under certain conditions but repel each other under others; the second rule is that the placing into contact of two identicals is significant insofar as one always prevails over the other.

In the case of incest of two "brothers" with the same woman, only one is the victim of it, generally the husband. Indeed, he is seen as the dupe, his powerlessness and blindness revealed, for if he were strong and clear-sighted he would have known what was happening. The most serious infraction occurs when a man's wife sleeps with her lover in the conjugal bed. In numerous societies, offenses of this type explain certain male illnesses: for example, when a man spits blood, the *pisa* disease among the Alladian, it is immediately ascribed to his wife's adultery on his own mat. Similarly, in numerous African societies, elephantiasis of the genitals is interpreted as clear proof of a wife's adultery with her husband's blood relation. It is the husband, the weaker, who bears the stigma of meeting his identical in the same womb: his bodily fluids are retained in his genitals, where his blood relation's semen has flowed as a result of the attraction of identicals.

To these two rules we may add a third: the equilibrium of opposites. Their proper balance is necessary to the world's harmony, social order, individual life, and the life of a person as undivided body and mind. Greek thought, for example, offers a systematic formulation of this. While the combination of the identical always causes an upset in equilibrium due to excess on one side to the detriment of the other, this excess will be sought elsewhere to cure certain illnesses, in rituals of inversion (for example, on occasions of royal succession, which is to say, after a death), or in carnivals. For a brief interval of time, what is ordinarily prohibited becomes possible, if not licit. For example, a new king may have sexual relations with his sister on the occasion of becoming a sovereign. In certain societies of the Ivory Coast, a particular slave is his master's double; on the sovereign's death, this slave will take his place during the transition period, before being put to death (usually) once the new king is installed. Shilluk princesses may have free unions (not marriages) with relatives, including agnatic half-brothers, but these unions must remain childless. And among the Zandé, women of the aristocratic Wungara clan have homosexual relations with each other even if they are sisters or cousins, for there are no potential male partners.[28] In this case, the combination of the identical in sex and kinship serves to enhance the extraordinary status of these princesses.

The mechanics of fluids, the attraction and repulsion of the identical and the different, will be examined next.

CHAPTER SEVEN

The Mechanics of Fluids

While the formal framework of the identical and the different may be considered universal, every population provides its own content and interpretation of it. Among the Samo of Burkina Faso, the central dualist category is the hot and the cold, and, correlatively, the dry and the wet, categories found in the discourse of lineage doyens, in myths, and in rituals. These particular categories, moreover, are frequently found in ethnographic literature. In the literature of seventeenth- to nineteenth-century hygienists, such as Julien-Joseph Virey, man is described as hot, dry, dark, vigorous, exuberant, and fiery, while woman is cold, wet, pale, weak, gentle, and tender, needing male semen to warm and dry her.[1] These conceptual associations seem to suggest that a woman requires a man's care — a father's, brother's, or husband's — and should be obedient. Weak, oppressed, and sensitive, women are naturally inclined to take care of children. Since the hierarchy of the first categories provides a ready-made value framework, it is not surprising that the categories themselves entail moral connotations. "Hot, dry, and fiery" connote honesty, courage, responsibility, and almost brutal determination; "gentle, tender, and weak" connote subtlety and fragility, but also spinelessness, lack of will, unpredictability, and so on.

239

Combination of the Identical

Among the Samo, bringing together two hot natures — putting hot on hot — dries out the body and the cosmos. This is a rather Aristotelian concept; indeed Aristotle explains that male heat results in ether, and that semen is not matter but ether: man fabricates semen through the inner concoction of his blood, and semen becomes ether, *pneuma*, just as boiling water turns to steam and not to stone. The drying out of the body, according to the Samo, means the draining of one's fluids (women's menstruation, men's sperm), as well as illnesses manifested by thinness or emaciation, possibly leading to death. The drying out of the cosmos means great climatic drought, groundwater sinking deeply into the earth, the barrenness of herds and soil. Placing cold on cold, on the contrary, triggers flows: excessive rains that ruin crops, flooding, hemorrhaging, diarrhea, and so on.

Combinations of the identical, whether conscious or unconscious, have repercussions in one of three registers: meteorological, biological, or social. A transgression committed in one register is not necessarily punished in the same register; it may be punished in any of them. Among the Samo, an offense of a purely social order, such as burying the remains of a *zama* —a pariah thought to be necrophilic, who is very hot since he incorporates the residual heat of dead bodies — is considered placing hot on hot, as the earth itself is hot. This offense may have dramatic meteorological consequences; in case of drought, when the earth's torrid emanations make rain evaporate before it reaches the soil, *zama* burial is one of the primary causes, along with incest, that will be sought through divination. A recently buried person might then be declared a *zama*. He will be disinterred and his remains left to rot between sky and earth in the branches of a tree. Since the taint is sexually transmitted and hereditary, the husbands or wives of these *zama* remains, as well as their children

240

and possible sexual partners, will be considered *zama*, too. There is always a *zama*-tainted body, therefore, to be implicated in case of misfortune, though the accusation is mythical (necrophilia being no more frequent in these societies than in our own); it is a myth whose curse is transmitted for generations.

I once saw a man accused of being *zama*. He was suspected of having had sexual relations with a *zama* Samo woman during a trip to Bamako (Mali). She warned him that she bore this fault, telling him she was "a big someone," the standard expression. When he returned to his village, he saw that everyone was avoiding him. No one would give him a daughter in marriage, and no work group would accept him. When he asked the reason for this ostracism, he learned to his consternation that he was thought to be *zama* and had to be prevented from contaminating the girls in turn. Fortunately, it is possible to absolve oneself of such an accusation; this rite involves retrieving an object from the bottom of a container of boiling oil without getting burned. After successfully completing this task, he went to all the villages where rumors of his affair had spread, accompanied by *griots* who told of his feat and proclaimed that he was not *zama*. Women approached and poured ashes over his head to show that he had been reintegrated into the community of the ordinary living. When he came to Dalo, where I happened to be, his joy was boundless.

The origin of the *zama* is found in a myth about the blacksmith lineage. Originally, men lived in the sky under the guidance of the earth master. They had so proliferated they could no longer live together. Food was eaten by voracious crowds before it could be cooked. The earth master therefore decided to send his people to earth, which was still soft, using a chain forged by the blacksmith and his brothers. He made clear that he would be the earth master there as well. After helping the ancestors of all known humanity descend, and discovering the potential wealth of the earth, the blacksmiths tried to appropriate it for themselves. Their leader thought up a scheme. He buried his younger brother in a ditch where people were descending and had him announce that the earth belonged to the blacksmiths. He organized a gathering of all those who had descended, and all went as planned. But the earth was hot and the brother started to burn up. He emerged from his pit, left the others, and headed toward the west. He is the ancestor of the *zama* and of the taint transmitted by descent, a living body buried before its time; absorbing and incorporating the earth's heat, he may no longer return to the earth, even after death.

In Samo thought, man comes under the category of the hot; he is thought to produce sperm continuously, through the internal decoction of his "bodily waters" located in bone marrow and joints. To conduct this process, he needs heat, which is located in the blood. A body emptied of its blood is cold. Sperm itself is considered to be extremely hot inasmuch as it is the most condensed form of blood. Man's blood is hot (*furu*) in all senses of the term: hot, impetuous, angry, violent, and dangerous.

The Samo had some idea of hematopoiesis. Noticing bone marrow's reddish color, they deduced that this was where blood came from via an alchemical process involving food. The blood would be purified through decoction in the spinal cord and transformed in the spermatic canals. Let us note in passing that the relationship between the brain, spinal cord, and spermatic canals has been established in numerous advanced civilizations. We find it in Chinese medicine (the theory of the three cookers)[2] and in Leonardo da Vinci, whose depictions of couples engaged in coitus show a clear link between the spinal cord and penis.

When a Samo man complains of shoulder, knee, or joint pain in the morning, the other men say he has "made a child," that his wife has conceived the night before. According to local representation, there is a gyrating ball in the female uterus, whose opening, when properly positioned and timed, has a strong suction that empties the man of his semen. It even sucks it out of his bones, which explains the morning pain and stiffness.

Sperm entering the female uterus brings blood to the child, necessary for birth. The mother's menstrual blood, which stops flowing, serves to constitute the child's body, skeleton, bone marrow, and flesh. The father must continue to have sexual relations with his pregnant wife until approximately the sixth month of pregnancy, so that the child will have enough blood to emerge from its lizard- or froglike fetal shape and take human form. On the other hand, if sex is extended beyond this period, the child may overheat in the womb, turn white-hot, and be born albino. Now, albinos come under the same category as the *zama*; they are not suspected of necrophilia, but they cannot be buried, for they, too, are very hot and likely to dry up the rains and groundwater due to their excessive heat. Similarly, children who are born covered in meconium (greenish feces composed essentially of bile discharged after birth) are not as readily accepted as the others, because their parents are thought to have continued having sex until the end of the pregnancy.

No one escapes these systems of interpretation. No one can be sure he has not committed some reprehensible act over an ill-defined period of time; and even so, there are other considerations. If a husband takes a trip during the last months of his wife's pregnancy, for example, she will be the one accused of adultery during this lapse of time. In a way, these systems of thought are totalitarian; they leave no gray area or doubt. To elude them is to be excluded from the community.

Among the Bobo, the Samo's neighbors, there are also those who cannot be buried: the "incestuous," those who have committed incest or are born of incest.[3] This is prohibited for the same

243

reason: to put them in the ground would be to combine the identical — to put heat on heat — thus, to dry up the rain and groundwater. The earth is hot, the incestuous, superheated.

The idea that semen transports blood, which is hot, is also popular in Western culture. When we say that blood is mingled in the union of a man and woman, it implies that male semen has the ability to convey blood from one organism to another. What allows us to say that children bear their father's blood, or that noble children have their father's blue blood, is the idea that blood comes from the father's sperm. Behind the words "flesh and blood" is the idea that paternal blood is found in sperm transmitted during sexual relations, providing the embryo with its share and giving it human shape throughout the pregnancy.

In the Samo system of representation, woman is categorized as cold for the simple reason that she loses her menstrual blood. She is hot before puberty because she does not yet lose it and hot after menopause because she no longer loses it. Having a sexual liaison with a prepubescent girl, therefore, is dangerous in terms of combination of the identical — placing hot on hot — particularly for the girl, who at that point is the weakest link and risks infertility if her internal sexual organs are burned. Prepubescent liaisons are not sins as we understand them, but dangerous acts given their consequences. The moment a woman gets her period, she becomes cold, *nientoro*. Her body's fluids are transformed into vaginal secretions and milk, through weaker decoctions than in men. Milk seems to be equivalent to sperm, though it is inferior as it has not attained the same degree of refinement in decoction. It has neither sperm's concentration, density, volatility, heat, nor odor; nevertheless it is of the same nature, and sperm may be harmful to milk as a result of combination of the identical, the one prevailing over the other.

An internal path in women's bodies allows different humors

244

to meet. Blood and sperm, which is of the same nature and origin as blood, have the characteristics of heat, strength, and odor, which "spoil" milk. A breast-feeding woman who begins menstruating again is thought to have milk whose consistency and odor displease the nursing infant. This is also thought to occur if a breast-feeding woman resumes sexual activity, which is why sexual relations during the breast-feeding period are commonly prohibited.[4]

Introducing sperm into the womb of a breast-feeding woman is equivalent to placing hot on hot, since during the breast-feeding period, the amenorrheic woman is hot herself in order to secrete milk. There may be a drying up of both the mother's milk, which may endanger the child's life, and the father's sperm, which may make him sterile. When children have fevers or turn away from the maternal breast, it is because "the bad smell spoiled the milk," because the milk came into contact with semen. This belief is traceable from Akkadian tablets to the present, by way of Ambroise Paré and hygienist doctors of the nineteenth century who recommended that nursing women space sexual relations as far as possible from feedings.[5] But the ban does not only aim to protect the child at the breast; it also aims to preserve the husband's virility. In a Mossi customary, it is said that if a mother lets a drop of breast milk fall onto her infant son's genitals, she causes irreparable damage.[6] An impotent man or an infertile one is considered the victim, as an infant, of such an accident. His mother inadvertently allowed a drop of milk to fall onto his genitals and, because of the infant's state of weakness, he could not tolerate the heat.

Mature women are therefore cold because they lose their blood, especially when they they are married since their husbands' sperm is again transformed into blood in their wombs. By nature, women are cold, except during pregnancy and breast-feeding, when they are hot, but less so than men, not surprisingly, for in these societies women rarely experience menstruation. As

245

soon as they reach puberty, they marry and have a child; after breast-feeding, they have another child, and their lives continue like this until they reach menopause.

When a woman is pregnant, the blood of her own father, her lineal blood, becomes the body of her child. But she does not give life; life, breath, and heat are given by paternal blood. And as we have seen, three generations will be necessary for the traces of blood, heat, and life to fade in her descendants. These come from her father, which she nevertheless transmits in recessive line to her children, who will transmit them residually, whereas her brothers transmit them as dominant stock.[7]

The inherent contradiction in this system is that boys and girls both receive their initial allocation of blood from their father and body from their mother. How, then, is sexual differentiation introduced? This is the flaw in systems of interpretation of reproduction which, like other interpretative systems, are not quite complete, cannot come perfectly full circle, despite aspiring to totalize the experience.

Any incestuous sexual commerce with a prepubescent girl or a menopausal woman constitutes an excessive accumulation of heat. The Samo say it expressly: incest "heats the body." If the prepubescent girl is dangerous because she has not lost her heat, the menopausal woman is dangerous because she no longer loses it. Consequently, both add their specific heat to that of male sperm. They cannot cool down either by losing menstrual blood or giving birth. In most societies, in fact, giving birth is considered a significant loss of heat for women. When the baby, which is hot *in utero*, is expelled, along with blood and other humors, the new mother's life is jeopardized. For this reason women who have just given birth take warm baths, sit by a fire, and stop up all openings to prevent wind, air, and even light from entering.

The menopausal woman who combines the heat she no longer

loses with masculine heat if she still has sexual relations may be suspected of sorcery. The woman having her period, by losing heat, attracts external heat to her (for example, the heat of cooking). Among the Nyakyusa, a pregnant woman or one who has just had sex with her husband must not visit a woman who has just given birth because the full attracts what remains of substance in the empty, and the new mother's life would be endangered.[8] Between these two women who are of the same nature, one weak and the other strong, it is not the strength of one that is transmitted to the other; it is, on the contrary, the fullness of one that attracts the other's remaining vitality.

As one can see, the same logic, the mechanics of fluids, may be translated in one sense or another, based on the society. The Samo woman who loses heat because she menstruates attracts the heat of certain fires to her, ruining the iron being fired if she passes the forge, or the poison being cooked for poison arrows. The cold attracts the hot; things of a different nature are paired. Inversely, among the Nyakyusa, who speak in terms of the full and the empty, as well as the hot and the cold, it is not the "empty" and cold woman who attracts the hot, but the woman with a superabundance of heat and corporal plenitude who attracts the new mother's weakness, emptiness, and coldness, endangering the life of the weak one. The hot attracts the cold, then, if attraction always occurs between objects of a different nature.

If we analyze these beliefs, we see that bringing together two identicals (positive or negative ions, to use pseudoscientific language) causes a kind of short-circuit. Instead of passing from positive to negative, there is an accumulation of the similar. Such short-circuits exist in many areas besides the sexual. Among the Samo, the rain master, the *lamu tyiri*, never cuts his hair, except at certain propitious moments in his life; it is then reverently kept in a pot that will be buried with him. His hair and head are thought to bring good rain. He is marked with the sign of the hot, and his heat is concentrated in his head and hair — in his head, because the head is a reservoir of semen, and therefore heat, and in the hair, the abundance of which is a sign of virility. There is nothing especially original in this; this symbolism of hair is found in the Greek world as well as in numerous primitive societies.[9] In a system where identicals repel each other and opposites attract, the hot attracts the cold and wet, and this is why the hot head of the sky-water master is thought to bring rain.

Men from rain master lineages marry earth masters' daughters. On a rain master's death, there is a sort of interregnum during which seers designate the woman who has married into this lineage and is pregnant (or will soon be pregnant) with the future *lamu tyiri*. This boy is taken at the age of seven to begin an entirely different life from the one he has known thus far. He will have to respect a series of injunctions: not looking others in the face because of his heat; not looking over walls (the heat of his gaze may inadvertently fall on weak people unprepared for it); walking with infinite precaution and sometimes being carried due to the risk of the intense union of his heat and the ground's heat; not sitting directly on the ground, for the same reason (he must sit on mats); finally, not eating from the same containers as others. If he is a good *lamu tyiri*, his head will bring rain; if he is bad, it is because his head is not hot enough: nothing can be done against him, but his death and replacement will be awaited impatiently. If his hair happens to touch the ground, this placing into contact of hot on hot immediately causes a short-circuit that will trigger drought and hot winds that are carriers of epidemics such as cholera and smallpox, and prevent wild and cultivated grasses from germinating. He must therefore never fall on the ground, which is why he is separated from other children, can no longer play games with them, and must walk very carefully. For the same reason, he cannot go out in the sun with his head bare, like the Mikado in Japan.

The Short-Circuit

The notion of short-circuit implies contamination through contagion or transmission. Emile Durkheim, who elaborated the notion of contagion, writes: "The properties of a being are propagated contagiously, especially when they are of a certain intensity.... We leave something of ourselves everywhere we go."[10] Among the Samo, if a man descends into a well to clean it when his wife is pregnant, he will cause her to miscarry. For a man to go down into a well, that is, to sink into the earth, is to accumulate heat; it is to add the earth's heat to his specific male heat through contagion. It is the husband's duty to contribute blood, heat, and life to the embryo, but if the earth's heat is added to his own heat, it will be too strong for the embryo and it will be burned from within. We might recall that frequent and prolonged sexual relations during the last months of pregnancy have the effect of "overcooking" the child, making it albino. Along these same lines, if a man descends to the bottom of the well while his wife is pregnant, the baby will emerge burned to ashes.

Inversely, if a Samo woman dies while pregnant or in labor, that is, while retaining heat, her husband will have the same characteristics through contagion. The Greeks thought that dying in labor was to women what dying in war was to men. To the Samo, a woman who dies while pregnant or in labor is particularly dangerous, for she will want to drag other pregnant women into her predicament. Consequently, pregnant women fear nocturnal apparitions, wear disguises, avoid going out at certain hours of the day, or go out with a knife so as to be able to confront the spirit of the woman who died in childbirth. As burying her would amount to putting hot on hot, since her baby is still inside her, and would thus cause a short-circuit, she is buried in a sacred place where she will not dry out the land, or after a post mortem caesarean. As her husband has been contaminated, he will later be buried in the same special place. As soon as his wife dies, his house is destroyed and all his goods distributed to gravediggers who specialize in the handling of these baleful cadavers. All traces are eradicated.

In addition to these cases of contamination through spousal identity where the dangerous element is excessive heat — that of the forge, poison, or pregnancy — there are others that do not concern human beings. For example, the material manifestations (the altars) of certain powers — those of the land or particularly powerful and hot gravediggers — may be dangerous. Wives who run off with a new partner are forced to return to their conjugal household when a fragment of one of these altars is deposited where the lovers have taken refuge; the local community, fearing maleficent effects, will pressure her to leave. But the most interesting case concerns plants. The sacred baobab, for example, situated on the road from one village moiety to another, is known to possess such internal force and heat that all persons in a state of weakness must avoid going near it, or risk being emptied of whatever strength they have (as among the Nyakyusa, in sum). Sudden deaths are explained this way, the tree's vital power sucking out the remaining force of the individual in a state of lessened resistance.

All these cases feature relationships established by the interaction of forces of attraction and repulsion between different orders of representation: the biological, the social, and the cosmic. Each of the terms of the whole that constitutes the short-circuit — contagion, contamination, propagation — connotes an aspect of the phenomenon, but, unfortunately, none connotes them all. The choice is made based on the cause to be treated, on the phenomenon to be explained. The short-circuit connotes the placing into contact of two identicals that should, on the contrary, avoid each other; propagation connotes the transfer of fluids; contamination and contagion connote danger. The Samo have a single general term for overheating, *fulõre*, whose root, *furu*, signifies heat, fever, anger, and danger.

These notions of short-circuit, contagion, contamination, and propagation-transmission allow us to understand the incestuous linking of two same-sex blood relations through the same sexual partner, or incest of the second type. This type of incest is a short-circuit, because two identicals — two sisters and their mother, two brothers and their father — come into contact. It is a contamination, or contagion, since the fluids of one infiltrate the other. In fact, the two blood relations are never of equal strength; one is for various reasons always slightly stronger than the other and therefore harmful to the other. Finally, incest of the second type is propagation, inasmuch as these fluids are transferred from one to the other through a carrier, a third person who comes out of it unscathed, unless the two blood relations are of equal strength, in which case their fluids will well up and accumulate in the third person. Generally, however, the third party is not affected: among the Baoulé, as we have seen, the two sisters, two female cousins, or mother and daughter must engage in a ritual of lustration with a sheep split in two, a ritual their common male partner escapes. Only one of the two blood relations, the weaker, is affected: we saw this in the case of genital elephantiasis, but it is also true of tuberculosis and spitting blood. Since blood is transformed, purified into sperm, reciprocally sperm is completely altered in the female body, turning into blood; consequently, a man's spitting blood is explained thus: his spermatic fluid cannot come out normally because it is impeded by an identical fluid in the same womb; it therefore flows back into the man's body and degenerates into blood, which has to come out one way or another.

251

In the Samo system, a man calls his real sisters (agnate or uterine blood relations) as well as his parallel female cousins (daughters of his father's brother or mother's sister or daughters of male and female cousins) "sisters." Now, if a man is suspected of engaging in secret relations with a "sister," in the broad sense, or with any of his wife's consanguineous female relatives or his wife's brother's wife, his wife leaves him immediately after learning of it — not out of anger, but because she is in danger. Her position as an unknowing third party places her in a position of weakness, and it is she who will be subjected to the maleficence of incest of the second type. She will return to her husband only after the illicit relationship has been broken off and the rituals of appeasement have been conducted. Her flight from the conjugal hut is not a sign of heartache or moral reproach, although these feelings are no more foreign to her than to any woman betrayed in any culture; it is truly a flight from danger, that of being placed in contact with her own substance.

Among the Nuer, the strongest identity is that of two agnate consanguineous men; that is, identity passes through men to the point of being conceived of as totally interchangeable.[11] Among the Samo, who prohibit the combination of the identical, two "brothers" of whatever sort cannot share their wives if both men are alive, while among the Nuer, on the contrary, it is absolutely licit to have a liaison with the wife of a "bull," that is, in this cattle-raising population, the wife of another male of the same lineage, outside the central core group (real father and brothers). The Nuer explain it this way: if a man sleeps with one of his father's wives, he is in fact placed into contact with his own mother through the intermediary of his father, and therefore finds himself in a situation of incest (of the first type). In the course of his sexual relations, the father transmits his wives' fluids from one to the other. By sleeping with one of them, the son

252

encounters his mother's fluids in her womb. And this unreal incest of the first type with his mother is doubled by an incest of the second type with his own father.

Among the Nambikwara, the homosexual activities between cross-cousins cease after their reciprocal marriage with the other's sister, as we have seen. Ethnologists explain this as a way not to confuse social roles: having become brothers-in-law, they are no longer cross-cousins. This explanation is undeniable, but it is not the only one. One must also take into account incest of the second type. If homosexual activities continued, each of the cousins would be placed into contact with his own sister through contagion. (See figure 45.)

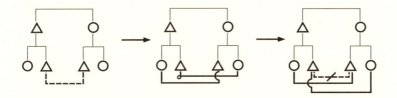

Figure 45.

This problematic of logical links between different processes can help us understand some of the disparate phenomena cited by Lévi-Strauss in the first chapters of *The Elementary Structures of Kinship*.

Lévi-Strauss mentions the Madagascan belief that when a household is sterile an incestuous relationship exists between spouses;[12] the Navaho belief in a fourth world where the sexes are separated and where monsters are the fruit of the masturbation to which each sex is reduced;[13] a Siberian group's assertion that patrilateral marriages make water flow back to its source;[14] the

Aleutian belief that a daughter may become blind or mute if her father sees her during her first menstrual period;[15] the belief among Malaysians that sundry acts — including incest, thoughtless speech, noisy games, the imitation of noisy games, and so on — will unleash storms and tempests.[16] Lévi-Strauss sees this as the consequence of a misuse of language. I ask a somewhat different question: Why would the misuse that incest constitutes have the power to unleash a tempest in Malaysia and inflict sterility on incestuous couples in Madagascar? More generally, what do these beliefs have to do with the remarkable events associated with the incestuous relationship (of both types) in different societies?

At issue is always the danger that results from excess of the identical in societies that have "opted" for a negative connotation of this excess. The Samo system I have attempted to explain is valid only as a paradigm: in other societies, the earth might be considered cold rather than hot; hot on hot might provoke floods rather than drought; another pair of categories might be substituted for the hot and the cold, or at least added to it, such as the empty and the full among the Nyakyusa. The latter consider new mothers cold and empty because they no longer carry the child (an accumulation of heat) and consider married, sexually active women full and hot from the marital semen; married women therefore cannot visit new mothers for they will endanger them, as we have seen. There does not seem to be a society that has chosen an entirely different categorical pair (such as light and dark or high and low) as the basis of their system of representation. The hot/cold pair is universally preeminent because it denotes the living body/dead body pair, allowing one to think immediately of the opposition of the living and the dead.

This may explain certain societies' reclusion of women in special huts for the duration of their menstrual periods. They only come out at night for they must protect themselves from the sun, whose excessive heat may sap their remaining vital force. They are in a state of lessened resistance due to the loss of heat, and the sun may empty them entirely of their blood. Likewise, in our societies, telling young girls to avoid contact with water during their periods comes from the fear that these periods will turn into constant hemorrhage (attraction) or, on the contrary, amenorrhea (repulsion): either blood is emptied from their bodies, or, on the contrary, flows back into their bodies. The sun has the same dual, flowing back and forth effect as cold water. Hot sun and cold water have the same attractive or repellent effects.

Masturbation constitutes the quintessential combination of the identical (male masturbation, that is, due to ejaculation). In Europe in the nineteenth century, restraining devices would be used on young boys to prevent them from masturbating at night, which was thought to provoke their wasting away or dehydration through the loss of substance and consumption by heat. It emptied them and turned them into half-wits. The underlying idea was that semen was located in the bones and a fair amount stored in the brain. Since earliest antiquity this whitish, spongy mass has been considered a sort of spermatic reservoir that allows semen to seep down along the spinal cord.[17] A modern reference might help to illustrate this. In Jean-Marie Périer's film *Sale rêveur*, Jacques Dutronc says to a friend who masturbates incessantly, "If you don't stop jerking off, you'll have nothing left in your head!" This forceful, if inelegant, sentence aptly explains the supposed relation between the brain as a reservoir of sperm and the stupefying effect of masturbation.

For the Navaho, masturbation does not make one sterile or stupid but leads to abnormal fertility and the engendering of freaks of nature — just as consanguineous incest is thought to do in our folk wisdom, despite the evidence of animal breeding and the example of societies that practice systematic consanguineous marriage, between cross-cousins, for example. Similarly, homo-sexuality can only be condemned in these interpretative systems as a form of combination of the identical.

The menstrual or parturient blood of primiparous women was particularly sought-after in traditional medicine for treating skin ailments and as youth cures. In the Christian liturgy, Christ's blood and sweat (for lack of semen, of course) cured leprosy, a disease also manifested on the skin. Thaumaturgic kings cured scrofula by the laying on of hands. Blood being antithetical to milk (spoiling it, as we have seen), it served to stop the inflow of milk as well as oozings of all sorts. All these cures attested to in various texts have a meaning; this is not a matter of chance but logic. In the terror that AIDS incites today, we find renewed interest in all the body's fluids again: blood, semen, milk, saliva, and sweat.

According to Rattray, one of the most serious sexual offenses among the Ashanti is raping a married woman in the bush, which is punished by death.[18] It is not a crime against women in general, because the woman must be married; it is not a crime against the institution of marriage, since it must occur in the bush; and it is not enough for it to occur in the bush, since the victim must be a married woman. It is the sum of these terms — rape, bush, mar-riage — that constitutes the danger, not only for the woman but for the entire community. Indeed, rape is a particularly hot act among the hot acts of coitus; the bush is a hot zone, and danger-ous because spirits inhabit it, as opposed to the village, a cold zone of harmony and security; lastly, the married woman is hot as a result of sexual relations with her husband. The rape of a mar-ried woman in the bush, therefore, represents an accumulation of heat with particularly harmful meteorological, climatic, and epi-demiological repercussions.

Aristotle

To conclude this chapter, I would like to comment on Aristotle's treatise *Generation of Animals*.[19] I will do so from an anthropologist's perspective, of course, and not as a historian of philosophy, that is, proceeding from the principle that there are certain essential modes of representation.

For Aristotle, the first aberration is female offspring. Ideally, if all unfolded as it should in the natural order of things, there would only be sons. The fact that daughters exist raises the fundamental problem of the existence of two sexes, of the identical and the different, and the requisite encounter between male and female in order to generate offspring. Unisexual reproduction does not exist in a directly visible way in nature. Why are daughters born? A fundamental *aporia*: Why do men and women exist?

We have mentioned several times that various societies perceive the problem of the existence of two sexes as a power struggle between seeds — a male seed and a female seed — and, strictly speaking, between the sexes. Among the Azandé, for example, semen and female mucus both contain *mbisimo,* the souls of children.[20] After puberty, these liquids thicken and take on consistency. The semen of young boys is thought to lack consistency; it is only an avatar of urine. If it does thicken, it is because children's souls have come to inhabit it. The gender of the unborn child depends on a ratio: if there are more souls of the female gender in the female mucus than of the male gender in the male semen, the child will be a girl, and vice versa. There is a statistical relationship, therefore, between these children's souls competing to come into world.

The Navaho see things differently. For them, a savage battle occurs during coitus. If the man dominates and imposes his fluids, the child will be a boy; if he is dominated and the woman imposes her fluids, which are hostile to procreation (contrary to our ideas that women exist solely to bear children), the coitus will remain fruitless; if the man dominates with a great deal of difficulty, the child will be a girl. The female nature is therefore considered to be hostile to reproduction; it must be forced into it by the male. In one case, the sex of the unborn child is determined by the ratio of the number of souls of each gender; in the other, it is determined by the power struggle between the male and female.[21]

Aristotle constructed one of the most beautiful explicative models of sexual difference, which one might call a savage genetics. His predecessor, Anaxagoras, simply believed that the father alone determined the child's sex: if semen came from the right testicle (the hotter one), he would have a son; if it came from the left testicle, he would have a daughter. Similarly, Empedocles explained the determination of the child's sex through the changing heat of the maternal womb during the menstrual cycle. During the menstrual period, the womb is cool because it loses blood, and will favor a girl; between periods, it accumulates heat because it does not lose blood and receives sperm, and therefore will favor a boy. Once again, the hot and the cold as a categorical pair are used to think about sexual difference. Aristotle criticized Empedocles and Anaxagoras on this point precisely: there is no objective reason why coldness would produce a uterus rather than testicles. Aristotle postulated that semen contributes no matter to the fetus, for matter is exclusively female. Semen is *pneuma*, breath and blood. Through his internal heat, the male is able to cause the blood's concoction and its transformation into semen. Aristotle writes that semen contains "the principle of form." By "principle" we should understand primary cause, source, origin. Aristotelian reasoning is a vicious cycle: the male can cause the concoction of blood because he is naturally hot; but he is naturally hot, because he can cause the concoction of blood. The woman has more blood than the man since she loses it regularly, unless she uses it to make an embryo, and she is cold since she does not transform it into semen. Another vicious cycle: woman is cold because she does not produce semen and she does not produce semen because she is cold.

Why does a man nevertheless engender daughters who sometimes even resemble their mothers? "For when the first principle does not bear sway and cannot concoct the nourishment through lack of heat nor bring it into its proper form, but is defeated in this respect, then must the material change into its opposite."[22] The conception of daughters is therefore the result of a partial impotence in the male. "Now the female is opposite to the male," therefore, they are not complementary but contrary.[23] "Observed facts confirm what we have said. For more females are produced by the young and by those verging on old age than by those in the prime of life."[24] Why is this so? "In the former the heat is not yet perfect [the male is too young], in the latter it is failing [the male is too old]."[25] They have less heat, they are incapable of concoction, their sperm is clearer: they have a liquid semen as opposed to a thicker semen. "Now all these characteristics come of deficiency in natural heat. Again, more males are born if copulation takes place when north than when south winds are blowing; for animals' bodies are more liquid when the wind is in the south, so that they produce more residue — and more residue is harder to concoct."[26]

Again we find a relationship between climate and the human body's fluids. In other words, this rational philosophical discourse is based on the same categorical grammar as that of the exotic thought systems we have already described. Likewise, according to Aristotle, the menstrual period occurs at the coldest and wettest moment, the waning of the moon, the wet attracting the wet. The nature of food also plays a part, since blood comes from food and semen from blood. Water temperature, too, is a factor: cold water encourages female births, hot water, male births. All these accidental causes are nevertheless efficient causes, for if only potential itself were in actuality, only males would be engendered. "The first departure indeed is that offspring should become female instead of male; this, however, is a natural necessity. (For the class of animals divided into sexes must be preserved....)"[27] Reproduction requires both male and female, but if the principle of the male did not alter itself such that it changed into its opposite, only males would be born. In other words, Aristotle is attempting to conceptualize the very duality of the identical and the different, which he reduces to a unity, that of the identical. The question then is how the different can come from the identical: through the alteration of the same into its opposite.

Aristotle distinguishes three elements in semen's potential, each of which can be changed into its opposite. First there is the male's generic potential which, if it does not dominate, is changed into its female opposite. Then, there is the male's individual potential which, if it is dominated when the generic potential is dominant, engenders a male that resembles the mother. If neither of these two potentials, the generic nor the individual, manages to dominate, to impose a male form in female material, the offspring is a daughter who resembles her mother. There can be no symmetry because there is no feminine potential, given that the feminine is matter and not form. The birth of daughters is explained by the failure of the masculine, which does not by any means imply a triumph of the feminine. The third element is movement, sexual motions that fashion the embryo. Movement may be sustained or may slacken as a result of male failure: the more it slackens, the more the child will resemble its distant ancestors.

The perfect model is immediately clear: generic male potential dominates and the child will be a boy; the father's individual potential dominates and his son will resemble him; movement is sustained and the resemblance will be total, or it slackens a bit and the boy will resemble his grandfather or his great-grandfather in paternal line. The imperfect model is also immediately clear: generic male potential is dominated and the child will be a girl; individual male potential is dominated and this girl will resemble the women in maternal line, more or less based on the quality of movement. Aristotle again envisages a number of intermediary models, but omits others, and these omissions are rather telling. In addition to the combinations mentioned earlier, if the generic potential is dominated but individual potential dominates, the offspring will be a girl who resembles her father or a distant male ancestor in paternal line, based on the intensity of the movement. But he omits the cases of resemblance to men in the maternal line (the mother's father, for example) or to women in the paternal line (the father's mother, for example). To account for it, a supplementary distinction would have to be introduced, between potential and actual movement: movement can be sustained potentially and relapsed actually, sustained or relapsed potentially and actually, relapsed potentially and sustained actually.

Daughters are only the first anomaly. Sometimes the offspring "appears finally to be not even a human being but only some kind of animal, what is called a monstrosity."[28] How are they engendered? "If the movements relapse" — potential and actual movements — "and the material is not controlled [by the generic or individual potential], at last there remains what is most universal, that is to say the animal."[29] The animal is therefore the apex of the feminine. Monstrosity constitutes the total defeat of masculine potential; it is the irruption of the raw force of the material, that is, an excess of the feminine. There is no excess unless it is feminine.

Monsters, then, are not hybrids born of the copulation between a man and a female animal; Aristotle holds this to be impossible: "All these monsters result from the causes stated above, but they are none of the things they are said to be; there is only some similarity [...]."[30] The monster may resemble an animal — a sheep, ram, calf, snake, or any other animal — but he only resembles it, he is not this animal, even partially. All copulation against nature is destined to sterility: "That, however, it is impossible for such a monstrosity to come into existence — I mean one animal in another — is shown by the great difference in the period of gestation between man, sheep, dog and ox."[31] A kitten takes three months to form, a human infant nine months, a baby elephant two years.

As for congenital malformations, extra limbs, or atrophied limbs, Democritus explained them through the conflict of two semens penetrating the same uterus, that is, incest of the second type or adultery. Aristotle saw things differently. The cause is not the male's volatile and pneumatic semen but the feminine material. Aristotle contests Democritus' argument because the masculine principle is a formal, never a material principle: "we must rather suppose that the cause lies in the material and in the embryo as it is forming" out of that material.[32] Indeed he observes that when the uterus is arranged lengthwise, as it is in snakes, whose eggs are arranged in a row, or when eggs are arranged in separate cells, as with bees, one does not encounter monstrosity. Therefore deformity has to do with the material itself, or more precisely with the arrangement of feminine matter in other species, particularly "in multiparous species, due to the difficulty of growing within the same organ," and in man, "since even in man, monstrosities occur more often in regions where the women give birth to more than one at a time, as in Egypt."[33] It was indeed believed that there was an overabundance of twins and triplets in Egypt. And by analogy he deduces monstrosity from multiparity, extra limbs from extra fetuses.

If the first anomaly is the birth of daughters, the second is multiparity, the proliferation of matter. "Whether the semen of the male contributes to the material of the embryo by itself becoming a part of it and mixing with the semen of the female, ... as the fig-juice does the liquid substance of milk..." which is to say, it concentrates it into a single mass.[34] "If the male emits more semen than is necessary [...] however much it is it will not make anything greater; on the contrary it will dry up the material and destroy it."[35] Desiccation thus emerges in Aristotle as being symmetrical to monstrosity. Monstrosity is the proliferation of feminine matter, which is not necessarily anarchic inasmuch as twins may be perfectly formed. Desiccation, caused by the proliferation of semen, is masculine heat consuming itself. Aristotle uses a beautiful metaphor: fire's excess violence does not make water hotter but makes it evaporate and disappear. The unnatural formation of supernumerary parts has the same cause as multiparity, "for the reason exists already in the embryo, whenever more material gathers than is required by the nature of the part."[36]

But such deformity exists only for humans. "For the monstrosity belongs to the class of things contrary to nature, not any and every kind of nature, but nature taken as what holds for the most part; nothing can happen contrary to nature considered as eternal and necessary...."[37] In the natural course of things in conformance to divine and social law, animals as well as men engender offspring who resemble them and have the characteristics of the genus and the species. For Aristotle, nature, like the earth and gods in myth and popular thought, can produce monstrosities that appear as such only in terms of man, his history, and his reproduction. Gods are not frozen in a contingent form; on the contrary, they change at will; no one has seen their faces.

Monstrosity is nothing more to Aristotle than the excess of the feminine: the birth of daughters, multiparity, anomalies, and deformities represent the crushing domination of the material, which is feminine and which man must fashion in his image, mastering it generically, individually, and dynamically. But what underlies this philosophical discourse is the same interaction of the opposition of the identical and the different — the heat that makes the concoction of fluids and therefore reproduction possible. It is the same discursive structure, imposed by the observation of nature, that we have described in more "primitive" or archaic forms of thought.

CHAPTER EIGHT

The Hidden Order of Things

By subsuming a set of marriage bans or simple sexual prohibitions under the category "incest of the second type" (eponymously, the prohibition of "two sisters"), I have not meant to suggest an order of prevalence: first, incest of the first type, with blood relations or affines to the degrees prohibited by local law; then, incest of a second type constituted by other forms of sexual prohibitions with more fluid contours. In fact, I believe just the opposite. I think it can be shown that if incest of the second type is not the very foundation of incest of the first type, it nevertheless provides the only coherent anthropological explanation for it. It also explains why other unions — with milk kin and godparents, for example — are prohibited as incestuous. Consequently, we can chart the extension of incest of the second type, looking back to sexual prohibitions concerning blood relations and relatives by marriage, and looking ahead to those concerning milk kinship and spiritual kinship. Our field of investigation can be extended further to include the relationship between this form of incest, which has been shown to be central, and other forms of sexual offenses, such as sodomy, homosexuality, zoophilia, and necrophilia.

Blood Kinship

Incest of the second type affects, rather than unites, two blood relations or two relatives by marriage through the intermediary of a common sexual partner. In the purest case, there is no consanguinity or alliance in the sexual relationships, strictly speaking: the common partner is not at all linked to one of the blood relations and none of them is married, which excludes any suspicion of adultery. This is the case of a man who sleeps with two sisters or a mother and daughter, to whom he is related neither by blood nor by marriage. In this case, the prohibition eludes traditional explanation.

Although not every society has a prohibition that expressly concerns two sisters — and some even recommend marriage with two sisters, or prohibit marriage with two sisters but oblige union with two twin sisters who are not only identical but one and the same thing, as we have seen in the case of the Mossi — incest of the first type can only be properly understood in terms of incest of the second type.

First we should note that, while incest of the second type (meaning the actual contact and not the prohibition) is not considered universal, this does not mean that it is not; it merely means that for one reason or another ethnologists have not always mentioned it, perhaps quite simply because they have failed to observe it. By contrast, incest of the first type is always attested; there is no society that does not explicitly decree the ban on a man's marriage or copulation with his daughter, sister, or mother, for this ban is related to the rule of exogamic alliance. Incest of the second type has nothing to do with either marriage or reproduction, and it often occurs without the partners even knowing. A man may have a liaison with a mother and daughter, or with two sisters, and be absolutely unaware of their kinship if he has met them in different places. The silence of ethnographic litera-

266

ture with respect to this phenomenon therefore does not in any way imply a lack of awareness of the particular relationship between two blood relations implicated in a love triangle.

There are several reasons to believe that the two types of incest always function together, indeed that incest of the first type could not exist without incest of the second.

The first reason is supplied by the famous case of Oedipus. What has always been seen — most recently through Freud's psychoanalytical interpretation, Lévi-Strauss's ethnological interpretation, and Vernant's historical interpretation, is incest of the first type, the marriage between a son, Oedipus, and his mother, Jocasta. This is the worst type of incest since the son returns to the place whence he sprang, which is obviously not the case with father/daughter or brother/sister incest. In *Oedipus the King*, after the revelation of Jocasta and Oedipus' infamy, the chorus pronounces the following words: "How, O how, have the furrows ploughed by your father endured to bear you, poor wretch, and hold their peace so long?"[1] Later, Oedipus raves: "Give me a sword, I say, to find this wife no wife, this mother's womb, this field of double sowing whence I sprang and where I sowed my children."[2] Commenting on this text, Nicole Loraux asked a pertinent question: "Do we find the father deep within the mother?" This question is at the core of incest of the second type.[3]

Indeed, Jocasta never tells Oedipus that he has slept with his mother, the chorus informs him that he has slept with his father: "How have the furrows ploughed by your father endured to bear you ... so long?" Laius is dead, of course, but he has left his mark, his trace, his furrows in the maternal body. The chorus does not accuse Oedipus of incest of the first type but incest of the second. And it reproaches Laius for failing to signal somehow that contact with his own substance was unbearable. The meaning of the Chorus' words to Oedipus are clear: How could your father bear to

cohabit with you in a womb where he left his trace and identity? Oedipus, too, refers to incest of the second type when he
says that he sowed the seed from whence he sprang. He is both
father and son in the same womb. Through a common partner,
two same-sex blood relations met when they should not have.
Consequently, even the canonical reference for incest of the first
type, *Oedipus the King*, makes mention of incest of the second
type, though the oblique reference to it has sufficed to mislead
commentators.

The second reason to believe the two types of incest always
work in tandem lies in the less remarkable but analogous case of a
man's union with his father's wife (for example, one of his wives
in a polygamous situation, or a second wife), perceived as double
incest of the first and second type. The incest of the second type
should be obvious now, since this man is placed in contact with
his father's substance through the intermediary of his father's
wife. But it is also incest of the first type, because the contact
with his father places him in a relationship with his own mother
as well: the father preserves her substantial mark, which he has
transmitted along with his own to the body of his other wife,
with whom the son is sleeping. Why forbid such a relationship
with a relative by marriage, if not because it implies an underlying doubly incestuous relationship with blood relations?

With the Council of Elvira, the church fathers became ob-
sessed by the need to justify the ban on incest with relatives by
marriage. If we deny the pertinence of incest of the second type
and the contact of identical substances, it is impossible to understand why the church fathers invented the notion of *una caro*.
Since two spouses form one flesh, a man's wife is one flesh with
him, so that Ego, in a liaison with his father's second wife, would
have contact with both the substance of his own mother, who
forms one flesh with his father, and with the substance of his

father, who forms one flesh with his second wife, in whom, consequently, the substance of the two wives mingles.

Milk Kinship

Incest of the second type allows one to understand that of the first, as well as even subtler kinship prohibitions, such as those based on milk kinship.[4] Milk kinship is most commonly practiced in the Islamic world (and I will refer to Soraya Altorki's work on it). Islam, however, did not invent milk kinship; it only codified earlier customs, giving it even greater scope.

One may recall that the Prophet, wishing to marry the wife of his adopted son Zayd, had the divine revelation that only biological paternity established filiation and the right to an inheritance. He inscribed it in law, that is, the Koran, thus eliminating the possibility of filiation by adoption. As Zayd's wife was no longer his son's wife, the Prophet was able to marry her, after Zayd divorced her. But this caused problems for followers who came to seek the Prophet's counsel. Among them was the wife of the adoptive father of a certain Salim. The childless couple adopted the young man long ago, in conformance with the custom of blood adoption which made him their full heir. The new law once again deprived them of descendants. Thus, in order to reestablish filiation, the Prophet ordered the mother to breast-feed Salim five times consecutively, though he was no longer a baby and she was infertile and had no milk. The mere gesture constituted a ritual that established a milk kinship between them. Adoption was no longer a matter of blood kinship but milk kinship.

Since then, milk kinship in the Muslim world has implied alliance prohibitions similar in all respects to those based on consanguinity. Three sorts of relationships are prohibited. First, those based on consanguinity, *nassab*: one cannot marry a direct ascendant or descendant, or the descendants of a relative (a brother

269

or sister, a nephew or niece). Secondly, those prohibited by alliance: one cannot marry an ascendant's wife, or a descendant's wife, or one's wife's ascendants or descendants, bans which can only be understood by means of incest of the second type. Finally, one cannot marry someone who is a relative by milk, and this prohibition concerns not only milk siblings but also the wet nurse and her blood relations, her children, their spouses, and their descendants.

The legal texts of both Hanafi and Malaki schools of Islamic law list the prohibited unions. A man (it is always a matter of men) cannot marry his wet nurse (1), his wet nurse's direct ascendants and descendants (2) (3), a daughter of the wet-nurse's grandparents (4), the wet nurse's milk daughter (5), an ascendant's wet nurse (6), an ascendant's milk sister (7), the milk daughter of a direct female ascendant or descendant (8) (9), the milk daughter of the wife of a direct ascendant or descendant (10) (11), the milk sister of a sibling (12), the daughter of a milk sibling (13), the direct ascendants of the wet nurse's husband and his sisters (14), the wives of the wet nurse's husband (15), the wet nurse's husband's direct descendants (16), nor a daughter of the wet nurse's husband's grandparents (17).

This list recalls the Chinese encyclopedias Michel Foucault spoke of in *The Order of Things*. One might wonder what all these people have in common. What relationship could there be between the wet nurse's husband's direct descendants and the wet nurse's milk daughter? While it seems sensible for a man to think of his wet nurse's daughter or another girl she breast-fed before or after him as a sister, it is less clear how close blood relations and other wives of the wet nurse's husband might be implicated.

The most interesting and unusual cases are those cited last, from the fourteenth to the sixteenth position, which involve the wet nurse's husband and his direct kin. Seven further prohibitions pertain to a man's wife's milk kinship: the man cannot marry his wife's wet nurse (1), his wife's wet nurse's mother (2), his wife's wet nurse's husband's mother (3), his wife's milk daughter (4), his wife's milk child's daughter (5), nor his wife's milk son's wives and descendants (6) (7).

There is an apparent coherence to this list. It begins with the wet nurse, goes to her ascendants, her direct descendants, and so on, then to the ascendants' wet nurses, the descendants', and so on, then to the wet nurses of relatives by marriage, and so on. But its true coherence is found in one line, implicit but indirect, which escapes scholarly observation because it can only be understood in popular thought in the form of a proverb or saying (Soraya Altorki even relegates it to a footnote): "Milk comes from the man." Milk comes not only from the husband but from all of a woman's sexual partners; a woman only has milk because she has sexual relations with a man. If a woman had no male sexual partners, she would not get pregnant or have any milk. Consequently, women's milk itself is denied as something that comes exclusively from women; even in this respect women are merely a temporary host. This proverb helps to explain why Muhammad was able to substitute milk adoption for blood adoption by ordering the mother to make the symbolic gesture, a simple simulacrum, of breast-feeding her adopted son. Although she had no milk, sexual relations with her husband made it seem as though she did; the important thing is the husband's semen. Once what people say is taken literally, the veil is lifted.

The saying "Milk comes from the man" also helps to explain the coherence of this list. A child who is breast-fed by a woman is considered this woman's husband's child, since her milk comes from him. In the last analysis, the child is nourished by the husband's milk. Therefore, two children with the same wet nurse, although born of different parents, have the same milk parents (which goes without saying); but, more subtly, a boy and a girl who are unrelated to each other, each breast-fed by the different wives of one man, are this man's children by milk, by "his" milk, and therefore consider themselves milk brother and sister even though they did not have the same wet nurse. The prohibition of marriage between them cannot be understood unless one acknowledges the saying. The children come from different families and have different wet nurses; they have only the wet nurses' husband in common, and the wet nurses obtain their milk from him.

Consider the case of a woman who divorces and remarries, and, while still lactating, nurses her second husband's child, born of his deceased wife. In this case, which is probably not very common but is nevertheless envisaged by Hanafi and Malaki jurisprudence, the first husband becomes the milk father of the second husband's child ipso facto, since the breast-feeding woman's milk comes from him, thereby establishing a whole series of prohibitions of alliance between this child and those the nursing woman's first husband may have had with other wives or milk children he may have had with other wives. This case fully underscores the importance of the proverb that says a mother's milk comes from the husband's semen.

Moreover, this saying illuminates the "structural incoherence"[5] in Muslim alliance prohibitions, that is, situations where the positions of various partners are homologous and might be represented by the same schemas with the exception of a detail. A man cannot marry his child's uterine sister or a daughter from his wife's earlier marriage. Note that the two cases are represented by the same schema. On the other hand, he can marry his child's milk sister, which is nevertheless a homologous situation; the wet nurse has no relation to him, which explains why he can marry his child's wet nurse's daughter or milk daughter. He may also marry his wife's milk child's sister, but not his wife's milk daughter. It soon becomes clear that the situations deemed licit are those in which his substance does not pass into the milk, but wherever it does, those situations will be illicit. (See figure 46.)

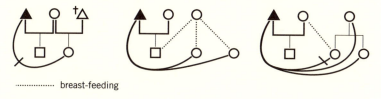

·············· breast-feeding

Figure 46.

Similarly, a man may not marry his agnatic sibling's mother, because the father's substance, which is also his, still exists there. On the other hand, he may marry his brother's wet nurse, though this is an homologous situation, for the male substance at the origin of the milk is different from his.

He may also marry his milk brother's mother or sister, again for the same reason: the paternal substance that is conveyed through these women is not his.

On the other hand, he may not marry his wet nurse's daughter, because she has drunk her mother's milk, as has he, and this milk comes from the same man. (See figure 47.)

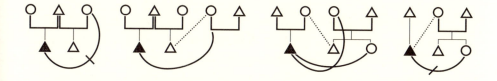

Figure 47.

A man may not marry his grandchild's mother (that is, his son's wife), but he may marry his grandchild's milk mother and the mother of his daughter's or his son's wife's milk child. These three situations are also equivalent; they represent people occupying the same key structural positions. (See figure 48.)

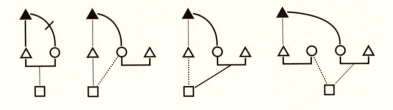

Figure 48.

Let us comment on these last schemas. A man may not marry his granddaughter because she is of the same substance as her father or her mother and they are of the same substance as him. In other words, incest of the first type (grandfather/granddaughter) is doubled by incest of the second type. He may not marry his son's wife without establishing incest of the second type between himself and his son. On the other hand, he may marry his grandchild's wet nurse, who is nevertheless in a situation homologous to that of his son's wife. He may also marry the mother of the milk child of his daughter or of his son's wife, who is nevertheless in a situation equivalent to that of his daughter or his daughter-in-law.

Likewise, he may not marry the grandmother of his children (that is, his wife's mother), for this falls under the prohibition against a mother and her daughter, but he may very well marry the grandmother of his wife's milk child, or the mother of the milk mother of his own child, who is nevertheless in an homologous situation to that of his child's grandmother. (See figure 49.)

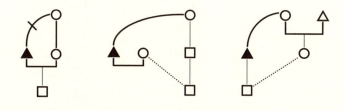

Figure 49.

A man may not marry his wife's sister — this falls under the prohibition of two sisters — but he may marry the mother of the milk child of his wife or the wet nurse of his child, who are nevertheless in an homologous situation. (See figure 50.)

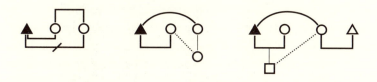

Figure 50.

A man may not marry his grandfather's wife, but he may marry the wet nurse of a sibling of one of his parents, who is nevertheless in an homologous situation. (See figure 51.)

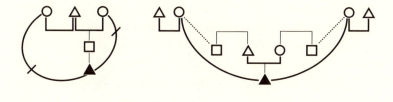

Figure 51.

275

Thus this catalog of apparent structural incoherence becomes coherent. Everything derives from the same organizational schema. A man may have several wives and will provide them with the milk necessary to feed his children. A woman may be a wet nurse to other people's children, whom she nurses with milk that comes from her husband. Any child may be nursed by a woman other than his mother. The breast-feeding relationship reinforces the agnatic relationship and extends it. Therefore, it is impossible to marry children nursed by co-wives of one's mother or wet nurse.

In Islam, when milk kinship is found to exist between spouses, the marriage is simply annulled. Muslim jurists have painstakingly sought to determine the age at which breast-feeding establishes an alliance prohibition (and specifically, the amount of milk that must be ingested). They believe the child's substance is definitively constituted around the age of two to two and a half, so any subsequent contributions of human substances can no longer alter it. Matrimonial strategies take advantage of this. If a man wants to prevent a familial marriage that would displease him — say, between his daughter and his brother's son — he need only ask his wife to breast-feed his nephew during this delicate period, even once. The two cousins then become milk brother and sister. The amount of milk may vary — one to three, five, or ten separate feedings. One cannot give the breast, withdraw it, then give it again, and so on, to meet the required number of feedings in one sitting. On the other hand, if the baby naturally pauses for breath, each time he takes the breast again counts as another feeding. For some jurists, milk kinship exists as soon as a baby has drunk one woman's milk five times from a container, but not if he has drunk milk collected at five different times all at once. For other jurists, it is exactly the reverse.

This casuistry — which is nevertheless interesting insofar as it shows the importance of milk kinship in the Muslim system of alliance — does not stop here. The texture of the milk is also an issue. Does the wet nurse's curdled or watery milk create milk kinship? In both cases, the materiality of the milk, a noble substance because it comes from sperm, is altered: in the first case it has congealed, in the second it has been diluted. Consequently, the question becomes whether such alterations preserve the spermatic nature of the milk.

A marriage could be annulled based simply on a wet nurse's testimony. Lacking this, testimony was required from two men, or from one man and two women, or from four women (in other words, the testimony of one man equalled that of two women). Nevertheless, despite divergences on the definition of a feeding and the nature of the milk (whole, curdled, or diluted), Muslim jurists all agreed on the essential thing, namely, the importance of this prohibition and the differences it introduced in homologous situations, differences that can only be understood in light of the belief that milk comes from semen.

In studies conducted by Altorki in contemporary urban communities, particularly among Saudi Arabia's elite,[6] most women had very few milk children but all of their grandmothers had them in the first third of this century. The Nadji of central Arabia observe all cases of the prohibition, while the Hijazi of the Red Sea province believe that a milk tie between two people also forbids marriage with their respective siblings, at least as far as younger siblings are concerned. A milk child's younger siblings therefore cannot marry their older sibling's wet nurse's children. (See figure 52.)

This is a curious detail since it supposes a sort of asymmetrical imprinting based on time within the group of siblings. There is no shared common substance from milk between the breast-fed child and his siblings, whether older or younger. Yet it seems

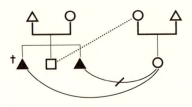

Figure 52.

logical that if there were such a thing as a "scent of milk," like a "scent of kinship," it would not affect the older children whose substance is already established, but the nursing infants who follow and whose unstable substance has yet to be constituted. Therefore, I cannot marry my older brother's milk sister, who is not my milk sister, though my older brother can marry my milk sister.

Imprinting goes forward, not backward in time. This strange extension explained by the notion of imprinting and the scent of milk between members of the same group of siblings only makes sense if one accepts that contact with a substance that is partially, imaginarily identical to an older sibling's would, without any direct sexual contact, place a man in a fraternal homo- or heterosexual incestuous relationship of the second type.

Up to the beginning of this century in Saudi Arabia, polygyny, on the one hand, and a high divorce rate and the common practice of brothers living communally, on the other, created households with many children, siblings, half-siblings, cousins, uncles, and nephews. Each of these relationships could be duplicated by a milk tie, which allowed the head of the family to construct subtle alliance strategies. For example, it was not unusual for a woman to suckle her husband's younger brother, the uncle of her own child. Uncle and nephew then became milk brothers, which led to matrimonial bans between their descendants. Their children would not be able to marry, whereas otherwise this would have been desirable. Similarly, marriage between first cousins, particularly with the father's brother's daughter, is a preferential marriage that can be prohibited if one is breast-fed by the other's mother. Milk kinship has also been a factor in women's (relative) liberation. Because young girls are required to wear a veil in the presence of blood relations they might marry, mothers contrived to multiply milk kinships, thus allowing their daughters to circulate freely in the house.

Every marriage between milk relatives constitutes a serious infraction of divine law, *zina*, even if it is agreed that the crime was not intentional. Altorki recounts the legendary case of two neighbors who, for fun, decided to create milk kinship between themselves, exchanging their nursing infants and taking turns breast-feeding them. Shortly thereafter, one woman left the neighborhood, and the friends lost touch. Much later, one of the infants, now a grown man, returned to his hometown; there he met the other, now a young woman, and unaware that she was his milk sister, married her. Several years went by before an old woman heard about the marriage and testified to seeing each mother breast-feed the other's child, thus revealing their milk kinship. The marriage was immediately annulled, but it had produced four children. Two sons were mute, one daughter lame, and the youngest daughter disfigured by smallpox. As far as everybody was concerned, this was divine punishment for transgressing the law against union between milk kin. One can only imagine the evils consanguineous incest would have brought!

Nevertheless, when a woman breast-feeds her husband's nephew (more precisely, her husband's brother's son), creating a milk kinship that prohibits subsequent union with her own daughter, the cause is clearly not paternal substantial identity since this already exists, the two fathers being brothers. Take the example of double parallel marriage followed by bilateral marriage: there are two brothers, one has two sons, the other two daughters, and they marry; one couple gives birth to a boy, the other to a girl, and they, in turn, marry. All the individuals in question share the same agnatic substance, boys as well as girls, due to their genitors as well as to being breast-fed, since their maternal milk came from the same paternal semen. This is an ideal marriage since there is only paternal substance, intensified by milk. However, if one mother had breast-fed the other's child, marriage between the cousins, now milk brother and sister, would be impossible. (See figure 53.)

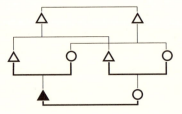

Figure 53.

To account for this, a hypothesis concerning a differential transfer of substance based on gender is necessary. Daughters would receive more substance or receive it differently from their mother than from their father, establishing their substantial identity, and vice versa for sons. Alliances are prohibited at the core of the identical, the *nassab*, which comprises the first, second, and third degrees Roman (mother, daughter, sister, and aunt, for a man). While a woman receives substances from her father and mother, as does her brother, she does not receive them in the same way, in the same arrangement. There would therefore be greater difference between first cousins than between brothers and sisters or uncles and nieces within a common substance, and this difference would be sufficient for union to be possible without combination of the identical. Reciprocally, certain unions would introduce an absolute differentiation in the identity the agnates share, which explains why these are prohibited; these are the prohibitions concerning the wet nurse's family and especially her husband.

Milk kinship introduces extremely efficient relationships of siblingship and consanguinity that are different from consanguinity of blood. While a number of prohibitions are added to those that concern blood relations (mother, daughter, sister, aunt), the spectrum is nevertheless infinitely vaster. It seems to me that it is based on a logic of relatedness of closest identicals (beyond the third degree), which controls even the smallest intrusions of lineal substance, because milk comes from the man. Neither the Koran nor the jurists say it explicitly. Only a common saying gives it voice. But the jurists take the trouble to list all the prohibited relationships that involve the wet nurse's husband particularly and that exceed the kinship relations prohibited in consanguinity and alliance — for example, the wet nurse's husband's grandparents' daughter, or the wet nurse's husband's father's sister (her status as a full sibling underscores the identity of substance between her and her brother).

While identity of substance should not be too perfect and not all marriages between cousins should take place, it "should not be excessively altered either, which would be the case if a man's contribution as co-wet nurse, accepted as a slight upset and displacement of identity, were reinforced in a man's descendants through the intermediary of a reduplicative alliance. A trace of the Other, or many others, is fine, but it should not be a chasm where identity is swallowed. In this perspective, marriage between cousins, which rearranges a puzzle of substances, is the ideal marriage."[7]

The sought-after redoubling of the identity of blood goes hand in hand with a repulsion for the reunification of foreign stocks, milk stocks understood not as women's specific contribution, obtained from their parents, but as the eminent contribution of a third blood, that of the wet nurse's husband. These are the traces that must not be reduplicated. The Samo system, after three generations, consolidates the residual maternal and grandmaternal traces (the closest of the different). Here, too, for three generations at most, the Samo refuse to consolidate the traces of foreign blood that pass through milk.

The practice of wet-nursing allows a certain amount of difference to enter a child in relation to the paternal substance. But it is not suitable for the foreign substance to be consolidated by subsequent unions to the point of altering the identity of the paternal group.

The belief that milk comes from semen is a development of the fundamental logic of bodily fluids, whose social circulation is clearly governed by systems of alliance prohibitions. Incest of the second type, moreover, is clearly evoked in the Koran, as we saw earlier, since it is not suitable to marry two sisters or the daughter of a woman with whom marriage has been consummated. The prohibitions regarding milk kinship are of the same order: if a man cannot marry his wet nurse's husband's daughter, he cannot marry any of this man's daughters, and therefore "two sisters." He cannot consolidate the wet nurse's husband's spermatic trace, found in milk, in his descendants, or establish a short-circuit between this secondary trace that he has in him and the same principal trace found in the wet nurse's husband's daughter, his milk "sister," or marry two sisters and make their common substance, similar to his, touch through him (figure 54).

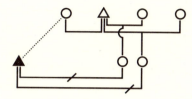

Figure 54.

Spiritual Kinship

Spiritual kinship, a completely different form of kinship established in the Christian world through the institution of the godfather and godmother on the occasion of baptism, creates alliance prohibitions that can only be explained by a sort of incest of the second type.[8] The institution confers an important social responsibility on the godfather and godmother, as they are expected to take the place of the parents in case of death, and a constant ritual responsibility, as they must celebrate the first tooth, the first nail trimming, the first haircut, the first pair of pants or dress, the First Communion, and so on. These rituals mark the many steps in the child's life until marriage, for which the godfather must bear the costs, and he is sometimes even expected to find the boy's wife.

In Albania and Greece, the midwife is frequently chosen as godmother (she has had intimate contact with the mother's blood and the child's placenta). In France, the husband's father and the wife's mother were traditionally chosen to be godfather and godmother for the first child, the wife's father and husband's mother were chosen for the second, the husband's older brother and the wife's older sister for the third, and so on, forming pairs that renewed the alliance between the families each time. The child's first names were those of his godfather and godmother. While this institution has become somewhat obsolete in French society, it is still alive in Hispanic societies, particularly in a number of Native American societies that were Christianized after the Discovery, where christening corresponded to a preexisting system of multiple relationships between the families involved in the birth of a child.

Yet the most important relationship is not the one between the godfather and godmother, but between the godfather and the mother of the child. Spiritual kinship induces a whole series of matrimonial prohibitions (in Sicily, Spain, central Europe, France, Latin America). The most common is the ban on marriage between the godfather or godmother and the corresponding godchild. The most significant ban forbids marriage between the children of the godfather or godmother and the godchildren. Godchildren of the same godfather or godmother cannot marry each other either, except in cases of ecclesiastical dispensation. Thus an equivalent, "spiritual" form of consanguinity exists among these individuals, which is most marked in the last case, forbidding marriage between godchildren of the same godfather or godmother. Just as among the Samo "two with the same maternal uncle" could not marry, these children are "two with the same godfather." Mystical substances and bodily substances amount to the same.

The prohibition against relations between the child's mother and godfather prevents more than just adultery; it prevents incest. Whatever the baby's gender, such a relationship would cause such condensation of heat and identicals (godfather/godson or mother/daughter) that the baby might die as a result.

In Sicily, where honor (particularly women's) is an extremely delicate subject, the godfather is the only man who can enter his godson's mother's house while she is breast-feeding. He may even display affectionate gestures, a kiss, a caress, that are never badly interpreted. This intimacy is only possible because the most severe prohibition bears on sexual relations between them. To transgress it would automatically bring misfortune on the child, the guilty parties, and the entire family. Such a transgression would be more serious than a godfather's daughter marrying the godson. Frequently, moreover, the mother will intentionally choose from among the husband's family or friends a godfather who is sexually attracted to her, so as to set up a solid barrier between them while still preserving a certain intimacy with him. Parents and godparents are therefore the object of both boundless trust and infinite suspicion, since they cannot transgress the prohibition without causing disaster, thus revealing the transgression, and since, reciprocally, any disaster that does happen to occur arouses the suspicion that they have transgressed the prohibition.

Insofar as the godfather is usually chosen from the husband's family, this prohibition typically involves incest of the second type — two blood relations would meet in the same partner, sexual for one, spiritual for the other. One could perhaps explain the homology between biological kinship and spiritual kinship by the homology between the Word and semen. In the Christian religion, the Word is the avatar of the semen of Christ. And just as in Oceanian societies, a man must nourish the child with sperm to bring it to maturity, in Christian societies, the godfather must ready his godson for marriage, thus, reproduction, by infusing him with the Word. The relations created by christening are also homologous to those created by breast-feeding, the Word substituting for milk to create a community of substance that, for example, prohibits godchildren with the same godfather from marrying each other.

Other Sexual Offenses

Finally, the last extension of the concept of incest of the second
type is directed toward other forms of sexual offenses. We have
seen that certain African societies used the same word to denote
several sexual offenses, causing problems for ethnologists because
consanguineous incest of the first type, homosexual incest of the
second type, and common adultery were associated pell-mell. To
understand this one must acknowledge the existence of chains of
logically or semantically linked concepts, which form co-structured sets of concepts that one may approach from any angle. For
example, the notion of fertility is associated with concepts of procreation, engendering, bodily fluids, pregnancy, lactation, food,
and menopause, but also, eventually, the concept of sterility,
which is immediately deduced as its opposite from the start. That
is why the order in which notions appear in discourse is not arbi-
trary; it is, on the contrary, often significant.

Leviticus 18:1–30 on marriage regulations and Deuteronomy
22: 1–23:5 elucidate this chain of concepts linked to incest of the
first and second type. For example, Deuteronomy 23:1 proclaims,
"He that is wounded in the stones [testicles], or hath his privy
member cut off, shall not enter into the congregation of the Lord."
Then in the following verse, "A bastard shall not enter into the
congregation of the Lord; even to his tenth generation shall he not
enter into the congregation of the Lord" (Deut. 23:2). Finally,
"An Ammonite or Moabite shall not enter into the congregation
of the Lord; even to their tenth generation shall they not enter
into the congregation of the Lord for ever" (Deut. 23:3). And so
on. One might wonder about the parallel established between a
eunuch, a bastard, an Ammonite, and a Moabite. What they have in
common is this: the eunuch cannot procreate, thus, he is not a man;
the bastard is born outside of marriage, thus, he is socially marginal; the Ammonites and Moabites are the nearest non-Hebrew

286

peoples. In other words, what they have in common is the otherness that excludes them from the congregation of the Lord.

In Leviticus 18, we find a series of prohibitions (which we discussed in chapter 2) marked by the refrain "Thou shall not uncover
the nakedness," which explicitly includes the prohibition of two
sisters: "Neither shalt thou take a wife to her sister, to vex her, to
uncover her nakedness, beside the other in her life time" (Lev.
18:18). Now the verse that immediately follows decrees the menstrual prohibition: "Also thou shalt not approach unto a woman to
uncover her nakedness, as long as she is put apart for her uncleanness" (Lev. 18:19). This parallel has a meaning, which is that all
the preceding prohibitions, whether they concern incest of the first
or second type, are aggravated if relations take place with a woman
who is menstruating, that is, losing her substance. The risks of
transferring the fluids of one to the other (her blood relation or
affine) are even greater, especially in the case of two sisters, making incest of the second type between them all the more likely.

The verses that follow condemn adultery ("Moreover thou
shalt not lie carnally with thy neighbour's wife, to defile thyself
with her" [Lev. 18:20]); apostasy ("And thou shalt not let any of
thy seed pass through the fire to Molech, neither shalt thou pro-
fane the name of thy God" [Lev. 18:21]); homosexuality ("Thou
shalt not lie with mankind, as with womankind: it is abomination" [Lev. 18:22]); and zoophilia ("Neither shalt thou lie with any
beast to defile thyself therewith: neither shall any woman stand
before a beast to lie down thereto: it is confusion" [Lev. 18:23]).
Through logical contiguity, a chain of concepts is developed that
goes from incest of the first and second type to menstrual impurity, to adultery, to apostasy, to sodomy, to zoophilia. All these
abominations incur the same punishment: being cut off.

Deuteronomy 27:15 says, "Cursed be the man that maketh any
graven or molten image, an abomination unto the Lord, the work

of the hands of the craftsman, and putteth it in a secret place" (that is, he who creates idols and worships them is cursed). The following verse says, "Cursed be he that setteth light by his father or his mother" (Deut. 27:16). Then, "Cursed be he that removeth his neighbour's landmark" (Deut. 27:17). Then, "Cursed be he that maketh the blind to wander out of the way" (Deut. 27:18). These crimes have an order: to renounce one's God; to renounce one's family; to violate the right to property; to violate the rights of an individual. In each case, the normal order of things is disturbed. Likewise, the following verse (Deut. 27:19) condemns he who violates the rights of the foreigner, orphan, and widow. Prohibitions immediately follow relating to incest of the second type between father and son through the intermediary of the father's wife, zoophilia, and once again incest of the first and second type, between a man and his agnatic or uterine sister and between a man and his wife's mother. This insertion of zoophilia illuminates all these bans: the man who transgresses them is behaving like an animal. Animals do not distinguish their own substance and copulate without concern either for kinship or alliance.

Consequently, all these offenses have this in common: not separating that which should be separated, mixing that which should be kept apart, and confusing genera, sexes, kinship, and alliance.

Various offenses may be compared by the terms used to denote them and the similarity of the biological, social, and cosmological sanctions they incur. Bestiality refers to the notion of *balal*, that is, mixture, the transgression of boundaries between the animal and the human. The word that denotes sexual relations with the sister, *heod*, implies all sexual relations outside of love. After this prohibition, being cut off is mentioned, which may mean ostracism, public execution, or death by God's hand. For example, the second book of Samuel presents the story of Absalom's death as an execution willed by God (2 Sam. 16:2–22, 17: 9, 20: 3). Meanwhile Leviticus states that in the case of prohibited relations with the uncle's wife or the brother's wife the guilty parties shall die childless, an assertion that implies either subsequent sterility or immediate death by divine punishment (Lev. 20: 20–21).

Relations with a sister-in-law, a brother's wife, or wife's sister are denoted by the same term as menstruation (uncleanness). A relationship with the brother's wife or wife's sister has the same meaning as with a woman having her period: there is a danger of mixing the identical fluids of two brothers or two sisters, and this danger is increased by the presence of blood. The prohibition of relations with a woman and her daughter or a woman and her granddaughter is called *zimat*, which means "crime" and generically designates all forms of incest and sexual impurity. In Ezekiel, *zimat* is to uncover the nakedness of one's father and to sleep with a woman who has her period: the issue is always the risk of aggravating contact between the father's and son's substances through the flow of blood.

In Deuteronomy 22:23–29 we find an equivalent of the supreme Ashanti crime: if a man rapes a woman who is married or engaged in town, they are both stoned to death; it is believed that the woman could have called for help and been heard, and that if no one came to her aid, she consented; if the rape is committed in the countryside, however, only the man is stoned, for the woman's cries might not have been heard. On the other hand, the rape of a virgin who is not engaged is not viewed in the same way and not punished by stoning, since she is not a man's property yet. This implies that the combination of the identical extends to simple adultery, where no consanguinity or alliance exists between the individuals, but where the seeds of two "anonymous" males meet in the same womb.

Benedictions — rain, fertility, abundance — come automatically when one acts in conformance with divine laws. Maledictions —

death, plague, wasting disease, fevers, inflammations, torrid heat, drought, skies of brass, earth of iron, dust, sand storms, ulcers, hemorrhoids, sores, scabies, delirium, blindness, plagues of locusts, and, finally, a trembling heart and languishing soul (in sum, burning scourges that lead to death and dereliction) — are the punishment of he who disturbs God's order.

The different sexual offenses constitute a confusion of genres that leads to veritable malediction. I would submit that most societies are aware of the links between these conceptual chains; the Bible represents only one canonical example, where, in the chapters relating to marriage, we find a whole series of sexual offenses that have little to do with marriage itself, such as sexual relations with a menstruating woman, with another man, or with an animal. The implicit relationship between all these sexual offenses, present indirectly to the Bible's authors and readers, is incest of the second type, the combination of the identical, but also, at the other end of the spectrum, the confusion of genres, the recourse to absolute otherness.

CHAPTER NINE

"De nobis fabula narratur"

We started this book with a quote from Michel Leiris and a passage from *Riche et légère,* Florence Delay's novel in which consanguinity, alliance, and purely sexual relations were intermingled. Despite their unsettling content, those sentences went almost unnoticed. They seemed so innocuous, but on reflection they were not. We asked what kind of incest was actually being discussed. We are now in a position to understand it.

Explaining his lack of desire for children, Leiris said jokingly, "Sleeping with their mother afterward would seem like committing incest." In a nutshell, he postulated the substantial identity of a mother and daughter (having a daughter and continuing to sleep with the mother would place all three in a doubly incestuous situation: father/daughter incest of the first type and mother/daughter incest of the second type) and also postulated father/son substantial identity (having a son and continuing to have sexual relations with the mother would also place the trio in a situation of double incest, mother/son and father/son). This would apply to sexual relations during pregnancy as well as after the children were born.

The sexual relationship *in utero,* considered nourishing in other societies, other texts, and other imaginations, is seen by

291

Leiris as an incestuous relationship. Naturally, sex during pregnancy has been practiced since the dawn of time without being questioned by couples who have engendered children, but it is not surprising that a mind as agile and complicated as Leiris's would have glimpsed what else might exist in the threefold relationship between the couple and between each partner with the conceived child.

A Culture Obsessed

Consider again the plot of Delay's novel.

Luz and Dorotea are agnatic half-sisters. Indio, their father, never married their respective mothers; they were his mistresses (he had a legitimate wife elsewhere). His close friend Iñigo has a daughter, Constance. She confides to Luz, the narrator, that she was sexually involved with her father, Indio. Constance was also caught sleeping with her matrilateral parallel first cousin, that is, with her mother's sister's son, a close relative since the two mothers are sisters. This would be enough to shock the family if these cousins hadn't also been born of the same father. In other words, Iñigo, Constance's father, had a relationship with Constance's mother's sister (an incestuous relationship of the second type) and a son was born. Consequently, the liaison between Constance and her "cousin" constitutes incest of the first type between agnatic brother and sister, and incest of the second type, between Constance and her mother and aunt, through Constance's identity with her mother and her mother's identity with her sister. Iñigo left the boy's mother when she was pregnant, palmed her off on a friend, who married her and legitimized the son, and then married her sister, who gave birth to Constance. (See figure 55.)

Luz later learns that Constance has had a lesbian affair with Luz's half-sister, Dorotea: "That summer, between London and

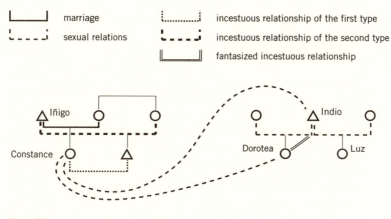

marriage

incestuous relationship of the first type

sexual relations

incestuous relationship of the second type

fantasized incestuous relationship

Figure 55.

Los Heraldos, Constance stopped in Madrid, in the apartment where I found myself that evening, placed her suitcase under the window where I had injured myself, slept in the bed I didn't want to sleep in. Enough time to make someone, my own sister, commit incest, as she did everywhere, as it was in her nature to do." Constance, who has already committed incest with her cousin (who is also her half-brother), has prompted Dorotea to commit incest as well because it is in her nature. "What kind of incest is this?" we asked.

This incest is Dorotea's incestuous relationship with her father Indio through the intermediary of the common partner that Constance represents. It is an incest of the second type that differs somewhat from the cases we have examined up until now, in that the homosexual and heterosexual relationships are reversed. Here, a homosexual relationship provokes heterosexual incest of the second type, whereas, generally, a heterosexual relationship results in homosexual incest. To tell this astonishing story, Delay dipped into our collective imagination, where relations between

293

identical (i.e., same sex) blood relations through the intermediary of a common partner are considered dangerous, and has arranged it in her own way.

This collective imagination, composed of notions not explicitly stated because they are naturally obvious, surrounds the mystery of sexuality and reproduction, through intimate bodily contact and the exchange of fluids: semen and vaginal fluids and blood thought to nourish the child in the womb. It characterizes the sexes and their bodily fluids as strong or weak, hot or cold, volatile or material, and so on. It also raises the question of the effects of an intermingling of fluids that possess the same essential qualities, that are identical substances. It reflects the difference between the sexes and posits a quasi-fusional consubstantial identity between blood relations of the same sex, which, in addition to any dreaded consequences, may more generally induce a confusion of sentiments.

Literature is not the only medium to address this issue (we have discussed only one example). Film and television soap operas have as well. While "two sister" incest is the object of social condemnation, it obsesses our culture.

I will cite two films precisely for their apparent banality: Marcel Carné's *Jenny* (1936) and Alberto Lattuada's *Venga a prendere il caffe... da noi* (1970).

In *Jenny*, Françoise Rosay plays a struggling "cabaret manager" who has an old flame (Charles Vanel), a young lover named Lucien, and a daughter, Danielle (Lisette Lanvin), for whom she has sacrificed everything. The young girl is a concert pianist and completely unaware of her mother's profession.

Lucien meets Danielle by chance. They fall in love and decide to marry. Danielle wants to run away with him but they have no money. In a later scene, Lucien is beaten up by his former associates and hospitalized. When Jenny visits him, she learns the

identity of her rival from his own lips. Devastated, she says nothing. In order to leave France with Danielle, Lucien needs money
and asks a friend to help him. The friend turns to Jenny for the
money. Jenny borrows the money from her former protector
(possibly Danielle's father?). Danielle leaves. Jenny has a nervous
breakdown.

Thus, we have a mother's passionate identification with her
child, who is adored to the point of sacrifice and deceit; the dual
relationship between one man and a mother and daughter, of
which two of the protagonists are unaware, leading to mother/
daughter incest of the second type; and a paternal or pseudo-
paternal contribution of money that adds a whiff of father/daughter
incest to the proceedings.

Alberto Lattuada's film *Venga a prendere il caffe... da noi*, a
1970 comedy with Ugo Tognazzi, tells the story of three sisters:
one is a nymphomaniac; the second, dim-witted; the third, pious
and hysterical. As though in compensation for their shortcom-
ings, they have inherited a considerable fortune from their father.
A family friend insinuates himself into their lives, marries one,
and effortlessly seduces the other two. Rather than feeling jealous, the sisters encourage him. Each sister receives his sexual
attentions, and each waits on him hand and foot. As they walk
past cafés and through public parks, the main character parades
arm in arm with his legitimate wife; she eventually allows another
sister to take her place; she, in turn, lets a third take her place,
and the dance continues for all to see. Able to satisfy three
women at once, the man is admired as virile.

One day after a lavish meal, he pleasures all three women in
succession (ordinarily, each would have had her appointed day).
Leaving the bedroom of the third, he sees the maid and decides to
add her to his list. She undresses; he follows her onto the stairway
and there, suddenly, has a stroke that leaves him paralyzed. The

295

next shot shows him in a wheelchair, which the women take turns pushing, parading their relations just as flamboyantly as before. Those who felt somewhat envious of his arrangement are now vindicated: he was punished for his immoderation.

The moral is clear: woe to those who transgress prohibitions, unless they are gods. At first admired for ostensibly transgressing the incest taboo of two sisters (in this case, three sisters) with impunity, he is revealed to be a common mortal who has sinned and is justly punished.

Unlike the tragic tone of Carné's film, this comedy might simply have told the story of a womanizer bragging shamelessly about his successes. The extra touch, in our phantasmic universe of incest, is that his conquests are sisters who live in the same place under the same roof and tend to his every need. The comic element of the story is that just when he wants to add banal adultery — an affair with the maid — to his sororal-conjugal trilogy, he is punished for his gastronomic and sexual excesses (three sisters gratified in a single day).

Let us now turn to *Les Coeurs brûlés*, a television series that was shown in France in the summer of 1992.[1] In the beginning, there are two fraternal pairs and a divorced couple. Marcel, a sailor, lives with his sister Geneviève, a clerk. She has a daughter, Isa, who was abused by her uncle Marcel when she was an adolescent and had a son, Tanguy, as a result. The second fraternal pair is also constituted by a brother and sister, Arnaud and Hélène. Arnaud is married to a famous singer, Julia, who has never wanted to consummate their union. Arnaud, we later learn, is Isa's father, which she had already learned from her uncle Marcel. Julia, however, fell in love with a black jazz musician during a tour, who fathered her daughter, Audrey, officially adopted by her husband Arnaud.

The divorced couple is Hélène (Arnaud's sister) and Marc, the dashing owner of a luxury hotel called La Réserve. Hélène is about forty-two. They have been divorced for ten years but both live at the hotel, where Hélène holds an important position. She has a lover, a banker who finances her ex-husband's operations. They have two children, Patricia and Christian, who refuses to succeed his father at La Réserve.

As the curtain rises, Isa, the biological daughter of Geneviève (and Arnaud), an ex-beauty queen, is working as a supermarket cashier and living with the handsome, penniless, and brutish Sylvain. (See figure 56.)

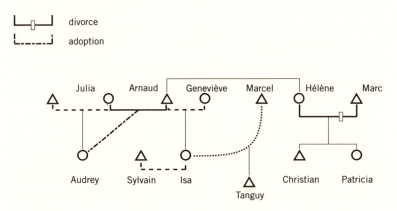

Figure 56.

The drama now unfolds: several incestuous relationships of the first and second type, an accident camouflaged as murder, a suicide, a murder attempt, a courageous sacrifice, a double redemption, and an attack involving acid that backfires against the attacker.

The stage is set, the actors in place. Isa's relationship with Sylvain gets worse; he takes her money, beats her, and wants to prostitute her. She breaks up with him, goes back to her mother, and looks for a new job.

Christian, Marc and Hélène's son, returns from sailing around the world to attend his sister's wedding. He clashes violently with his father, who wants him to take over the business. Patricia has learned of her fiancé's homosexuality during their engagement party and cancels the wedding. Christian meets Isa, whom he picks up hitchhiking on the road, and is moved by her beauty. Isa forgets her purse in the car. Christian returns it and must confront Sylvain. Isa is hired as a maid at La Réserve. She crosses paths with Christian several times. He is more and more taken with her. His parents see this love in a positive light, something capable of keeping him on dry land. Unfortunately, Christian tries to kiss Isa by surprise — an awkward attempt that reminds her too much of her uncle Marcel's and Sylvain's assaults — and she rebuffs him, though under other circumstances she would have consented.

After a scene involving a deceitful old hotel guest, Hélène fires Isa, but Christian, then Marc, intervene. The young woman is hired by Julia, who is preparing a lavish party. During this event, the singer takes some drugs, permanently ruins her voice, and retreats into apparent madness. We are to believe she is in the United States receiving treatment, but in fact she has remained in town under her husband's care.

Sylvain blackmails Isa (threatening to tell Tanguy who his father is) in order to obtain a key and take pictures of Julia. He is caught and betrays Isa, who is fired. She decides to take action. She knows that Marc finds her attractive. One day they meet in town, and she tells him her life story. Marc is touched; instead of leaving on a safari, he moves Isa into a secret apartment and they start a relationship. Hélène finds out. She tries to bribe Isa, offering her money to disappear; the young woman accepts the check, but only to show it to Marc. On Christmas Eve, when the two families gather, Marc gives Hélène the check in a jewelry case and announces his marriage to Isa.

During their honeymoon in the mountains, Marc falls and becomes a quadriplegic. He begs Isa, then Hélène, to kill him. Hélène asks an old nurse to perform this task, whom she sends to Canada afterward.

Isa is accused of her husband's murder. She accepts the accusation but is absolved at the trial, thanks to the nurse's unexpected return and her confession in a letter to the judges. Before killing herself, she sends a note to Isa, revealing Hélène's involvement, which allows Isa to obtain what she wants — power at La Réserve. She now controls it with her son Tanguy, whom Marc recognized as his son when they got married.

In the meantime, Patricia has met a kind-hearted businessman whom she loves, though he is confined to a wheelchair, paralyzed from the waist down. Out of love for her, he refuses to marry her, pretending to be involved with another woman. In despair, Patricia begins leading a wild life and taking drugs. One evening, she speeds down the highway intent on killing herself. But she is saved by Sylvain on his motorcycle, who reveals his heart's true nature. He becomes her devoted suitor.

Several things have occurred in the meantime. Marcel, the incestuous uncle, his deeds revealed to his sister Geneviève, kills himself at sea. To humiliate Isa, Hélène has recruited Sylvain as a swimming instructor. But seduced by the young man's good looks, she takes him as a lover and soon falls prey to him. Audrey, Julia's daughter and Arnaud's adopted daughter, has returned. She has a beautiful voice like her mother, but does nothing with her talent. She falls in love with Christian, who marries her.

The relationship between Sylvain and Hélène is discovered by the banker, Hélène's jealous lover, who withdraws his financial protection. Furious and desperate, Hélène decides to take revenge by revealing Tanguy's origins to him. She leaves the island in a speedboat and comes across the child on a Windsurfer. She tries to kill him by crashing into him, but changes her mind at the last minute. The child is toppled in the wake and disappears. Intense searches begin; Isa is frantic. Sylvain and Christian reconcile after much fighting and find the little boy alive.

Isa succeeds magnificently in running the company. She organizes a big party at which a famous singer is expected to perform but does not show up. Audrey fills in for her at the last minute at the request of her mother, who rediscovers her maternal love and regains the sanity she supposedly lost. She recognizes herself in her daughter.

Before the concert, Christian thinks he sees Isa in the garden from behind. He professes his love to her in the moonlight. He says he regrets their ruined lives, but the woman who turns around is actually Audrey. She generously grants him his freedom.

Meanwhile, Isa is looking for Hélène and finds her with Sylvain. He has come to ask Hélène why she tried to take Tanguy's life. A violent scene ensues, during which Hélène attacks Isa with acid to ruin her beauty. Sylvain stops her and Hélène is splashed with the acid.

In the final episode, Hélène receives a visit from Isa and her children at the hospital. She is calm. They inform her that she is permanently blind.

The hotel is sold. Christian, Isa, and Tanguy, finally reunited, sail around the world on Christian's new sailboat. Patricia stays with Sylvain. Audrey will duplicate her mother's career, and the former diva will accept her fate and manage her daughter's career.

Let's break this melodrama down into its various parts, exchanges, intersections, compositions, and recompositions. Its

force has to do with the apparent obviousness of all the relationships, only one of which is explicitly incestuous, namely Isa's
forced relationship with her maternal uncle Marcel, of which
Tanguy is the product. His is an insignificant role in the script,
but a driving element of the story.

Outside of this incest of the first type, we find several other
relationships that could be catalogued as incest of the second
type:

- Incest between a paternal aunt (Hélène) and her niece (Isa),
  who share the same husband:

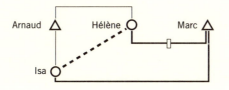

Figure 57.

(Recall that Isa has "always known" who her father was, namely
Hélène's brother.)

- Incest between a mother and daughter through the intermediary of a common partner: Hélène and Patricia, who have both
  "known" Sylvain:

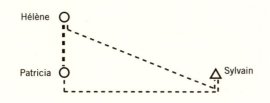

Figure 58.

- Actual incest between the father's wife (Isa) and the husband's son (Christian) and a fantasized father/son incest (Marc and Christian):

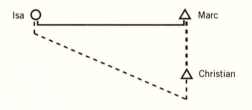

Figure 59.

- In addition to the fantasized mother/daughter incest, a step-mother/stepdaughter incest, doubled by a fantasized father/daughter incest of the first type through the intermediary of mother and stepmother:

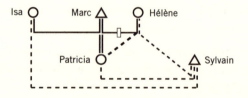

Figure 60.

- Moreover, Christian marries his "cousin" Audrey, his mother's brother's adopted daughter, with no problem. But legally she is also Isa's half-sister, who is Arnaud's natural daughter. By separating from Audrey to marry Isa or live with her, he puts them in an (approximate) situation of incest of two sisters.

302

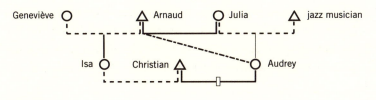

Figure 61.

- Finally, Christian finds himself with both his sister-in-law (his wife's half-sister) and his stepmother, his father's widow.

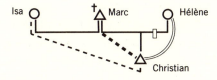

Figure 62.

- Christian will raise his wife's son, Tanguy, who is also legally his brother (recognized by Marc) and his cousin (Isa's son is also Arnaud's, Hélène's brother's, grandson). Patricia, the innocent victim, enters a vaguely incestuous situation with Sylvain (the lover of her stepmother and her mother), after having twice been denied the chance for a sexual relationship with a man: of her successive fiancés, one was homosexual, the other paralyzed from the waist down. Her quasi-platonic union with Sylvain is also presented as a quasi-brother/sister incest. "After Tanguy's disappearance, a strange complicity is established between the two men,"[2] a complicity the writer attributes to the affection they share for Tanguy, though the two men have fought, damaged each other's property (Sylvain set

303

Christian's boat on fire), and always hated each other. This "strange complicity" does not stem from shared affection for the boy, but instead from the fact that Sylvain is Christian's sister's lover and has been the lover of Christian's future wife.

Figure 63.

Sylvain has also been Hélène's lover, which puts him in a quasi-father-in-law relation to Christian.

Finally, one can say that Isa marries her almost-son, the son of her husband and co-wife Hélène. The allusion is all the more pertinent since Marc has recognized Tanguy as his son, thereby implying maternal feelings, or at least maternal behavior, on the part of his wife Isa toward his own children, in return, maternal behavior that actually exists between Isa and Patricia and that has taken an amorous, thus incestuous, turn with Christian.

In this confusion of sentiments and situations, it becomes astonishingly clear that the plot is motivated by incest of the second type, in all its possible forms, including approximation. Only one incestuous relationship corresponds to an ordinary incest: that of the uncle raping his niece as a child. I don't believe the writers were necessarily aware of this in their efforts to "spice up" the plot: a father and son in love with the same woman, whose own lover is a brute who will become the father's first wife's lover and then their daughter's lover.

In this sulfurous situation, there is the *frisson* of audacity, an expectation of gratified urges. We carry these fantasies within us, perhaps in our limbic system, unaware of them, just as we are supremely unaware of their existence in law. Only when a particular situation uses or attacks the fantasy — such as the alliance sought by a notable Englishman with his deceased wife's sister — are passions unleashed (in England, judicially; in France, by gratifying the transgressive fantasies of television viewers). There is no need for words to express it or for detailed and explicit analysis to illuminate the links and possible developments. Everyone "knows" in his heart of hearts whether he is within a hair's breadth of incest, or whether he is committing it.

Hélène is blinded by her own hand, like Oedipus. But why must Hélène–Jocasta punish herself? This shift might be enough to remind us of Oedipus, but other developments in the script are more explicit. It is she who causes her substance to touch her son's through the double intermediary of Marc, her husband, and Isa, her husband's wife, and then her son's wife. There is an evocative sequence in which, despite their divorce and shortly after Marc's marriage to Isa, Marc and Hélène make love, thus exchanging intimate substances and creating a bodily fusion, the murky, vague, and inexpressible suggestion of which provides the basis for both the fear and appeal of incest of the second type, inserted into the lives of otherwise ordinary people.

Another component of this story should be underscored: a mother's fusion and identification with her daughter, illustrated by Julia and her daughter Audrey. The mother rejected this child, who was half-black and whom her husband adopted so that she would not be abandoned. Although for years the mother takes no notice of it, the beauty of her daughter's voice and her talent as a singer eventually causes Julia to identify with Audrey and push her onto the stage in her place. She encourages her to dissolve her marriage in order to devote herself entirely to the realization of the maternal desire.

What I call the confusion of sentiments takes the form of a

mother-daughter fusion. More primal and specific than generic mother/child fusion, the incarnated object that fits into another becomes a singular being, and is in its form identical to the mother, like Russian dolls. While fusion and maternal love, in the sense of relations uniting the mother to the daughter and not the daughter to the mother, may take on aspects of devotion and sacrifice, as was the case in *Jenny*, they may also take on the aspect of living vicariously through a double, who is made an intermediary and manipulated to this end.

Based on identity of gender within consanguinity, incest of the second type is the primordial incest, as I wrote earlier. I would now add that in all the basic forms it may take — mother/daughter, father/son, aunt/niece, sister/sister, brother/brother, uncle/ nephew, and so on — the founding form is that of the mother/ daughter relationship, for in addition to the identity of gender, there is the physical fact of the reproduction of the same form in the same mold. The mold and its product are identical. This also applies to the identity of two sisters. If the father/son and brother/brother identity involves the identity of gender induced by the force of the nourishing spermatic substance, it is inferior in the absolute sense to the perfect mother/daughter identity. What is surprising is that nature in its most secret and most recently identified mechanisms provides for this ideal discrimination of form and matter, mingled in the female sex: all fetuses are female at first, and half of them will become male as the result of a hormone. Nature does not lead to fantasy, but fantasy is based on the great cornerstones of autonomous thought, impossible to shift or circumvent: the difference between the sexes, sexual reproduction, and the gestation-childbirth-lactation cycle.

In my eyes, the fundamental incest, so fundamental that it can only be expressed approximately, in texts as well as behavior, is mother/daughter incest. The same substance, the same form, the same sex, the same flesh, the same destiny, one issued from the other, *ad infinitum*, mothers and daughters live out this relationship in complicity or rejection, love or hate, always in tumult. The most normal relationship in the world is also one that may be cloaked in the greatest ambiguity.

Living through the daughter is an attenuated but real form of mother/daughter incest. Psychiatrists and judges can speak of this better than I. I will cite three brief examples.

The first is a psychiatrist's account of a young woman's existential crisis: Amelia sought something she could not define in her various marriages.[3] Starting in adolescence, her mother would buy her makeup, lingerie, and clothes to make her as attractive as possible. The two women's main activity was having Amelia try on clothes, makeup, hairstyles, and poses. When she was seventeen, her mother began to advise her on her romantic choices and successive marriages, and each time the mother came to live with the couple. To the psychiatrist, the mother used her daughter's beauty to live the life she did not have. And the young woman manifested the very clinical symptoms indicative of a victim of physical incest: dissociation, distance, destruction. Adulated but manipulated like a puppet, it had become impossible for her to experience an authentic romantic relationship.

Social Condemnation

In an issue of *Marie-Claire,* an article on mother/daughter relations told of a forty-year-old mother, still youthful and attractive, her twenty-year-old daughter, and the girl's fiancé, who was in his thirties.[4] One day, the woman's future son-in-law came over and the two of them slept together, wordlessly. "What about my daughter?" she later asked. The man coldly replied that she had "nothing to do with this!" The relationship ended there, but the mother confided to the journalist that she no longer felt comfortable with her daughter because she had "known her intimately" as a mother never should. She no doubt meant to say that she could now imagine her daughter's sexual relations in detail, assuming their experiences were similar. But, much more profoundly, it seems to me, the mother came into contact with her own daughter's carnal, substantial intimacy, as she felicitously put it, an incestuous fusion of the second type, the evanescent idea of which she could only reject.[5]

The second case was a story told to me by a juvenile court judge, who was troubled by certain situations and discussions he had encountered and for which he saw no explanation, while sensing the importance of the thing left unsaid, unknown but shared by all the partners.

This judge, in a town in northern France, had a twelve-year-old girl before him, whose bearing and behavior made him suspect that the problem was more complex than the minor offense with which she had been charged. He ordered a psychological evaluation, which revealed an "incestuous climate" in the family. The judge summoned the family — authoritarian father, self-effacing mother, and the little girl, who was ill at ease, too grown-up, awkward, badly dressed — and without mincing words read them the report suggesting incest. Instead of responding, the father turned to his wife and yelled, "See! I told you we should've been more careful!" The judge was not as surprised by the implicit confession of incestuous relations with the daughter as intrigued by what the precautions might have been.

The father then explained that his wife knew about his relations with their daughter, but refused to leave the conjugal bed. It was even her condition for keeping it secret. She therefore continued to have conjugal relations when she knew that her husband wanted to end them. What he called "being careful" was this: having sexual relations only with his daughter, not with the

daughter and mother simultaneously. This man had an unconscious idea of incest of the second type; it seemed less serious to
him to commit only incest of the first type, without adding a second violation. What worried him was the simultaneity of his relations with his wife and their daughter.

The mother probably insisted on preserving her conjugal relations because she wanted total fusion, total identity with her
daughter. Of course, she could not explain it; in fact, she offered no
explanation at all. It was simply suggested by the fact that the girl
was wearing clothes unsuitable for her age, because she was made
to wear her mother's clothes. With this detail, the mother indicated her desire for identity with her daughter; she claimed incest
of the second type as her own. While the father desired incest of
the first type with his daughter, the mother desired a fusional incest of the second type by sharing the same sexual partner with her
daughter: the mother's husband, who was the daughter's father.

The third case is that of Woody Allen's affair with Soon Yi
Previn, the adopted daughter of his companion Mia Farrow and
her ex-husband André Previn. Farrow had had a child with Allen
and had adopted several other children, including this young
Korean girl, who had been adopted prior to Farrow's union with
Allen. For months the affair was the talk of the town; it was scandalous due to the fame of the participants, but especially, it seems,
due to the evocation of incest in its successive approximations,
incest of the second type, which, I would submit, still saturates
our individual and collective imagination.

Even though Allen and Farrow were not married, they had
been living together for some time. Allen nevertheless defended
himself against ever having been "a father [...] in any sense of the
term. [...] I did think that, well, she is the adopted daughter of my
previous girlfriend, but that didn't mean anything to me. It didn't
manifest itself in any significant way. She was a grown, sophisti-

cated person. [...] I didn't feel that just because she was Mia's daughter, there was any great moral dilemma. It was a fact, but not with any great import. It wasn't like she was my daughter."[6]

He explained that his romance with Soon Yi began with conversations when he went to see Farrow, that it became more torrid at the end of 1991, and that he had said nothing to Farrow since it might have turned out to be nothing but a brief fling for the young girl as well as for him. In other versions, Allen is said to have stated: "Well, it's true. She's my old girlfriend's adopted daughter, but she's not my daughter. I don't feel guilty and our relationship doesn't pose a big moral problem for me. As soon as the reporters go away, we'll do the things we like to do."[7]

If this affair caused such a scandal, it is not because it was original, but because it caused something unimaginable, unthinkable, unheard-of to come to the surface. By succumbing to the charms of Soon Yi, Allen brought the fantasy of the transgression of the most ancient taboo into the public arena for all to see. If this prompted excitation rather than merciless condemnation, it was because the case seemed marginal from every standpoint.

Allen was right to stress that he was neither the young woman's biological father, as he had not engendered her, nor her social father, as he had not adopted her. Nevertheless, the fact remains that between Mia Farrow and Soon Yi there was a mother-daughter link, a social if not biological link. The sexual intrusion of Woody Allen immersed them in incest of the second type. The fact that Farrow was only his girlfriend and not his actual wife — a point he emphasized — changes nothing. The prohibition of incest of the second type bears solely on a man's sexual relations with a daughter and her mother, regardless of whether there is a legitimate union with one.

Allen pleads distant kinship: it is not really a mother and daughter but an American mother and her adopted Korean daughter; it

is not really a man and his wife, but a couple who were living together; it is not really a man and his adopted daughter, but a man
and the adopted daughter of his former girlfriend. The psychol-
ogy professor's phrase summed it up perfectly: "It's incestuous
even if it's not incest." Simply put: it is incest of the second type,
even if it isn't incest of the first type, and it is approximate. This is
enough to inflame public opinion and the collective imagination.

What was once present in consciousness and expressible was
buried away, yet continued to manifest itself; it simply could not
be formulated. We recall the young woman of Montaillou who
told her suitor that she could not be with him for she had already
had a liaison with his first cousin: "You may not touch carnally
what already touches you naturally." Whether articulated or not,
it is still latent in our minds. This is what can be heard in Allen's
words. If he is seeking to introduce the most distance possible
in their relations as a threesome, it is indeed to deny that his
romance was a combination of the identical. Likewise, by invok-
ing the fact that Allen, although not Soon Yi's biological father,
"spoke like a father" and seemed "almost exemplary" as a father
"even an unconventional [one]," a columnist in *USA Today* only
echoes traditional beliefs that shared food and speech create a link
of paternity as strong as blood.[8]

By defending himself against incest of the first type, Allen
does not wash his hands of the opprobrium and simmering interest attached to incest of the second type, which he never seems
aware of except perhaps subconsciously.

Thus, while it is the object of social condemnation, incest of the
second type — incest of "two sisters," and mother/daughter incest — continues to obsess our culture in daily life. Like the plots
of the fictional works it engenders, we must learn to decipher it.

311

Conclusion

Ay, that incestuous, that adulterate beast,
... won to his shameful lust

The will of my most seeming-virtuous queen.

Let not the royal bed of Denmark be
A couch for luxury and damned incest.[1]

Hamlet, too, is a story of incest of the second type that ends in blood. It is less a question of the father's murder by his brother, Claudius, than Claudius' seduction of Queen Gertrude. Hamlet's father asks his son for vengeance, but he also asks him to spare the queen, who was the intermediary, the point of contact between the brothers:

But, howsoever thou pursuest this act,
Taint not thy mind, nor let thy soul contrive
Against thy mother...[2]

As among the Baoulé, the incest is *between the brothers*, and it is between them that the reparation must be made, or kinship severed. The methods of the murder are characteristic, too, of the effects of this particular incest. The poison (or poisonous word?) is poured by Claudius "in the porches of [his] ears,"

> That swift as quicksilver it courses through
> The natural gates and alleys of the body,
> And with a sudden vigor it doth posset,
> And curd, like eager droppings into milk,
> The thin and wholesome blood. . . .[3]

The King dies from a terrible leprosy that ruptures his skin (a result of the mechanics of fluids). The contact of the two brothers' fluids in the same womb makes the fluids of the weaker — the one being deceived, the one who does not know — flow back into his body, and resurge as vile purulences on his skin.

At stake is the "illicit collusion" between identical fluids, collusion between two brothers through the intermediary of the same woman, collusion between two sisters through the intermediary of the same man. Death awaits the weaker of the two. This is a matter of bodily fluids.

From the beginning of our inquiry, the question has not so much been why the incest prohibition concerns exogamy as why it also extends to relatives by marriage. In the case of Christianity, a doctrine was formulated that made spouses "one flesh" (a phrase repeated by Hamlet: "man and wife is one flesh"[4]), which presupposes the total fusion of bodies through sexual relations and the mingling of fluids. But why is the same prohibition present well before the church offered its own explanation for it, and also present in places untouched by Christianity? I think I have supplied an answer that, in both its simplicity and complexity, accounts for both varieties of incest as well as for other forms of social avoidance.

The facts show the existence of this profound interrogation based on the classification of bodies as identical to or different from one's own, as repellent or attractive, something which cannot be expressed by the edict of a social rule (the classic prohibition of incest) except when it becomes necessary: when identity vacillates at the threshold of difference, when bodies entwine and fertilization occurs. The incest prohibition, when it begins to exist, opens the field to exogamy and to the institution of social links. But what is absolutely unthinkable — perhaps because, like masturbation, homosexuality, relations during the menstrual cycle, zoophilia, or necrophilia (all explicitly condemned), it does not lead to reproduction — is the sexual relationship between perfect identicals. Unthinkable evil, unthinkable ideal.

Identity is unproductive. Difference, tempered with a bit of identity, as among the Samo, or identity, tempered with a bit of difference, as among the Arabs, is necessary for biological as well as social reproduction.

Thus, at the origin of the social link are very abstract symbolic conceptions drawn from the observation of what was most visible in the human body anatomically and physiologically: the difference between the sexes. It is not because the human being witnessed the regulation of the female's fertile period that it was necessary to establish the taboo against incest of the first type and construct social regulations. This prohibition comes from, or rather is included in, the other, which dazzlingly marks the primacy of the symbolic, founded on an astonishingly, universally complete discourse drawn from the premises of the identical and the different.

Primary incest, the prototypical incest, then becomes the imagined possibility of mother/daughter incest, where identity of form and matter is total. Many symbolic mediations, many reasonings based on the observation of the circulation of fluids and their circulation from one body to another, sometimes mediated by a third body, were necessary for the texts to indicate clearly that a man may not have relations "with two sisters" or with a sister and her mother, i.e., the impossibility of joining two identicals even if only through the intervention of a third party.

The incontestable and irreducible character of sexual difference is at the origin of the various reflections and directions each society has taken. These cover an entire spectrum, but use the same language to make sense of unsettling exceptions (royal incest, Pharaonic incest, that of ordinary Egyptians) and various modes of matrimonial alliance, from the simplest (i.e., Arab marriage) to the most complicated.

Notes

INTRODUCTION

1. As quoted in a paper given by Jean Jamin at the "Manhood" seminar at the Collège de France, May 18, 1993.

2. Florence Delay, *Riche et légère* (Paris: Gallimard, 1983), p. 219.

3. Reo Fortune, "Incest," in the *International Encyclopaedia of the Social Sciences* (New York: Macmillan, 1932), vol. 7, pp. 115–22. Fortune observes that "The prevailing emphasis on incest taboos as they are related to the regulation of marriage has resulted in an almost total neglect of homosexual incest..." (p. 118).

4. E.E. Evans-Pritchard, "Nuer Rules of Exogamy and Incest," in *Social Structure: Studies Presented to A. R. Radcliffe-Brown*, ed. Meyer Fortes (London: Clarendon, 1949), pp. 85–103.

5. Emmanuel Le Roy Ladurie, *Montaillou: The Promised Land of Error*, trans. Barbara Bray (New York: George Braziller, 1978), p. 185.

6. J.S. Slotkin, "On a Possible Lack of Incest Regulations in Old Iran," *American Anthropologist* 49 (1947), pp. 612–17; Ward H. Goodenough, "Comments on the Question of Incestuous Marriages in Old Iran," *ibid.*, 51 (1949), pp. 326–28; J.S. Slotkin, "Reply to Goodenough," *ibid.*, 51 (1949).

7. See, e.g., Norbert Bischof, "Comparative Ethology of Incest Avoidance," in *Biosocial Anthropology*, ed. Robin Fox (New York: Wiley [ASA Studies], 1975), pp. 37–67.

8. Sir James Frazer, *Totemism and Exogamy: A Treatise on Certain Early Forms of Superstition and Society* (London: Dawsons of Pall Mall, 1968), vol. 4, p. 97.

9. Brenda Seligman, "The Incest Taboo as a Social Regulation," *The Sociological Review* 27.1 (1935), pp. 75–93.

10. Emile Durkheim, "La Prohibition de l'inceste et ses origines," *L'Année sociologique* 1 (1898), pp. 1–70.

11. Edward Burnett Tylor, *Primitive Culture* (London: H. Murray, 1871).

12. Claude Lévi-Strauss, "The Family," in *Man, Culture and Society*, ed. Harry L. Shapiro (New York: Oxford University Press, 1971), p. 350.

13. Margaret Mead, *Sex and Temperament in Three Primitive Societies* (New York: William Morrow, 1935), p. 84, quoted by Lévi-Strauss in *The Elementary Structures of Kinship* (Boston: Beacon Press, 1969), p. 485.

14. Françoise Héritier, "Symbolique de l'inceste et de sa prohibition," in *La Fonction symbolique: Essais d'anthropologie*, eds. Michel Izard and Pierre Smith, (Paris: Gallimard, 1979); "Sur l'inceste," in *L'Inceste* (Caen: Cahiers du LASA, 1985); and "Inceste," in *Dictionnaire de l'ethnologie et de l'anthropologie*, eds. Pierre Bonte and Michel Izard (Paris: Presses Universitaires de France, 1991), pp. 347–50.

CHAPTER ONE: LONG AGO IN THE DISTANT EAST

1. Richard Haase, "Der Inzest in den sog. hethitischen Gesetzen," in *Die Welt des Orients* 10 (1977), p. 33.

2. See the glossary at the end of this volume for a definition of this and subsequent terms.

3. E. Neufeld, *The Hittite Laws* (London: Luzac, 1951).

4. Godfrey Rolles Driver and John C. Miles, *The Assyrian Laws* (Darmstadt: Scientia Verlag Aalen, 1975), p. 401.

5. Andries van Praag, *Droit matrimonial assyro-babylonien* (Amsterdam: Noord-Hollandsche Uitgevers Maatschappij, 1945).

CHAPTER TWO: WHAT DO GREEK PHILOSOPHY, THE BIBLE, AND THE KORAN SAY?

1. In French law, when siblings share the same father and mother, they are called *germains de lit entier* (literally, "siblings from a single bed"); this, of course, is redundant since being "siblings" means having the same mother and father. Otherwise they would be half-siblings, with either the same mother or the same father, but not the same two parents.

2. Aristotle, *Generation of Animals,* in *The Complete Works of Aristotle: The Revised Oxford Translation*, vol. 1, ed. Jonathan Barnes, trans. A. Platt (Princeton, NJ: Princeton University Press, 1984).

3. Françoise Héritier-Augé, "La costruzione dell'essere sessuato, la costruzione sociale del genere e le ambiguità dell'identità sessuale," in *Maschile e Femminile: Genere e ruoli nelle culture antiche*, ed. Maurizio Bettini (Rome: Laterza, 1993), pp. 113–39.

4. *The Republic* in *The Collected Dialogues of Plato*, ed. Edith Hamilton and Huntington Cairns, trans. Paul Shorey (Princeton, NJ: Princeton University Press, 1961), p. 798.

5. *The Laws*, trans. A.E. Taylor, in *The Collected Dialogues of Plato*, p. 1403.

6. I would like to thank Jean-Pierre Vernant and Giulia Sissa for bringing to my attention certain lesser-known texts.

7. *The Metamorphosis of Ovid*, trans. Allen Mandelbaum (New York: Harcourt Brace & Co., 1993), p. 225.

8. *Sophocles I, Three Tragedies*, ed. David Grene and Richmond Lattimore (Chicago: University of Chicago Press, 1991 [2nd ed.]), *Oedipus the King*, trans. David Grene, pp. 30 and 28.

9. Artimedorus, *Oneirocritica: The Interpretation of Dreams*, trans. Robert J. White (Park Ridge, NJ: Noyes Press, 1975).

10. Aeschylus, *The Suppliant Maidens*, trans. Seth G. Benardete, in *The Complete Greek Tragedies*, vol. 2, eds. David Grene and Richmond Lattimore (Chicago: University of Chicago Press, 1992), p. 185.

11. Jean Racine's *Phaedra* cannot be overlooked when examining Greek thought through literature. See Racine, *Phaedra*, act 1, scene 3, in *Brittanicus,*

Phaedra, Athaliah, trans. Richard Wilbur (San Diego: Harcourt Brace Jovano-vich, 1986).

12. *Metamorphosis of Ovid*, pp. 198–99.

13. Ibid., p. 199.

14. Andocides, *On the Mysteries*, in *Greek Orators*, vol. 4, ed. and trans. Michael Edward (Warminster, UK: Aris and Phillips, 1995), pp. 77–79.

15. All quotations from the Bible are taken from the King James version. In the French, Héritier used Edouard Dhorme's annotated edition of the Old Testament (Paris: Gallimard/La Pléiade, 1966) — TRANS.

16. Cf. Anthony Phillips, "Uncovering the Father's Skirt," *Vetus Testamentum* 30.1, pp. 38–43. Stephen F. Bigger, "The Family Laws of Leviticus 18 in their Setting," *Journal of Biblical Literature* 98.2 (1979), pp. 187–203.

17. W. Kornfeld, "Mariage. I. Dans l'Ancien Testament," col. 906–26, in *Supplément au Dictionnaire de la Bible* (1929). G.J. Wennan, *The Book of Leviticus,* The International Commentary on the Old Testament (Grand Rapids: B. Erd-man, 1979).

18. See Dhorme's annotation to Lev. 20:17–18.

19. Reuven Yaron, "Duabus sororibus coniunctio," *Revue internationale des droits de l'Antiquité* (1963), pp. 115–36, a fundamental text in the exegesis of the law of the ancient Orient, the Bible, and the Talmud.

20. *The Koran*, translated with notes by N. J. Dawood (Harmondsworth, UK: Penguin, 1972).

21. Biological paternity is not as important as social paternity, since shared food produces the same blood, even if based negatively on specific prohibitions concerning a particular animal or plant. These vary from group to group but start with a basic diet that is the same for everyone. As Spinoza said, determination involves negation; identity is defined by subtraction.

22. Julien-Joseph Virey, *De la femme, sous ses rapports physiologique, moral et littéraire* (Paris, 1823); *De l'éducation* (Paris, 1802); *Dictionnaire des sciences médicales* (Panckoucke, 1811–22).

23. Françoise Héritier, "Le Sang du guerrier et le sang des femmes," in *L'Africaine: Sexes et Signes, Les Cahiers du GRIF* 29 (Winter 1984–85), and "Iden-

tité de substance et parenté de lait dans le monde arabe," in *Epouser au plus proche: Inceste, prohibitions et stratégies matrimoniales autour de la Méditerranée*, ed. Pierre Bonte (Paris: Editions de L'EHESS, 1994).

CHAPTER THREE: ONE FLESH

1. Paul Ourliac and Jehan de Malafosse, *Histoire du droit privé*, vol. 3, *Le Droit familial* (Paris: Presses Universitaires de France, 1968), p. 168.

2. Emile Benveniste, *Indo-European Language and Society*, trans. Elizabeth Palmer (London: Faber, 1973), and "Termes de parenté dans les langues indo-européennes," *L'Homme* 5 (1965), pp. 5–16.

3. For example, the wife's maternal grandmother in the first case, or the husband of the niece (the sister's daughter) in the second.

4. Basil the Great, epistle 160, *Patrologia graeca*, vol. 32, col. 621.

5. According to Reuven Yaron ("Duabus sororibus coniunto," *Revue internationale des droits de l'Antiquité* [1963]), who assembled and critiqued all the sources, this is indeed an equivalent of the imprinting theory. The couple's one flesh, created in their conjugal life, continues after death. Christian law might also have wanted to distinguish itself from Hebraic law, he says, or it may have feared that permitting the union after the first spouse's death might encourage deceit and even murder.

6. *The Theodosian Code*, trans. Clyde Pharr (Princeton: Princeton University Press, 1952).

7. *The Syro-Roman Lawbook*, trans. Arthur Vööbus (Stockholm: ETSE, 1983), pp. 23–24.

8. Peter Damian, *De parentelae gradibus* in *Patrologia latina*, vol. 145 (Paris: Migne, 1963 [1853]), cols. 191–208.

9. *Ibid.*

10. Nowadays, biological kinship seems to prevail over social kinship, and genetic proof of paternity to take precedence over the *is est pater quem nuptiae demonstrant* of civil law. Curiously, while the biological paternity of the mother's husband can be contested, paternity established by adoption is not contestable. Thus, two adoptive children of one couple could never marry each other, even if

there is no biological tie between them. They are brother and sister, and this social link takes precedence over all biological considerations.

11. Georges Duby, *The Knight, the Lady and the Priest*, trans. Barbara Bray (New York: Pantheon, 1983), p. 73.

12. *Ibid.*, p. 79.

13. *Ibid.*, p. 91.

14. *Ibid.*, p. 175.

15. The historian Gérard Delille, who discovered Manduria's marriage registers, mines this extremely rich data in his forthcoming *Le Maître et le prieur: Pouvoir central et pouvoir local en Mediterranée occidentale (XVe–XVIIIe siècle).*

16. Martine Segalen, *Quinze générations de Bas-Bretons: Parenté et société dans le pays bigouden, 1720–1980* (Paris: Presses Universitaires de France, 1985).

17. Sybil Wolfram, "Le Mariage entre alliés dans l'Angleterre contemporaine," *L'Homme*, vol. 1 (1961), pp. 47–71, and *In-Laws and Outlaws: Kinship and Marriage in England* (London and Sydney: Croom Helm, 1987).

18. A. R. Radcliffe-Brown and Daryll Forde, eds., *African Systems of Kinship and Marriage* (London: Oxford University Press, 1950), pp. 62–63.

19. Julien-Joseph Virey, *De la femme, sous ses rapports physiologique, moral et littéraire* (Paris, 1823); Yvonne Knibiehler, "La Nature féminine au temps du code civil," *Annales* 31.4 (1976).

20. In 1940, an ecclesiastical commission decided not to recognize the law allowing a man to marry his deceased wife's sister.

21. Bronislaw Malinowski, "A Sociological Analysis of the Rationale of the Prohibited Degrees of Marriage," Appendix 3 to the Church of England Commission, *Kindred and Affinity* (1940).

22. Andreï Pandrea, "Le Mariage et la résidence à Boisoara (Tara Lovistei)," in Paul H. Stahl, "Le Mariage: Recherches contemporaines sur des populations balkaniques," *Buletinul Bibliotecii Române* 8.12 (1981), pp. 61–134.

23. What of the relationship represented in figure 16? Is the (5)–(6) marriage possible? If it is, would a subsequent (1)–(4) marriage be possible after the death of their respective spouses?

CHAPTER FOUR: TWO SISTERS IN AFRICAN SOCIETIES

1. Samo country is located northwest of Burkina Faso, formerly known as Upper Volta.

2. Françoise Héritier-Augé, *L'Exercice de la parenté* (Paris: Le Seuil-Gallimard, 1981).

3. Claude Lévi-Strauss, "The Future of Kinship Studies," in *Proceedings of the Royal Anthropological Institute of Great Britain and Ireland* (London, 1965), pp. 13–22 (outlined in the preface to the second edition of *The Elementary Structures of Kinship*).

4. This is a prime example of the subtle variations that exist in a single society. The ban on "making two brothers meet in the same womb" applies only if both brothers are still alive, as we shall see among the Samo and other African societies with similar rules. Must the very representation of the sexual act be relied on to understand this difference between two sisters and two brothers? The social and economic reasons already expressed in the Assyrian laws are certainly helpful in explaining this difference in a strongly patrilineal society. It is important to note that variations may occur over time, as we have seen, but may also exist concurrently in a single society.

5. Héritier-Augé, *L'Exercice de la parenté*, ch. 2; "Systèmes omaha de parenté et d'alliance: Etude en ordinateur du fonctionnement matrimonial réel d'une société africaine," in *Genealogical Mathematics*, ed. Paul Ballonoff (Paris and The Hague: Mouton, 1974); "L'ordinateur et l'étude du fonctionnement matrimonial d'un système omaha," in *Les Domaines de la parenté*, ed. Marc Augé (Paris: F. Maspero, 1975), pp. 95–117; "Contribution à la théorie de l'alliance: Comment fonctionnent les systèmes d'alliance omaha?," *Informatique et Sciences Humaines* 29 (1976), pp. 10–46.

6. Lineal agnatic substantial identity (both women are of the same lineage) is different in its carnal nature from that which unites a mother and daughter, as we shall see further on.

7. Particularity of symmetry is explained thus: in a figure symmetrical to another, the sex of the intermediary positions must be changed only if made necessary by marriage. It is not necessary when taking into account collaterality.

8. Héritier-Augé, *L'Exercice de la parenté*, pp. 110–13.

9. Pierre Etienne, "Les Interdictions de mariage chez les Baoulé," *L'Homme* 15 (1975), pp. 3–4.

10. Since colonial occupation and independence, lineal and village legal institutions continue to function, but war is no longer waged and captives no longer taken.

11. In a lineage, all individuals from the same genealogical level call each other "brother" and "sister" without, of course, all being descended from the same parents. The children of "brothers" are once again "brothers" to each other.

12. This is not to say that women remember twelve generations, but that the genealogies reconstructed by computer show a discrepancy between the length of the purely agnatic, purely uterine, and mixed lines.

13. See above, note 4.

14. Starting with masculine Ego and feminine Ego, on positions of consanguinity and affinity, and also on the blood relations of relatives by marriage (affines) and on relatives by marriage of blood relations. In all plausible cases, I verified whether marriage was possible or not between Ego and Alter.

15. Cowries are little oval-shaped shells used as money in small exchanges, in funerary rituals, and as decorations on dance costumes. They have a central striated slit on their flat side and are thus frequently considered symbolic of the female sex.

16. Héritier-Augé, *L'Exercice de la parenté*, ch. 1.

17. See also, *ibid.* ch. 2.

18. Pierre Etienne, *Les Interdictions de mariage chez les Baoulé* (Abidjan: ORSTOM, 1972), p. 41. See also *ibid.*, n. 12, and Pierre Etienne, *Essai d'analyse des interdictions de mariage Baoulé* (Abidjan: ORSTOM, 1973).

19. A relationship in which a man gives his sister as a wife to a man whose sister he receives as a wife in return.

20. R. Dubois and R.P. Fihavanana, *Approche de la spécificité malgache*, 1972.

21. Françoise Héritier, "Symbolique de l'inceste et de sa prohibition," in *La*

Fonction symbolique: Essais d'anthropologie, ed. Michel Izard and Pierre Smith (Paris: Gallimard, 1979), pp. 219–20.

22. Elisabeth Copet-Rougier, "Mariage et inceste: L'Endogamie dans une société à fortes prohibitions matrimoniales," *Bulletin de la Société d'anthropologie du Sud-Ouest* 15.1 (1980), pp. 13–53; *Nguelebok: Essai d'analyse de l'organisation sociale des Mkako Mbogendi* (Paris: Université de Paris X, 1977); and Françoise Héritier-Augé, *Les Complexités de l'alliance*, vol. 1, *Les Structures semi-complexes* (Paris: Editions des Archives Contemporaines, 1990).

23. Danielle Jonkers, "Le Système de parenté minyanka est-il de type Omaha," *L'Homme* 23.2 (1983), pp. 79–96.

24. Bernard Juillerat, *Les Bases de l'organisation sociale chez les Mouktele (Nord-Cameroun): Structures lignagères et mariage*, Mémoires de l'Institut d'ethnologie (Paris, 1971); Jeanne-Françoise Vincent, "Utérins et maternels: De la parenté au soupçon (Mofu, Cameroun du Nord)," in *Femmes du Cameroun d'hier et d'aujourd'hui* (Paris: Ed. Karthala, 1980).

25. See Françoise Héritier-Augé and Elisabeth Copet-Rougier, *Les Structures semi-complexes*, n. 28, for more examples as well as a more in-depth discussion of the renewal and nonrenewal of alliance by same sex blood relations. See also Jean-Claude Muller, "Straight Sister-Exchange and the Transition from Elementary to Complex Structures," *American Ethnologist* 7 (1980), pp. 518–28; Antonio Viveiros de Castro, "Structures, régimes, stratégies," *L'Homme* 33.1 (1993), pp. 117–37; Elisabeth Copet-Rougier and Françoise Héritier-Augé, "Commentaires sur commentaire: Réponse à A. Viveiros de Castro," *L'Homme* 33.1 (1993), pp. 139–48; Antonio Viveiros de Castro, "Une mauvaise querelle," *L'Homme* 34.1, pp. 181–91.

26. Robert Rattray, *Religion and Art in Ashanti* (Oxford: Clarendon Press, 1927); Meyer Fortes, "Kinship and Marriage Among the Ashanti," in *African Systems of Kinship and Marriage*, ed. A. R. Radcliffe-Brown and Daryll Forde (London: Oxford University Press, 1950).

27. Meyer Fortes, *The Web of Kinship Among the Tallensi* (London: Oxford University Press, 1949).

28. E. E. Evans-Pritchard, "Nuer Rules of Exogamy and Incest," in *Social*

Structure: Studies Presented to A. R. Radcliffe-Brown, ed. Meyer Fortes (Oxford: Clarendon Press, 1949).

29. Jack Goody, "A Comparative Approach to Incest and Adultery," *British Journal of Sociology* 7 (1956), pp. 286–305.

30. Bronislaw Malinowski, *The Sexual Life of Savages* (London: Routledge and Kegan Paul, 1929), p. 447.

31. Goody, "A Comparative Approach to Incest and Adultery," p. 305, n. 3.

32. It was quite some time before I heard the Samo word for incest: *dyilibra*, "doglike act," "the way dogs act" (*dyili*). Incestuous acts are not common occurrences. To speak of incest theoretically always involved using the periphrasis "to sleep with." The word was not uttered in conversation until a case of incest was committed in the bush (an aggravating circumstance) and the term was then used by men drinking millet beer at nightfall.

33. The Mossi also have an Omaha system of alliance and terminology. But their treatment of the identical is one of the possible variants already mentioned: joking and flirting with the older brother's wife (whom one may marry if the brother dies) is possible. Similarly, while marriage with two sisters is normally impossible, it is obligatory with two twin sisters.

34. P.P. Howell, *A Manual of Nuer Law* (London: Oxford University Press, 1954) p. 164.

35. *Ibid.*

36. *Ibid.*

37. Goody, "A Comparative Approach to Incest and Adultery," p. 300.

CHAPTER FIVE: FROM MATRIMONIAL LOGIC TO HUMAN REPRESENTATION

1. E.H. Winter, *Bwamba: A Structural-Functional Analysis of a Patrilineal Society* (Cambridge: W. Heffer, 1956).

2. Claude Levi-Strauss, "Preface to the second edition," *The Elementary Structures of Kinship* (Boston: Beacon Press, 1969), pp. xxxvii, xxxviii.

3. For readers interested in the theoretical and practical possibilities of these marriages, see Françoise Héritier-Augé, *L'Exercice de la parenté* (Paris: Gallimard/Le Seuil, 1981), p. 113.

4. Emmanuel Le Roy Ladurie, *Montaillou, village occitan, de 1294 à 1324* (Paris: Gallimard, 1975), pp. 79, 216, 252, 267.

5. For a schema that elaborates on all these implications, see Françoise Héritier, "L'Ordinateur et l'étude du fonctionnement matrimonial d'un système omaha," in *Les Domaines de la parenté*, ed. M. Augé (Paris: Maspero, 1975), pp. 95–117. See also, Héritier-Augé, *L'Exercice de la parenté*, p. 111.

6. Héritier-Augé, *L'Exercice de la parenté*, p. 115.

7. Françoise Héritier, "La Paix et la pluie: Rapports d'autorité et rapport au sacré chez les Samo," *L'Homme* 13.3 (1973), pp. 121–38.

8. Françoise Héritier, "L'Identité samo," in *L'Identité*, a collection of papers delivered at a seminar conducted by Claude Lévi-Strauss (Paris: Grasset, 1977), pp. 51–80.

9. Françoise Héritier, "Résumé des cours et travaux," *Annuaire du Collège de France* (1985–1986), pp. 527–42; "Semen and Blood: Some Ancient Theories Concerning their Genesis and Relationship," in *Zone 5: Fragments for a History of the Human Body* (New York: Zone Books, 1989); *Nouvelle Revue de Psychanalyse* 32 (1985), pp. 111–22.

10. In a way, in recognizing bone marrow's ability to provide blood to the organism during its entire life, the Samo have found and constructed a theory of hematopoiesis based on empirical observations relating particularly to color.

11. Herbert Maisch, *L'Inceste* (Paris: Robert Laffont, 1970), p. 33.

CHAPTER SIX: THE IDENTICAL AND THE DIFFERENT

1. See Gerald Holton, *The Scientific Imagination* (Cambridge and New York: Cambridge University Press, 1978*)*.

2. Peter Damian, *De parentelae gradibus* in *Patrologia latina*, vol. 145 (Paris: Migne, 1963 [1853]), cols. 191–208.

3. Bronislaw Malinowski, *The Sexual Life of Savages* (London: Routledge and Kegan Paul, 1929).

4. Torben Monberg, "Fathers Were Not Genitors," *Journal of the Polynesian Society* 85.2 (1976), pp. 243–55.

5. Françoise Héritier-Augé, "Résumé des cours et travaux," *Annuaire du Collège de France, 1984–1985* (Paris, 1986).

6. The principle that bears the name of the chemist Henri Louis de Chatelier (1850–1936) concerns the stability of physico-chemical equilibrium: "Any modification of one of the parameters of a system in stable balance provokes a process that tends to oppose this modification," *Compte-rendus de l'Académie des Sciences* (Paris, 1907).

7. G.E.R. Lloyd, "The Hot and the Cold, the Dry and the Wet in Greek Philosophy," *Journal of Hellenic Studies* 84 (1964), pp. 92–106.

8. Claude Lévi-Strauss, "The Effectiveness of Symbols," in *Structural Anthropology* (New York, Basic Books, 1963). Pierre Smith, "Aspects de l'organisations des rites," in *La Fonction symbolique*, ed. Michel Izard and Pierre Smith (Paris: Gallimard, 1979).

9. Henriette Diabaté, *Le Sanwin: Un Royaume akan de la Côte-d'Ivoire (1701–1901)* (doctoral diss., Paris, Ecole des Hautes Etudes des Sciences Sociales, 1984).

10. Françoise Héritier-Augé, "Semen and Blood: Some Ancient Theories Concerning Their Genesis and Relationship," in *Zone 5: Fragments for a History of the Human Body* (New York: Zone Books, 1989).

11. Françoise Héritier, "Sterility, Aridity, Drought," in *The Meaning of Illness: The Anthropology, History and Sociology of Illness*, eds. Marc Augé and Claudine Herzlich, trans. Katherine J. Durnin et al. (Philadelphia: Harwood Academic Publishers, 1991).

12. Françoise Héritier, "Symbolique de l'inceste et de sa prohibition," in *La Fonction symbolique*, ed. Michel Izard and Pierre Smith (Paris: Gallimard, 1979), pp. 209–43.

13. Claude Lévi-Strauss, *The Elementary Structures of Kinship*, trans. James Harle Bell and John Richard von Sturmer (Boston: Beacon Press, 1969), p. 128.

14. Françoise Héritier, *L'Exercice de la parenté* (Paris: Seuil, 1981), p. 47.

15. *Ibid.*, p. 50.

16. *Ibid.*, pp. 44–67.

17. Rodney Needham, "Remarks on the Analysis of Marriage and Kinship," in *Rethinking Marriage and Kinship* (London: Tavistock, 1971), pp. 10–11.

18. *Ibid.*

19. R. Tom Zuidema, "The Inca Kinship System: A New Theoretical View," in *Andean Kinship and Marriage*, eds. Ralph Bolton and Enrique Mayer (Washington, D.C. : American Anthropological Association, 1977); "Une Théorie inca d'alliance matrimoniale et politique," in Françoise Héritier-Augé and E. Copet-Rougier, eds., *Les Complexités de l'alliance matrimoniale*, vol. 1, *Les Systémes semi-complexes* (Paris: Editions des Archives Contemporaines, 1990).

20. Richard Huntington, "Bara Endogamy and Incest Prohibition," *Bijdragen tot de taal-, land-en volkenkunde* 134.1 (1978), pp. 30–62.

21. Judith Huntsman and Antony Hooper, "Male and Female in Tokelau Culture," *Journal of Polynesian Society* 84.4 (1975), pp. 415–30 and "The 'Desecration' of Tokelau Kinship," *Journal of Polynesian Society* 85.2 (1976), pp. 257–73.

22. Reo Fortune, "Incest," article in the *International Encyclopaedia of the Social Sciences* (New York: Macmillan, 1932), vol. 7, p. 118.

23. Maurice Barry and Adélaïde Johnson, "The Incest Barrier," *Psychoanalytic Quarterly* 27 (1958).

24. Herbert Maisch, *L'Inceste* (Paris: Robert Laffont, 1970).

25. Lévi-Strauss, *Elementary Structures of Kinship*, p. 484.

26. *Ibid.*, p. 480; Honoré de Balzac, *Louis Lambert* in *Oeuvres complétes* (Paris: Gallimard/La Pléiade, 1937), vol. 10, pp. 366 and 382.

27. Raymond C. Kelly, *Etoro Social Structure: A Study in Structural Contradiction* (Ann Arbor: University of Michigan Press, 1977); David M. Schneider, "The Meaning of Incest," *Journal of the Polynesian Society* 85.2 (1976), pp. 149–69; Edward L. Schieffelin, *The Sorrow of the Lonely and the Burning of the Dancers* (New York: St. Martin's Press, 1976); and Maurice Godelier, *La Production des grands hommes* (Paris: Fayard, 1982).

28. Luc de Heusch, *Essais sur le symbolisme de l'inceste royal en Afrique* (Brussels: Institut de Sociologie Solvay, 1958).

CHAPTER SEVEN: THE MECHANICS OF FLUIDS

1. Julien-Joseph Virey, *De la femme, sous ses rapports physiologiques, morals et littéraires* (Paris, 1823).

2. P. Huard and Wing, "Médecine chinoise," in *Dictionnaire archéologique des techniques*, vol. 2 (Paris: Editions de l'Accueil, 1964).

3. *Les Bobos-oulés, I. Droit civil, II. Droit criminel*, anonymous customary, s.é.n.d., CVRS, Ouagadougou.

4. Françoise Héritier-Augé, "La Mauvaise odeur l'a saisi," *Le Genre Humain* 15 (1987), pp. 7–17.

5. René Labat, *Traité akkadien de diagnostics et pronostics médicaux, I. Transcription et traduction*, Paris, Académie Internationale d'Histoire des Sciences (Leiden: E.J. Bail, 1951); *Oeuvres de Ambroise Paré de la Val du Maine* (Paris, 1585); Antonin Bossu, *Anthropologie ou étude des organes, fonctions, maladies de l'homme et de la femme, comprenant l'anatomie, la physiologie, l'hygiène, la pathologie et la thérapeutique* (Paris: Baillière, 1849).

6. Robert Pageard, *Le Droit privé des Mossi: Tradition et évolution*, 2 vols., Paris and Ouagadougou, CNRS and CVRS (*Recherches voltaïques*, vols. 10 and 11), 1969.

7. Françoise Héritier-Augé, "L'Identité samo," in *L'Identité*, a collection of essays presented at the eponymous seminar conducted by Claude Lévi-Strauss (Paris: Grasset, 1977), pp. 51–80.

8. Monica Wilson, *Rituals of Kinship Among the Nyakyusa* (Oxford: Oxford University Press, 1957).

9. Richard Broxton Onians, *The Origins of European Thought about the Body, the Mind, the Soul, the World, Time and Fate: New Interpretations of Greek, Roman and Kindred Evidence about some Basic Jewish and Christian Beliefs* (Cambridge: Cambridge University Press, 1951).

10. Emile Durkheim, "La Prohibition de l'inceste et ses origines," *L'Année Sociologique* 1 (1898), pp. 1–70, esp. p. 56.

11. E.E. Evans-Pritchard, "Nuer Rules of Exogamy and Incest," in *Social Structure: Studies Presented to A.R. Radcliffe-Brown*, ed. Meyer Fortes (London: Clarendon Press, 1949), pp. 85–103.

12. Claude Lévi-Strauss, *The Elementary Structures of Kinship*, trans. James Harle Bell and John Richard von Sturmer (Boston: Beacon Press, 1949), p. 9.

13. *Ibid.*, p. 40.

14. *Ibid.*, p. 449.

15. *Ibid.*, p. 22.

16. *Ibid.*, p. 495.

17. Françoise Héritier-Augé, "Semen and Blood: Some Ancient Theories Concerning their Genesis and Relationship," in *Zone 5: Fragments for a History of the Human Body* (New York: Zone Books, 1989); Serge Sauneron, "Le Germe dans les os," *Bulletin de l'Institut Français d'Archéologie Orientale* (1960).

18. Robert Rattray, *Religion and Art in Ashanti* (Oxford: Clarendon Press, 1927).

19. Aristotle, *Generation of Animals* in *The Complete Works of Aristotle: The Revised Oxford Translation,* vol. 1, ed. Jonathan Barnes, trans. A. Platt (Princeton, NJ: Princeton University Press, 1984).

20. C.R. Lagae, *Les Azandé ou Niam-Niam: L'Organization zande, croyances religieuses et magiques, coutumes familiales*, Bibliothèque Longo, vol. 18 (Brussels: Uromant, 1926).

21. Flora L. Baily, *Some Sex Beliefs and Practices in a Navaho Community* (Cambridge, MA: Harvard University, Peabody Museum of American Archaeology and Ethnology Papers, vol. 40, 1950).

22. Aristotle, *Generation of Animals*, p. 1185.

23. *Ibid.*, p. 1185.

24. *Ibid.*, p. 1186.

25. *Ibid.*

26. *Ibid.*

27. *Ibid.*, p. 1187–88.

28. *Ibid.*, p. 1191.

29. *Ibid.*

30. *Ibid.*

31. *Ibid.*

32. *Ibid.*

33. *Ibid.*, p. 1192.

34. *Ibid.*, p. 1194.

35. *Ibid.*

36. *Ibid.*, p. 1195.

37. *Ibid.*, p. 1192.

CHAPTER EIGHT: THE HIDDEN ORDER OF THINGS

1. Sophocles, *Oedipus the King*, trans. David Grene, in *The Complete Greek Tragedies*, vol. 2, eds. David Grene and Richmond Lattimore (Chicago: University of Chicago Press, 1942), lines 1211–13. C. Stein, "Oedipe roi selon Freud," preface to the new edition of Marie Delcourt's *Oedipe ou la légende du conquérant* (Paris, 1981). Jean-Pierre Vernant and Pierre Vidal-Naquet, *Myth and Tragedy in Ancient Greece* (New York: Zone Books, 1988).

2. *Oedipus the King*, lines 1255–58.

3. Nicole Loraux, "L'Empreinte de Jocaste," *L'Ecrit du Temps* (1986).

4. Françoise Héritier-Augé, "Identité de substance et parenté de lait dans le monde arabe," in *Epouser au plus proche: Inceste, prohibitions et stratégies matrimoniales autour de la Méditerrané*, ed. Pierre Bonte (Paris: Éditions de l'EHESS, 1994), pp. 149–64.

5. Soraya Altorki, "Milk-kinship in Arab Society: An Unexplored Problem in the Ethnology of Marriage," *Ethnology* 19 (1980), pp. 233–44.

6. Soraya Altorki, "Family Organization and Woman's Power in Urban Saudi Arabian Society," *Journal of Anthropological Research* (1977), pp. 277-87.

7. Héritier-Augé, "Identité de substance et parenté de lait dans le monde arabe," p. 163.

8. Salvatore d'Onofrio calls it "incest of the third type." Salvatore d'Onofrio, "L'Atome de parenté spirituelle," *L'Homme* 118, 31 (2); pp. 79–110.

CHAPTER NINE: "DE NOBIS FABULA NARRATUR"

1. Edith Valter, *Les Coeurs brûlés*, from an original screenplay by Jean-Pierre Jaubert and Jean-Charles Audrumet (Paris: TFI Editions, 1992).

2. *Ibid.*, p. 226.

3. John Bradshaw, "Incest: Living Her Mother's Fantasy," *Lear's*, December 1992, p. 43.

4. *Marie-Claire*, November 1993.

5. "There are days I wish my daughter would break up with Vincent, so the problem would disappear on its own.... [W]hen a man sleeps with a mother and daughter, it creates a link that's, how can I say this ... against nature. It forced me to think about my daughter's sexuality, to know her intimacy in a way that doesn't concern me.... I've encroached on my daughter's territory..." (*ibid.*, p. 114).

6. Walter Isaacson, "The Heart Wants What It Wants," *Time*, Aug. 31, 1992, pp. 59–60.

7. *Le Nouvel Observateur*, Aug. 27–Sept. 2, 1992.

8. Joe Urschel, "Woody Allen Again Redefines Our Terms," *USA Today*, Aug. 20, 1992.

CONCLUSION

1. *Hamlet,* act 1, scene 5, lines 42–83.

2. *Ibid.*, lines 84–86.

3. *Ibid.*, lines 63–70.

4. *Ibid.*, act 4, scene 3, line 52.

Glossary

AFFINITY, AFFINES: Kinship, relatives by marriage. The term *affines* refers to all blood relatives of Ego's spouse and spouses of Ego's blood relatives. Thus, in the first case: the wife's father, or, for a woman, the husband's mother's brother; in the second case, the father's sister's husband, a nephew's wife, and so on.

AGNATIC BROTHER, SISTER: Siblings engendered by the same father.

AGNATIC DESCENT, FILIATION, KINSHIP: That which passes through men exclusively in direct line as well as collateral line. The father's father (paternal grandfather), the father's brother (paternal uncle), the father's brother's son (first cousin, or more precisely, patrilateral parallel cousin), and so on, are agnatic relatives (see *parallel/cross*, *uterine*, *cognate*, *patrilineal*).

ALTER: Designates the position of kinship which marks the end of a particular genealogical chain starting with Ego; thus: "my father's sister's son" is a formula that, starting with me (Ego), "declines" a series of positions of kinship that end in designating Alter (see *Ego*).

335

APICAL, POINT, ANCESTOR: The most distant ancestor known to a line or to several lines of descendants.

COGNATIC, DESCENT, FILIATION, KINSHIP: A relationship that unites individuals through chains that include men as well as women: for example, my father's sister's son (patrilateral cross-cousin, first cousin) and my father's mother's brother (great uncle, with no other specification) are cognates of Ego (see *parallel/cross*, *patrilateral*, *uterine*, *patrilineal*).

CROW AND OMAHA KINSHIP SYSTEMS: Kinship systems characterized by particular terminology to designate relatives, a system of unilineal filiation and prohibitive rules of alliance that forbid, rather than recommend, certain choices. Omaha systems are characterized by a rule of patrilineal filiation, Crow systems by a matrilineal rule. In both cases, matrimonial prohibitions pertain as much to particular individuals (cognate kinship, alliance, rival) as to entire groups defined by the rule of filiation, from which Ego's mothers and grandmothers descend, in the Omaha system, fathers and grandfathers in the Crow, which forbids cousins from marrying. In kinship appellation, these systems are characterized by an oblique imbalance. While parallel cousins (issued from two brothers or two sisters) call each other "brother" and "sister," this is not the case for cross-cousins (descended from a brother and sister). In the Omaha system, Ego calls the mother's brother's children "uncle" and "mother" (they call Ego "nephew" and "son" reciprocally) and the father's sister's children are nephews and nieces for masculine Ego (whom they call "uncle" reciprocally). Inversely, in the logic of Crow appellation, the father's sister's children are called "father" and "aunt" and those of the mother's brother are "children." (See also *unilineal*.)

336

DEGREES OF KINSHIP: The number of relationships in direct line, or through collateral lines, that unite two individuals. There is one degree of kinship in direct line between a parent and a child, two degrees in direct line between a grandparent and a grandchild, and so on. In collateral lines, degrees are counted on each line until the closest common ancestor. Two siblings or half-siblings, that is, two brothers, two sisters, a brother and sister, are second degree; a degree is counted between each of them and their common father or mother. It follows that an uncle and his nephew are third degree; two degrees unite the "nephew" to his grandfather, who is united in a first degree relationship to his son, the "uncle" in the relationship. Two first cousins are fourth degree, and so on.

This is the formula used in civil and roman law, and it is used in this book. The calculation is different in canon law; there it is based on the number of generations that separate the two relatives concerned from the common ancestor by establishing itself on the longest line of descent.

EGO: Term of reference that designates the speaker or situation of reference in relation to which all possible situations of kinship are described.

ENDOGAMY, EXOGAMY: To marry within/to marry outside a group defined by a social rule (clan, lineage, village, etc.). Local endogamy is marrying in an area of familiarity in the vicinity of one's home.

EXTENDED FAMILY: Any two or more nuclear families joined by a parent-child link, e.g., a married couple and their married daughter and her husband and children.

FIRST-DEGREE ASCENDANT: Ego's father and mother.

INVERSE CASE: Ego changes places and goes from one end to the other in the chain called symmetrical. This is the reciprocal case of the symmetrical case.

LEVIRATE: An institution that suggests or requires a widow's remarriage to a real or classificatory "brother" of her deceased husband.

LINEAGE: All persons who can be linked to a common ancestor, a founding forebear; in patrilineal descent, this occurs through the intermediary of men exclusively, as daughters belong to their father's lineage but do not transmit filiation to their children. In matrilineal filiation, this occurs through the intermediary of women exclusively, as sons belong to their mother's lineage but do not transmit filiation.

LINE: A line of descent among others within a lineage, in relation to the common ancestor or intermediary ancestors.

MATRICLAN: A group of relatives, including the dead, who can trace their ancestry back to a common, real, or mythical originating ancestor through matrilineal descent, i.e., through their mothers only.

MATRILATERAL CROSS-COUSIN: A child of one's mother's brother.

MATRILINEAL SYSTEM: A kinship system which is characterized by recognition of matrilineal descent in group formation and the recognition of ancestors.

338

PARALLEL/CROSS-COUSIN, RELATIONSHIP: Without going into detail, we will say that parallel cousins are those children issued from two brothers or from two sisters (that is, two siblings of the same sex), and that cross-cousins are the children issued from a brother and a sister respectively (that is, from two siblings of the opposite sex). The parallel/cross relationship is used to describe and analyze other kinship relations besides those of cousins. But there is no simple and universal criterion for what the objectively parallel or cross character of a consanguineous relationship would be beyond the level of first cousins.

PATRILATERAL, MATRILATERAL: On the father's side, on the mother's side. A "patrilateral parallel cousin" is the son of one of the father's brothers; "matrilateral cross-cousin" describes the relationship that unites Ego to his mother's brother's son.

PATRILINEAL, MATRILINEAL, SYSTEM OF FILIATION: Unilineal system of filiation which in the first case includes only blood relations linked by chains of kinship composed exclusively of men (e.g., my father's father's brother's son's daughter); daughters do not convey the filiation they obtain from their father to their children; the children will obtain it from their own father. The matrilineal system of filiation includes only blood relations linked by chains composed exclusively of women (e.g., my mother's mother's sister's daughter's son, matrilateral parallel cousin of the sixth degree); sons do not transmit the filiation they obtain from their mother to their children; the children will it obtain from their own mother. (See also *unilineal*.)

POLYGAMY: A social system that allows an individual to have several spouses. *Polyandry* is used to refer to a woman with several husbands, *polygyny* to a man with several wives.

RECIPROCAL CASE: The chain of kinship is the same as in the first schema but Ego changes places and goes from one extremity to the other.

SEGMENTARY: An adjective applied to unilineal descent groups, which can be seen as one huge unit with a distant apical ancestor or as the aggregate of a number of discrete groups such as clans, or an even larger number of smaller discrete groups such as lineages, which may share apical ancestors with other lineages. The society is said to be made up of a number of segments which can join together or separate for different social and ecological functions.

SORORAL POLYGYNY: An institution that allows a man to have two sisters as wives at the same time. (See also *Sororate*.)

SORORATE: An institution that allows or compels a man to marry his deceased wife's sister.

STOCK: A non-technical word referring to members of a kinship group who feel themselves to be related by any mechanism of consanguinity (i.e., blood relatives through either males and/or females).

SYMMETRICAL CASE: The figures at each end of the chain change in gender as do the intermediary figures necessary in cases of alliance.

SYSTEMS OF ALLIANCE: The set of rules by which the kinship groups in a society are joined together through repeated marriages, e.g., matrilineal or patrilineal cross-cousin marriage or parallel cousin marriage.

UNILINEAL FILIATION: A system that recognizes as belonging to the same group of filiation, with the same rights, only individuals linked to each other either through men (patrilineality) or through women (matrilineality).

UTERINE, DESCENT, KINSHIP: What passes through women in direct line as well as collateral line, especially through the mother or grandmothers, due to the rule of filiation. In a patrilineal system, the mother, the mother's brother, the mother's brother's son, are uterine relatives of Ego, as are the mother's mother and her agnatic relatives. (See also *Agnatic, Cognatic, Patrilineal/ matrilineal.*)

UTERINE BROTHER, SISTER: Born of the same mother.

Designed by Bruce Mau
with Barr Gilmore and Louis-Charles Lasnier
Typeset by Archetype
Printed and bound by Maple-Vail on Sebago acid-free paper